SOCIAL JUSTICE AND SUBSIDIARITY

SOCIAL JUSTICE AND SUBSIDIARITY

LUIGI TAPARELLI
AND THE ORIGINS OF MODERN CATHOLIC SOCIAL THOUGHT

THOMAS C. BEHR

The Catholic University of America Press
Washington, DC

Copyright © 2019
The Catholic University of America Press
All rights reserved

Library of Congress Cataloging-in-Publication Data

Names: Behr, Thomas, 1958- author.
Title: Social justice and subsidiarity : Luigi Taparelli and the origins of modern Catholic social thought / Thomas C. Behr.
Description: Washington, DC : Catholic University of America Press, 2019. | Includes bibliographical references and index.
Identifiers: LCCN 2019020755 | ISBN 9780813231181 (hardcover)
Subjects: LCSH: Social justice—Religious aspects—Catholic Church. | Subsidiarity—Religious aspects—Catholic Church. | Taparelli d'Azeglio, Luigi, 1793-1862. | Christian sociology—Catholic Church. | Catholic Church—Doctrines.
Classification: LCC BX1795.S62 B44 2019 | DDC 261.8088/282—dc23
LC record available at https://lccn.loc.gov/2019020755

TABLE OF CONTENTS

Acknowledgments   vii
Abbreviations   ix

INTRODUCTION: SOCIAL JUSTICE RECONSIDERED - TAPARELLI'S REALIST SOCIAL SCIENCE   1

I – TAPARELLI AND THE AGE OF IDEOLOGY   17
   The Religious Question from the Middle Ages to the Nineteeth Century   19
   Traditionalists and Liberals in the Restorationist Period   23
   Eclecticism and Taparelli's "Conversion" to Scholastic Philosophy   32

II – TAPARELLI AND THE REVIVAL OF SCHOLASTIC NATURAL LAW REASONING   39
   The Scholastic Revival: The Appeal of Thomism   39
      Metaphysics and Epistemology   40
      Psychology and Anthropology   45
      Natural Law and Politics   48
   Metaphysics and Methodology in the *Saggio teoretico*   55
      Reading the *Saggio*   55
      Two Philosophies   58
      Dialectic of Theory and Fact   61
      Application   64
   Taparelli and the Development of Modern Catholic Social Teaching   65
      Pius IX and *Civiltà Cattolica*   69
      Leo XIII from *Aeterni Patris* to *Rerum Novarum*   74

III – SOCIAL JUSTICE AND SUBSIDIARITY   81
   The Problem of Social Justice   83
   Introduction to Subsidiarity   93
   Genealogy of the Idea of Subsidiarity   98

Natural, Voluntary, and Dutiful Societies   113
Authority and the Common Good   122
Principles of Subsidiarity in Practice   131

IV – SOCIAL JUSTICE AND SUBSIDIARITY AS COMPLEMENTARY PRINCIPLES   141
A Coherent Account of Social Justice   141
    Natural Right to Subjective Rights   144
    Social Justice Rightly Understood   149
Social Justice and Subsidiarity Applied: Social Economics   154
    Compared with Naturalistic Economic Thought   155
    Principles and Objectives   159
    Scope and Limits of State Intervention   164

CONCLUSION – TAPARELLI'S REALIST SOCIAL SCIENCE   174
    Summary of the Argument   176
    The Development of Catholic Social Teaching   193

Charts
    1. Self-Interest Rightly Understood: The Three Motors of Human Will/Action   197
    2. Subsidiarity: Sociality and Hypotactical Society   198
    3. From Natural Right to Subjective Rights to Social Justice   199
    4. Social Justice, Subsidiarity, and Social Economy   200

Appendix. Luigi Taparelli, SJ, "Treatise on Subsidiarity"   201
Bibliography   233
Index   247

ACKNOWLEDGMENTS

I am most deeply grateful to my wife, Francesca D'Alessandro Behr, for her encouragement, patience, and occasional assistance, whether in fighting my tendency towards the Teutonic in writing, or in figuring out some particular tortuous Taparellian turn of phrase. I thank her also for being exactly who she is, passionate, serious, hardworking, but also a lot of fun—namely, for laughing at my jokes. I thank also my sons, Gervin and John-Paul, to whom, along with my dear parents, Gervin and Berenice, and Francesca's dear parents, Luigi and Giuliana, I dedicate this book.

Profuse thanks go to my mentor in the study of intellectual history, the late Prof. Georg G. Iggers at SUNY Buffalo, and to his gracious wife, Wilma (also now deceased), for spreading out the tea and cakes every week for our seminars in their home. I thank the late Prof. Frank Annunziata at Rochester Institute of Technology for the encouragement, and adjunct courses, during my recuperation from gastric and esophageal cancer—and, from the same period, I thank Rick and Paola Price of Experience Plus Bicycle Tours for the opportunity to work on 31 bicycle trips in Italy, which undoubtedly contributed to that recovery.

I thank Prof. Russell Hittinger, as the outside reader on my dissertation, for his insights and suggestions. I thank my friends at the Acton Institute, Fr. Robert Sirico and especially Sam Gregg, for their encouragement and support, and my friends at the Institute for Humane Studies, especially the late Leonard Liggio, and also Alex Chafuen, for their encouragement and support. Special thanks go to Winston Elliott, III, of the Free Enterprise Institute in Houston, for his encouragement and very practical support while I was Resident Scholar there.

At the University of Houston I must thank those friends who brightened my time there, especially the late Ross Lence, my Liberal Studies friends, Luca Oliva, Taylor Fayle, and Tamara Cobb, and most of all, my eventual Chair, Lois Zamora, without whose encouragement and generosity, along with her late husband Steve, this book would not have been possible. To (former) Associate Dean Sarah Fishman, who had invited me to create and direct the Liberal Studies degree program at UH, and who has been a model of integrity, I owe undying gratitude.

I have been blessed to have encountered so many other persons of principle, whose friendship has been instrumental one way or another over the years, whom I wish also to thank—beginning with my brothers and sisters, Terry, Cathy, Betsy, Barbara, Larry, David, Gregory, and including all of my good friends of today: you know who you are.

I want to thank the research and funding organizations that have made this work possible: SUNY Buffalo-Technische Universität Darmstadt Exchange Fellowship; United States-Italy Fulbright Fellowship; Calihan Research and Travel Grant (Acton Institute); Notre Dame University Erasmus Institute Seminar; History and Economic Research Grant (Atlas Network), Hayek Research and Travel Grants (Institute for Humane Studies), and Free Market Economics Mini-Grant (Acton Institute).

And then there are the editors! I mentioned already my thanks to my dear wife, Francesca. My colleague Luca Oliva also read over the manuscript and made valuable suggestions. I owe a special thank you to Prof. Joe Trabbic, at Ave Maria University, who directed my attention to specifications concerning St. Thomas's philosophy that resonated with Taparelli's search for a method in establishing a normative social science. I thank Greg Black, of Black Language Consulting, for his patience and persistence in the multiple rounds of editing that we had. His legal schooling and bit of Italian language made him a very good fit for this job! And lastly, I thank CUA Press acquisitions editor John Martino who has been very kind and helpful at every step of the way.

ABBREVIATIONS

ACC—Archivio della Civiltà Cattolica

CC—*Civiltà Cattolica* (1850-present), cited by Series (ser. III), Volume (vol. 4), Year (1856), and Page numbers, in segments, sometimes distributed over two volumes.

CST—Catholic social teaching.

NE—Aristotle, *Nicomachean Ethics*, cited by Book (X), and Chapter (3).

Saggio—Luigi Taparelli, SJ, *Saggio teoretico di dritto naturale appoggiato sul fatto* (§§ 1-1685) cited by Section number (§685), and occasional "Notes" (Note XLVII).

SCG—St. Thomas Aquinas, *Summa Contra Gentiles*, cited by Book (I, II, and so on), chapter

ST—St. Thomas Aquinas, *Summa Theologiae* (*Theologica*), cited by Part (I, I-II, II-II, III), Question (q.91) Article (a.1), sometimes Objection or Reply to Objection (obj.2 or ad.2) within an Article.

INTRODUCTION

SOCIAL JUSTICE RECONSIDERED – TAPARELLI'S REALIST SOCIAL SCIENCE

"**M**AN IS BORN FREE; AND everywhere he is in chains." Thus begins Rousseau's *Social Contract*, as he sets himself the task: "How did this change come about? I do not know. What can make it legitimate? That question I think I can answer." Luigi Taparelli, SJ (1793–1862), with his characteristic style when in polemical mode, slams the abstractions of the *ginevrino* (little Genevan, as he calls him) as *sofismi*[1] (sophisms) and self-contradictory *paralogismi*[2] (paralogisms)—more poetry than philosophy. And he describes Rousseau's supposedly salutary casting off of those chains, with individual wills dissolving into a "general will," a romantic *metempsicosi*[3] (metempsychosis). In his magisterial *Saggio teoretico di dritto naturale appoggiato sul fatto* (Theoretical treatise of natural right based on fact), Taparelli lays out that far from being born free, except as pure abstraction, man is everywhere born totally dependent, subject to the anterior facts of history and concrete circumstances. How could the social contract theorists be oblivious to such facts? How had "natural right" become the justification of the modern state? Taparelli claimed that the modern political theorists—Hobbes, Locke, Rousseau, and their descendants—were not interested in questioning the foundations and tendencies of Leviathan, but rather in theoretically legitimizing its exercise of power.

---

1 Luigi Taparelli, *Saggio teoretico di dritto naturale appoggiato sul fatto*, §276. For complete citation information, see n. 8 below. Referred to hereafter as "*Saggio.*"
2 *Saggio*, Note XLVII, "On Independence."
3 *Saggio*, §469.

It was against the background of the catastrophic, murderous excesses of the French Revolution and Napoleonic Empire, which exhibited the worst tendencies of the modern state, that Taparelli elaborated his neo-scholastic theory of social order, including the natural law principles of social justice and subsidiarity. These terms, especially "social justice," are almost part of everyday political speech in the Western world, and yet their origins have been ignored or obscured, along with their meaning. In Taparelli's generation, the political question, the social question, and the religious question were all contested in competing ideological visions of the future. Taparelli was of a generation of social theorists who saw the collapse of the old order with varying degrees of trepidation or welcome, but none without a vision of their hoped-for future society. Among John Stuart Mill, August Comte, Karl Marx, and Alexis de Tocqueville, only Tocqueville remained agnostic about the direction that the social forces he analyzed would take. Mill, Comte, and Marx proposed not only their versions of a true future according to impersonal laws of history, but also of new religions to give that future purpose and broad appeal.

Luigi Taparelli inaugurated a realist social science, an Aristotelian-Thomistic sociology in the full sense of the term. As Raymond Aron explains, "Sociology marks a moment in man's reflection on historical reality, the moment when the concept of the social, of society, becomes the center of interest, replacing the concept of politics or of the regime or of the state."[4] As a science, sociology must offer both an empirical and theoretical focus for that part of social existence identified as "society" and the relationship of "society" to that social existence. The tendency toward the analytical or instead toward the global and historical reflects the duality of the sociologist's ambition; for the latter, that ambition leans in the direction of theories and laws of social evolution. Aron does not, however, address the tendency of analytical sociological reasoning to end in positivistic confirmation of unexplored assumptions. Thomas Kuhn in *The Structure of Scientific Revolutions* makes the case that science is impossible without a preexisting paradigm comprised of theory and assumed facts that makes research and hypotheses possible. All sociologists are theoretically

---

4 Raymond Aron, *Montesquieu, Comte, Marx, de Tocqueville: The Sociologists and the Revolution of 1848*, vol. 1 of *Main Currents in Sociological Thought* (Garden City, N.Y.: Anchor Books, 1968), 9.

informed and motivated by these paradigms, which Kuhn defined as "accepted examples of actual scientific practice—examples which include law, theory, application, and instrumentation together—provid[ing] models from which spring particular coherent traditions of scientific research."[5]

Aron states that "[if] one defines the aim proper to sociology as the combination and reunion of the study of the part with the study of the whole," then sociology's place within the other social sciences becomes clear, and Taparelli's corpus as a sociological enterprise likewise becomes clear.[6] The study of the role of the individual element within the totality of social existence; that is, empirical analysis of individual facts so as to locate their dialectical significance in relationship to the whole of social existence, synchronically and diachronically, is at the heart of Taparelli's project. And indeed, as Aron suggests, "If sociology's specific intention is to analyze and comprehend the social as such, both as element and as entity, then countless questions inevitably arise concerning the relations between sociology as such and the other social disciplines."[7] Taparelli's theoretical and methodological approach to sociology has, broadly speaking, fundamental significance for the social sciences in the areas of politics, economics, and history.

In his *Saggio teoretico*,[8] published from 1840 to 1843, Taparelli elaborated the sociological ideas that fundamentally shaped modern Catholic

---

5 Thomas Kuhn, *The Structure of Scientific Revolutions*, 2nd ed., in *International Encyclopedia of Unified Science*, vol. II, no. 2 (Chicago: University of Chicago Press, 1970), 10.

6 Aron, *Montesquieu*, 10.

7 Ibid.

8 The *Saggio teoretico di dritto naturale appoggiato sul fatto* [Theoretical treatise of natural right based on fact] (Palermo: Stamperia d'Antonio Muratori, 1840–43; Rome: Civiltà Cattolica, 1855 and 1949) is Taparelli's major work. Published originally in Palermo between 1840 and 1843 in five volumes, this work appeared in a number of subsequent Italian editions and reprintings, including the definitive fourth edition of 1855 published in Rome in two volumes, considerably updated and reorganized by the author. References herein are to the edition of 1949, which was based on the 1855 text. This 1949 edition has an expanded index, additional footnote references to Taparelli's *Civiltà Cattolica* work, and a summary outline of the whole work, the "Epilogo ragionato." There are also editions of the work in German (1845), French (1857), and Spanish (1866–67). The work is divided according to a hierarchy of books ("*dissertazione*") and then chapters, articles (not in all chapters), and sections. Because the sections are numbered continuously throughout (§1–§1685), numbering that is carried over in foreign language editions, it will be convenient to refer primarily to them rather than to page numbers. There are also frequent elaborations on topics following certain chapters or articles, labeled as "Notes," and designated with continuing roman numerals I–CXLV.

Social Teaching (hereafter CST), which had its magisterial origins in Pope Leo XIII's 1891 encyclical *Rerum Novarum*.[9] Taparelli's theories on social justice, and especially on subsidiarity, were given even more emphasis in Pius XI's 1931 encyclical *Quadragesimo Anno*, delivered on the fortieth anniversary of *Rerum Novarum*.

In European historical scholarship, Taparelli is largely remembered as a Jesuit reactionary enrolled in the alleged campaign of Pope Pius IX to push back against the march of progress, and his works are virtually unknown in the English-speaking world. Efforts to study his work have largely been undertaken by fellow Italian Jesuits, especially from the circle of writers for the *Civiltà Cattolica*, the journal he co-founded in 1850. Very few English-speaking scholars have read and made an effort to understand the *Saggio*, relying, much to the detriment of their understanding, on the commentary of others, the best of which is Robert Jacquin's sympathetic and exhaustive 1943 biography in French.[10] However, Jacquin's interests influenced his appreciation and interpretation of aspects of the *Saggio*, and it was only with some difficulty that he overlooked Taparelli's eclectic intellectual formation and erratic style of presentation, shifting at times, between philosophical, didactic, and polemical modes, even in a single passage. The key implications of Taparelli's hylomorphic social theory for culture, politics, and economics are his description of the origin of subjective rights following on moral reflection and his development of the principle of subsidiarity as the natural law of society versus the rationalizing and centralizing tendencies of the modern state. Both of these escape Jacquin's notice to varying degrees. Although Taparelli's contribution to the principle of subsidiarity as enunciated in *Quadragesimo Anno* had come to light before the publication of his biography, Jacquin did not make the connection between subsidiarity (the theoretical foundation for a flourishing social order in conjunction with a limited governmental state) and the *dritto ipotattico* ("hypotactical right"), a term coined by Taparelli. Jacquin was more interested in this "hypotactical right" as pointing toward the desirability of world government, and he appeared to appreciate only one

---

9 Of course the Church had taught about social realities from the beginning; see note 3 of chapter 1 on the dawn of "modern" Catholic Social Teaching.
10 Robert Jacquin, *Taparelli* (Paris: Lethielleux, 1943).

aspect of Taparelli's economic thought: his criticism of the laissez-faire liberal school's one-dimensional emphasis on self-interest.

Although the chief drafter of *Quadragesimo Anno*, Oswald von Nell-Breuning, SJ, borrowed Taparelli's theoretical formulations in enunciating the principle of subsidiarity, the scholarly literature has remained largely silent on Taparelli's role. Scholars on both sides of the Atlantic have mostly been unaware of how Taparelli's definition of social justice is connected to subsidiarity,[11] even though subsidiarity has become a widely applied principle in social organizational theory, notably as an important protocol in Article Five of the Maastricht Treaty, the governing law of the European Union, adopted in 1992.[12] The terms "subsidiarity" and "social justice" are interdependent in Taparelli's theoretical framework. Social justice is the personal virtue of rendering due regard and support, employing appropriate means, for the fulfillment of the duties and exercise of the abstract rights of individuals and of their associations within the given, concrete, historical facts of existence.[13] Subsidiarity is the principle that determines the appropriate means of effecting social justice while respecting personal and associational liberty. Subsidiarity is the principle of "hypotactical" right, of the rights that pertain to persons and to the intermediary associations they form in pursuit of happiness and flourishing as composite material, social, and rational beings. These associations—social, economic, cultural, and political—extend horizontally

---

11 See Thomas C. Behr, "Luigi Taparelli D'Azeglio, SJ (1793–1862) and the Development of Scholastic Natural-Law Thought as a Science of Society and Politics," *Journal of Markets and Morality* 6, no. 1 (Spring 2003): 99–115; see also the in-depth study by Ilenia Massa Pinto, "La Concezione Antica dell' Origine dello Stato e il Principio di Sussidiarietà: Luigi Taparelli d'Azeglio" [The ancient conception of the origin of the state and the principle of subsidiarity: Luigi Taparelli d'Azeglio], chap. 4 in *Il Principio di Sussidiarietà: Profili Storici e Costituzionali* [The principle of subsidiarity: Historical and constitutional profiles] (Naples: Casa Editrice Jovene, 2003).

12 See Robert Schütze, "EU Competences: Existence and Exercise," chap. 4 in *The Oxford Handbook of European Union Law*, 5th ed., ed. Anthony Arnull and Damian Chalmers (Oxford: Oxford University Press, 2015). See especially section IV, "Subsidiarity: Safeguarding Federal Values."

13 Taparelli has long been credited with coining the term "social justice," but scholars have rarely given anything more than cursory attention to his formulation of its contents. See Thomas C. Behr, "Luigi Taparelli and Social Justice: Rediscovering the Origins of a 'Hollowed' Concept," in *Social Justice in Context* 1 (2005): 3–16. Cf. Michael Novak and Paul Adams, with Elizabeth Shaw, *Social Justice Isn't What You Think It Is* (New York: Encounter Books, 2015), for a comprehensive overview of the critique of the term.

and vertically in their comprehensiveness, from the family and village up to the nation-state, and indeed beyond the nation-state to theoretically encompass a "wise cosmopolitanism."[14]

Nell-Breuning is reputed to have said, probably in class to his students, "Tell me what your image of man is, and I will tell you what your notion of social order is."[15] With this dictum, Nell-Breuning summarized the development of Taparelli's argument as laid out in the guideposts of his treatise: first, "from the germ of anthropology, [we can derive] the ontological idea of the human act and the laws of individual human action," and second, "from the nature itself of man, the general idea of society will be shown."[16] At each step Taparelli's ideas would be informed by facts, and theories would be confirmed by facts, and abstract conclusions would be applied to facts—because it is in the facts of concrete existence that the interplay of universals and material circumstances takes place. Only in that hylomorphic union do abstractions "exist," to be apprehended by reason as formal cause. Starting from this understanding of human nature and from the concept of "society" it implicates, Taparelli then turns to an investigation of the natural laws of human "cooperation" applied in the formation of concrete societies, which yields the principles of subsidiarity.

The focus of this present work is to provide an introduction to Taparelli's realist social theory, beginning with the context of its origins, then examining its main theoretical and methodological tenets, and concluding with some implications for social scientific research, including an explanation of how the terms "social justice" and "subsidiarity" relate to each other in theory and practice. In particular, this work will show how Taparelli's social scientific concepts and natural law reasoning on subjective rights, not to mention his dialectical method based on thesis-and-hypothesis (a method that infuriated contemporary liberals), have become central pillars of modern CST. Selections of the *Saggio* dealing with the laws of social formation, and those governing both horizontal and vertical relations between associations, with their respective rights,

---

14 *Saggio*, §937.
15 Thomas O. Nitsch, "Social Economics: The First 200 Years," in *Social Economics: Retrospect and Prospect*, ed. Mark A. Lutz, 5–90 (Dordrecht: Kluwer, 1990), 90n84.
16 *Saggio*, "Partizione dell'Opera," p. 10.

namely *dritto ipotattico*, are attached hereto in an Appendix, under the title "Treatise on Subsidiarity."

Aron identifies Montesquieu, the author of *The Spirit of the Laws*, as not just a precursor to modern sociological thinking, but indeed as one of sociology's great, and first, theorists. "He sought to understand historical truth. But historical truth appeared to him in the form of an almost limitless diversity of morals, customs, ideas, laws, and institutions. . . . The goal of the inquiry should have been the replacement of this incoherent diversity by a conceptual order. . . . On what level and by what means does one discover the intelligible order?"[17] Montesquieu sought to answer that question by studying the interplay of the two "general causes" of historical variety—the moral and the physical. Montesquieu's research culminates with his organizing historical diversity into political, historical, and geographical contexts, with political contexts and regime forms largely reflecting classical categorizations. Reflecting on what he sees as his predecessor's laudable sociological enterprise, of value even today, Aron sees Montesquieu's essential liberalism, characterized by his theory of political order based on a balance of power between people, nobility, and king, as the guarantee of moderation and liberty.[18]

Taparelli admired Montesquieu's attention to historical "accident" (empirical facts) in the search for a general theory of societal organization; however, he disagreed with what he saw as the conclusion-driven nature of Montesquieu's project—namely pro-republicanism—and faults him for his overly Cartesian anthropology. Taparelli reasoned from an Aristotelian-Thomistic anthropology of composite human nature, inextricably material, social, and rational, and from the resulting natural law of social obligation, always starting from and reflecting back upon the facts of history and life. In this regard, if Montesquieu is more of a sociologist than August Comte, as Aron pointedly suggests, then Taparelli is more of a sociologist than Montesquieu.[19]

---

17 Aron, *Montesquieu*, 11–15.
18 Aron, *Montesquieu*, 60–62.
19 Taparelli's participation in the development of a Catholic sociology has occasionally been recognized, but has not been very much explored. For example, Gianfanco Legittimo, in the chapter "Sistemazione dottrinaria e programmatica," in *Sociologi Cattolici Italiani* (Rome: Il Quadrato, 1963), 30–50, sketches out Taparelli's main sociological insights and provides 120

Taparelli took much of his theoretical starting point from Montesquieu—not from the slew of natural law theorists and popularizers to whom the few scholars who write about Taparelli (but who have only scratched the surface of the *Saggio*) tend to point. In preparing to teach a course on natural law, Taparelli studied, at least to some degree, many of those theorists—Grotius, Pufendorf, Wolff, Hobbes, Locke, Rousseau, and Bentham, for instance—and a number of their mainly Italian language popularizers, but found himself primarily pointing to their limitations or outright errors. He came to realize that Aristotle and Thomas Aquinas could be taken as reliable guides to his research, and he consulted other Scholastic theorists on important points. Taparelli appreciated Montesquieu's contributions but also criticized his failings. He sought to evaluate the potential elements of truth contained in modern social and political theory generally but did not hesitate to scathingly criticize what he saw as false premises or illogical conclusions. He at times extends to authors the backhanded compliment that at least their illogical conclusions reflect some residual morality or unconscious avoidance of unacceptable logical consequences. Less tongue in cheek, there are authors whom Taparelli sees as deliberately engaging in deception—obscuring premises, distorting reasoning, ignoring the practical implications of their theories—in the quest for acclaim and personal advancement.

His overall assessment of Montesquieu is mixed. He thought that Montesquieu's categorization of governmental types as republican (democratic or aristocratic), monarchical, and despotic, was akin to qualifying "types" of individuals as "male, female, and handicapped." After all, despotism in classical political models is not a regime form per se, but the degeneration of one, namely of democracy. He saw Montesquieu's conclusions as reflecting defective axioms concerning human nature, inadequate methodology, and above all a distorted agenda. He did, however, appreciate that Montesquieu began to bring political theory into relationship with social theory and historical contingency:

> That notwithstanding, by that loyal impartiality which we profess even toward the enemies of truth, we must recognize that the *Spirit*

---

pages of relevant excerpts from the *Saggio*.

of the Laws was a transition of social right from the abstract to the concrete; and if the impiety then reigning had not stripped the author of [religious faith]; if his mind, distorted by republican doctrines, had not perverted the ideas that his genius suggested to him; the thought of researching in the *individuality* of every people the basis of the *individuality* of its laws would have merited him recognition on the part of political philosophy. But he fell into the pure empiricism then reigning, and instead of seeing in individual conditions *a determining fact* of universal and immutable laws of nature, seeming at times (though elsewhere he contradicts himself) to wish to bury in this material element human liberty and virtue and justice, deducing from such elements every [bit of] morality, or at least subjecting it to these.[20]

Together with Mill, Comte, and Marx, Alexis de Tocqueville, the intellectual heir of Montesquieu, was the other great nineteenth-century sociological thinker. His comparative study of the social, cultural, and political differences between America and Europe in his day is brilliant, and provocative still today; it is a shame Taparelli did not study either *Democracy in America* or *The Old Regime and the French Revolution*. There are several dimensions of Tocqueville's understanding of American society that would have struck Taparelli as breakthrough contributions on the dialectical nexus of culture, social existence, and politics. Taparelli would not have taken issue with Tocqueville's argument that history in the Western world, together with its progress in material civilization, had produced an increasing leveling of social conditions, or that those conditions involve moral tendencies, even in America, that lean toward tyranny.[21] Taparelli would have been very receptive to Tocqueville's analysis of the confusion between the ideas of liberty and equality,[22] and of the temptations of soft despotism faced by "democratic man."[23] Tocqueville's "discovery" in America of how the principles of "self-interest rightly understood" are learned in the "school of association," would have invited

---

20 *Saggio*, Note LXV.
21 Alexis de Tocqueville, *Democracy in America*, trans. Harvey C. Mansfield and Delba Winthrop (Chicago: University of Chicago Press, 2000).
22 Tocqueville, *Democracy in America*, 479–82.
23 Tocqueville, *Democracy in America*, 661–65.

more serious discussion by Taparelli, as will be seen in this study of Taparelli's own conception of "self-interest rightly understood."

Tocqueville's reflections on the course of history in *Democracy in America* would have appealed to Taparelli, from its "Introduction" sketching out the march toward "equality of conditions" across "the Christian universe" with a seeming providential inexorability, to the concluding chapter, positing an uncertain future.[24] But Tocqueville's seeming providentialism is rhetorical, not theoretical. Tocqueville implies a role for human will in the ultimate choices ahead: "Whether equality leads them to servitude or freedom, to enlightenment or barbarism, to prosperity or misery," these are choices present within the "fatal circle around each man that he cannot leave."[25] And yet the ground for the exercise of free will remains unclear, and Tocqueville's attitude seems one of stoic fatalism. Taparelli's providential thinking is instead theoretical and not merely rhetorical. He presents a natural law of moral agency and social order, of persons in concrete society, that could well be summed up by one of Marx's lesser-known dictums that "men make their own history, but they do not make it as they please; they do not make it under self-selected circumstances, but under circumstances existing already, given and transmitted from the past."[26]

Tocqueville's appreciation of how religion in the United States makes political liberty practicable, how the "spirit of religion" and the "spirit of freedom" combine marvelously there, would also have been interesting to Taparelli. For Tocqueville, the spirit of political freedom and experimentation was grounded in the moral stability provided by religious belief.[27] However, Taparelli would have had unkind things to say about

---

24 "The gradual development of equality of conditions is therefore a providential fact." Ibid., 3–6.
25 Tocqueville, *Democracy in America*, 676.
26 Karl Marx, *The Eighteenth Brumaire of Louis Bonaparte* (New York, Berlin: Mondial, 2005), 1.
27 Marx, *Louis Bonaparte*, 43. In the chapter in *Democracy in America* entitled, "On Religion Considered as a Political Institution," Tocqueville has laudatory, "unexpected" (as he says), things to say about Catholics in America:
> These Catholics show great fidelity in the practices of their worship and are full of ardor and zeal for their beliefs; nevertheless they form the most republican and democratic class there is in the United States. This fact surprises one at first approach.... Among the different Christian doctrines, Catholicism appears to me, on the contrary, one of the most favorable to equality of conditions. Among Catholics, religious society is composed of only two elements: the priest and the people. The priest alone is raised above the faithful: everything is equal below him.

Tocqueville's conception of religion as a passive, unreflective metaphysical security blanket, strangely detached from the practical reasoning of economic and political life. For example, Tocqueville identifies a Catholic spirit of liberty and justice in America, which he evidences with a speech by a Catholic priest seeking to raise funds for support of the Polish independence movement. Tocqueville relates the speech with apparent admiration but makes no attempt to account for the content of the "dogma" that specifically explains where such a regard for liberty and justice comes from.[28] He merely quotes the priest's invocation: "Lord, who have created all men on the same model, do not permit despotism to come to deform thy work and to maintain inequality on earth."[29] If Tocqueville had had a greater appreciation for how the ideal content of religious belief affects in an ongoing practical manner the development of conscience and morality, he would have come close to Taparelli's own theory of human rationality and action. It is unclear how Tocqueville reconciles the practical effect of religious belief described in the chapter in *Democracy in America* titled, "On Religion Considered as a Political Institution," with his theory of "self-interest rightly understood," from the habit of masking calculations of material self-interest behind apparent benevolence. He merely reiterates the utilitarian aspect of religious belief as a restraint on human tendency toward excess, a concept with which he began his great work.[30]

Tocqueville, *Democracy in America*, 275–76.

28 Taparelli's essay, "The Influence of Catholic Prayer on Civilization," *Brownson's Quarterly Review*, vol. II (New Series), 1848: 345–80, addressed the social-psychological effect of particular religious belief and is the only of his writings translated into English prior to my translation of Taparelli's 1857 article "Analisi critica dei primi concetti dell'economia sociale" in "Critical Analysis of the First Principles of Political Economy," trans. Thomas C. Behr, *Journal of Markets and Morality* 14, no. 2 (Fall 2011): 613–38.

29 Tocqueville, *Democracy in America*, 277.

30 "[The spirit of religion] abjures doubt; it renounces the need to innovate; it even abstains from sweeping away the veil of the sanctuary; it bows with respect before truths that it accepts without discussion." Tocqueville, *Democracy in America*, 43, and, "[Freedom] considers religion as the safeguard of mores; and mores as the guarantee of laws and the pledge of its own duration." Ibid., 44. Note that Tocqueville assumed that the practical effect of religious belief was bound to wane with the advancement of material civilization—at least in Europe: "Do you not perceive on all sides beliefs that give way to reasoning, and sentiments that give way to calculations? If in the midst of that universal disturbance you do not come to bind the idea of rights to the personal interest that offers itself as the only immobile point in the human heart, what will then remain to you to govern the world, except fear?" Ibid., 228.

Tocqueville diagnosed the problem of religion in France as one of having linked its destiny to the powers of the old order—but he did not appreciate the complicated history of the "Throne and Altar" ideology, and he seemed to assume that religion in America was somehow unchanging while irreligion in Europe was in linear ascendance. This is no doubt a shortcoming caused by his limited experience in America and his singular attention to the facts of the French revolutionary experience. In neither case would Taparelli have found such conceptual inflexibility tenable, first and foremost because Taparelli does not see religion as only the social-psychological phenomenon that Tocqueville seems to. Also, significantly, Taparelli understood that culture and social order are dialectically related and not fixed in any permanent arrangement. Religious values and culture in general are variables in every generation, inextricably part of a dynamic historical matrix.

No point of contact between the theories of the two thinkers would have been more provocative than what is widely regarded as one of Tocqueville's most important themes—the role of associations as the "schools" of "self-interest rightly understood," and as a bulwark against despotism. Taparelli would have been moved by Tocqueville's genius and his powerful rhetoric, and he would not have been able to agree more strongly with his diagnosis that the principal root of despotism is selfishness.

> Despotism, which in its nature is fearful, sees the most certain guarantee of its own duration in the isolation of men, and it ordinarily puts all its care into isolating them. There is no vice of the human heart that agrees with it as much as selfishness: a despot readily pardons the governed for not loving him, provided that they do not love each other.[31]

But disagreement would have arisen between the two over the causes of selfishness and especially concerning its cure. Tocqueville sees individualism being overcome in the experience of political liberty and participation in the public affairs of society. Taparelli would have heartily agreed but would regard political liberty as a necessary but not sufficient cause of human flourishing. Tocqueville finds a paradoxical, almost ironic, materialist mechanism at work: in free participation in public affairs, people

---

31 Tocqueville, *Democracy in America*, 485.

find practical success and advancement by attracting the esteem of others. Political associations in particular are "great schools" of the "general theory of association." Associations of all kinds, from the lending library to the fire department, characterize the radical American difference from the European tendency to rationalization and centralization as the surest means of ameliorating every condition.[32] The "science of association" is for Tocqueville the "mother science": "Among the laws that rule human societies there is one that seems more precise and clearer than all the others. In order that men remain civilized or become so, the art of associating must be developed and perfected among them in the same ratio as equality of conditions increases."[33]

Tocqueville offers a "general theory" as to how Americans come to "combine their own well-being with that of their fellow citizens," and of what he calls the "doctrine of self-interest rightly understood," by means of which man is made virtuous not "through the will," but rather by bringing them "near to [virtue] insensibly through habits."[34] As he argues:

> The free institutions that the inhabitants of the United States possess and the political rights of which they make so much use recall to each citizen constantly and in a thousand ways that he lives in society. At every moment they bring his mind back toward the idea that the duty as well as the interest of men is to render themselves useful to those like them; and as he does not see any particular reason to hate them, since he is never either their slave or their master, his heart readily leans to the side of benevolence. One is occupied with the general interest at first by necessity and then by choice; what was calculation becomes instinct; and by dint of working for the good of one's fellow citizens, one finally picks up the habit and taste of serving them.[35]

Taparelli would have vigorously agreed with Tocqueville on the indispensability and beneficent effects of social cooperation across a whole range of

---

32 Tocqueville, *Democracy in America*, 489.
33 Tocqueville, *Democracy in America*, 492.
34 Tocqueville, *Democracy in America*, 500–3.
35 Tocqueville, *Democracy in America*, 488.

associations that people establish or find themselves in; and he could not have agreed more, following the basic ideas of Aristotle as developed by Aquinas, that virtues are learned in the doing and strengthened by habit so that they become part of a person's character. But he would have pointed out that Tocqueville offered little (beyond an analysis of the operation of certain kinds of associations) that formed the basis for an actual science or theory of association, let alone a normative theory of the duties and rights inhering in each individual and in the social relationships all people form and cultivate in the pursuit of human flourishing and happiness. Tocqueville refers to some facts from the English political tradition and from the Christian faith, and he points to the geographic isolation of the recently founded United States as enabling a case study of one flourishing democratic experiment, at least for the time being, but one may well ask how the experience gained from studying that society has theoretical application elsewhere. Tocqueville declared that "[a] new political science is needed for a world altogether new."[36] He offered an extraordinarily detailed and insightful analysis, but his attempts at theoretical explanation are constructed around a largely one-dimensional, materialist conception of human nature. Tocqueville called for a science of associations, and Taparelli, upon a very a different metaphysical and anthropological basis, offers exactly that.[37]

The current study is a work of intellectual history, or to be more precise, a study of ideas in context—an examination of historically effective ideas, with an elaboration of the ideas in terms of their essential forms, their ideal-typical character, along with their axioms, reasoning, supporting evidence, methodologies, chief conclusions, and practical implications, from which their historical effectiveness derives. The "ideas in context" approach regards intellectual paradigms (metaphysical, anthropological, and ethical views) as a vital part of the life of persons and societies that exist in a dynamic matrix of historical contexts.

36 Tocqueville, *Democracy in America*, 7.
37 It is lamentable that Taparelli did not address Tocqueville's work in his treatise or in his *Esame critico degli ordini rappresentativi nella società moderna* [Critical examination of the representative orders in modern society] (Rome: Tipografia della *Civiltà Cattolica*, 1854), his collected *Civiltà Cattolica* articles on the theory and limitations of popular sovereignty—a collection that sealed his reputation as a political reactionary because of his use of the dialectical thesis-and-hypothesis methodology, an approach that was almost incomprehensible to his critics.

Chapter One is a survey therefore of the relevant contexts in which Taparelli's realist social theory was elaborated over the first half of the turbulent nineteenth century, often referred to in the textbooks as the "age of revolution" or the "age of ideology."

Chapter Two examines the relevant particulars of the philosophy of Thomas Aquinas, which first attracted Taparelli's attention as early as 1816 and which Taparelli saw as a way back to intellectual and moral coherence. It was primarily the natural law philosophy of Aquinas that provided the grounding for Taparelli's science of society and provided the church and the Catholic faithful with a theoretical model for engagement with the challenges of modernity. Chapter Three is a close study of the meaning and applications of the terms "social justice" and "subsidiarity." Taparelli's realist social theory established the concepts and practical application of these pillars of modern CST. His understanding of the human person and natural sociality is the foundation for his normative social science, based as it is on a respect for the duties inhering naturally in human persons, and for the subjective rights extended in conscience toward others in society. Human rights and duties are applicable then also to the range of human associations formed as means in the pursuit of natural felicity and true happiness.

Chapter Four takes Taparelli's conception of subjective human rights and elaborates how the difference between abstract theory and concrete fact applies in conscience to establish the precepts underlying social justice rightly understood. Then, in combining the complementary principles of social justice with those of subsidiarity, and of human action in general, Taparelli's project of founding a new, normative social science (sociological, economic, and political) is sketched out in its implications. Based on Aristotelian-Thomistic paradigms of composite human nature, Taparelli's work poses a challenge to positivistic, supposedly value-free, and empirical social science in order to address the holistic and eudemonic end of personal and social existence. Taparelli argued that his theory should inform social scientific research and practical reasoning on political, cultural, and economic policies in order to promote equally the material and the moral progress of humanity. A true social science would have a research agenda, for which Taparelli sets the paradigm with the laws of the "three motors of human action"—material interest, interest in social order, and interest in truth.

Some European scholars have begun to express interest in reexamining the writings of Taparelli, particularly in order to recover his contribution to the tradition of classical liberalism from a Catholic perspective, and looking beyond the caricature of him as a reactionary that was drawn by liberal Catholics of his time.[38] Taparelli has been a well-known figure in the revival of Thomistic and neoscholastic studies since his own time. But an historical exegesis of Taparelli's social scientific theories and methodologies, and their impact on the development of CST, is comprehensively presented here for the first time to English-speaking scholars.[39] It is my hope that this introduction to Taparelli's realist social theory will stimulate additional research, translations of his works, and forays into the kind of social scientific research that Taparelli launched.

---

38   For example, Paolo Heritier, "Le personalisme libéral catholique dans l'Italie du XIX siècle" [Catholic liberal personalism in nineteenth-century Italy], in *Histoire de libéralisme en Europe*, ed. Philippe Nemo and Jean Petitot, 567–94 (Paris: PUF, 2006). Heritier was moved by Friedrich Hayek's critique of Taparelli's use of the term "social justice" to look at Taparelli's articles in which social justice finds certain applications to economics, and he concludes that there are classical liberal dimensions of the term that can be appreciated with further study. Raimondo Cubeddu, *Margini del liberalismo* [The margins of liberalism] (Soveria Mannelli (CZ): Rubbettino Editore, 2003), 54–58 points out Taparelli's distinction between natural right based on a moral understanding of obligation and the modern natural rights theories of the social contract theorists, and how Taparelli's position based on a moral understanding of obligation supports a different view of market morality than the laissez-faire position of certain Catholic Liberal thinkers, for example Bastiat, whose positions could not be distinguished from those of atheistic liberals. See also, António Almodovar and Pedro Teixeira, "The Ascent and Decline of Catholic Economic Thought, 1830–1950s," *History of Political Economy* 40 (annual supplement, 2008), 62–87, especially 72–74. Note that in all these authors, subsidiarity as the natural law of social organization, a concept that Taparelli adds to the concept of social justice, is not known, nor is the extent of his influence over the shape of modern CST. Moreover, his differences with what his protégé Matteo Liberatore later elaborated on economics, or how the German Jesuits Heinrich Pesch and then Oswald von Nell-Breuning turned his theories in a more corporatist direction, for instance, topics that are only touched upon briefly in this study, remain areas meriting further research.

39   As will be seen in Chapter Three, the evaluation of Taparelli's idea of social justice by, for example, Rommen, Hayek, Fortin, and Novak, has been incomplete. On subsidiarity, Russell Hittinger gives detailed and illuminating attention to the concept, noting Taparelli's contribution, in his chapters "Introduction to Modern Catholicism" and "Pope Leo XIII (1810–1903)," Introduction and Chap. 1 in *The Teachings of Modern Roman Catholicism on Law, Politics, and Human Nature*, ed. John Witte and Frank Alexander, 1–38 and 39–75 (New York: Columbia University Press, 2007), and "Social Pluralism and Subsidiarity in Catholic Social Doctrine," in *Annales Theologici* 16 (2002):385–408. Also, there is the insightful study of subsidiarity and social justice, with attention to Taparelli's contribution to subsequently developed CST, in Patrick McKinley Brennan, "Subsidiarity in the Tradition of Catholic Social Doctrine," in *Global Perspectives on Subsidiarity*, ed. Michelle Evans and Augusto Zimmerman, 29–47 (Dordrecht: Springer, 2014).

CHAPTER I

TAPARELLI AND THE AGE OF IDEOLOGY

THE DEFEAT OF NAPOLEONIC FRANCE in 1815 did nothing to halt the march of economic, social, and political modernization in the European and wider world. In ripping to shreds historical liberties, privileges, immunities, laws, and customs in the name of *liberté*, *égalité*, and *fraternité*, the French revolutionaries of 1789 most assuredly made possible an expansion and centralization of state power and an acceleration of economic and technological development that the Sun King himself could only have dreamt of. Waxing and waning but inexorably advancing, tidal forces of economic, social, and political modernization birthed the industrial bourgeoisie and proletariat, as well as international clashes and shifting alliances, truly making the nineteenth century an age of revolutions. It was also an age of new and competing ideologies. The old paradigms of God, man, and society that had once informed the European social and political imagination were declared dead, without any authority in place to anoint new ones apart from the modern state with its relentless rationalizations of power. The church, the Roman Curia, the hierarchy, the clergy, and the lay faithful all struggled to come to terms with the radically new political conditions in which the very survival of the Catholic faith was at stake.

In the midst of the revolutionary instability and paradigm interregnum of the times, Luigi Taparelli elaborated a science of economic, social, and political life based on natural law. Taparelli's major work, *Saggio teoretico di dritto naturale appoggiato sul fatto* (Theoretical treatise of natural right based on fact), published from 1840 to 1843,[1] rapidly became the standard natural law textbook in Catholic schools and universities and in Jesuit seminaries in Italy, France, Spain, and Germany. He played a pivotal role in the neoscholastic philosophical revival, promoting study of Thomas Aquinas as early as the 1820's from his position as rector of the Collegio Romano. He wrote scores of essays applying his natural law social scientific concepts to topics of economy, society, and politics in the *Civiltà Cattolica*, the journal of Catholic intellectual engagement, which he co-founded in 1850. He enjoyed the added celebrity of being the brother of one of the leading nationalists and Liberals in Italy, the eventual prime minister of the Kingdom of Sardinia (Piedmont), Massimo D'Azeglio.

The Catholic Church—including the hierarchy, clergy, religious, and lay faithful—was forced to grapple with these birth pangs of modernity, and it is in that context that we encounter Taparelli's foundational work. After a host of serendipitous turns in his life, Taparelli set himself to the audacious task of redeeming those parts of the new empirical and experimental sciences that were valid and useful and could be employed to promote the common good. It was his intention to refute the materialistic and idealistic philosophical assumptions of the modern theorists, but at the same time baptize, so to speak, some of their conclusions in creating a modern social science refounded on classical and neoscholastic premises. His ideas, as they developed from the 1820s through the 1850s, engaged with the dramatic course of political events, were influential on the pontificate of Pius IX, and became a pillar of modern CST with the pontificate of Leo XIII and the publication of Leo's encyclical *Aeterni Patris* (*On the Restoration of Christian Philosophy*) in 1879 and of the "magna carta" of modern CST, *Rerum Novarum* (1891, often titled in English *On the Conditions of the Working Class*).[2]

1. See Introduction, note 8, for full citation information.
2. For works referencing Taparelli's contribution to modern CST, see Russell Hittinger, "Introduction to Modern Catholicism" and "Pope Leo XIII (1810–1903)," in *The Teachings of Modern Roman Catholicism on Law, Politics, and Human Nature*, ed. John Witte and Frank Alexander, 1–38 and 39–75 (New York: Columbia University Press, 2007); Ernest L. Fortin, *Human Rights, Virtue, and the Common Good*, vol. 3 of *Ernest L. Fortin: Collected Essays*, ed. J. Brian Benestad (Lanham, Md.: Rowman & Littlefield, 1996), especially the essay "Sacred and Inviolable: *Rerum Novarum* and Natural Rights," 191–222. Also see Jacquin's standard biographical study

Rerum Novarum is often referred to as the magna carta of modern CST precisely because of Pope Leo's explicitly parallel biblical and natural law argumentation—a turning point in the church's approach to the modern world.[3]

The Religious Question from the Middle Ages to the Nineteeth Century

The "religious question" in the unfolding of nineteenth-century European events involved not just addressing relations between church and the modern state, but ultimately required a deep evaluation of the nature and proper spheres of both. In practical terms, securing the legal protection and autonomy of the church was the first priority for the hierarchy and for all faithful Catholics as the church emerged from under the rubble of revolution and empire. Dioceses and monasteries had been seized, bishops exiled, religious orders suppressed; confraternities, artisan guilds, and charitable associations had been eradicated. Pius VI's person had been abused—he had been arrested and exiled for five years, and he died while under arrest.

---

of Taparelli and the collected letters and complete bibliographical list in Pietro Pirri, *Carteggi del Padre Taparelli d'Azeglio* [The letters of Father Taparelli d'Azeglio] (Torino: Bocca Librai, 1932). Also, Thomas C. Behr, "The 19th Century Historical and Intellectual Context of Catholic Social Teaching," in *Catholic Social Teaching: A Volume of Scholarly Essays*, ed. Gerard Bradley and E. Christian Brugger, 34–65 (Cambridge University Press, 2019).

3. Leo XIII, Encyclical Letter *Rerum Novarum* (May 15, 1891). The church's teaching on social, political, and even economic issues did not begin, obviously, with Leo XIII, and for that matter extends through every period of church history back to the teachings of Jesus, with references throughout the Hebrew Bible. Earlier eighteenth- and nineteenth-century popes were forced to confront the manifold circumstances of the revolutions (economic and political) in Western societies; cf. Michael Schuck, *That They Be One: The Social Teaching of the Papal Encyclicals 1740–1989* (Washington D. C.: Georgetown University Press, 1991), but it was only after Leo XIII and with the comprehensive analysis of the social order in *Rerum Novarum* that natural law and divine revelation, taken together, become viewed as the "unshakeable foundation" of political morality, as described by Pius XII in his Encyclical Letters *Summi Pontificatus* (October 20, 1939) and *Humani Generis* (August 12, 1950). The emphasis on the harmony of faith and reason was an important theme when it was taken up by Pius IX in the mid-nineteenth century, already revealing the influences of the neoscholastic revival. Specifically, the harmony of natural and divine law represents a development of doctrine, and it is treated repeatedly by Leo XIII, not only in *Rerum Novarum*, but in his Encyclical Letters *Libertas* (June 20, 1888) and *Sapientiae Christianae* (January 10, 1890), for example. See also John Paul II's extended treatment of this double foundation of universal morality in his Encyclical Letter *Veritatis Splendor* (August 6, 1993).

In the history of church-state dynamics, the effort of the political sphere (regime, class, ideology) to subsume or instrumentalize the religious sphere (hierarchy, clergy, faith) in the service of political ends is a persistent, worldwide historical tendency. The idea of the separation of church and state, arguably a Catholic social teaching from the beginning ("Render unto Caesar"[4]), was radically new in world historical terms and contributed in unscripted ways to the advancement of the liberty and intellectual and material progress that are hallmarks of Western civilization. Battles were fought between these two spheres in Christendom from the time of the declining Roman Empire through the high Middle Ages, at times with force of arms. More often, arguments were mustered, theological and philosophical theories were advanced, legal arguments and lawyers were deployed, letters and pamphlets flew back and forth, counselors and clerics were trained for the battle, abuses were reformed, and treaties and charters were signed. It is perhaps easy to underestimate the unique historical dynamic of this conflict, which contributed significantly to the evolution of the institutions upon which Western civilization has been built.[5]

With the advancement of economies and material civilization throughout the Middle Ages came the rise of new opportunities for wealth and power, and the centralizing governments of Europe (whether dynastic princes or parliaments) arose to make use of them. The phenomena of bureaucratic rationalization, with its efficient pursuit of power and profit, required church doctrines and institutions to submit to *raison d'état*.[6] For centuries before the rise of atheistic, revolutionary ideologies, church institutions, and the papacy in particular, had been subjected to waves of intimidation, and at times open violence, by German, Italian, French, English, Dutch, and Spanish state-builders competing

---

4. Mt 22:15–22, Mk 12:13–17, and Lk 20:20–26.

5. Focused on what he calls the "Papal Revolution of 1075–1122," or the "Gregorian Reformation," Harold Berman makes the case that "in the West, modern times—not only modern legal institutions and modern legal values but also the modern state, the modern church, modern philosophy, the modern university, modern literature, and much else that is modern—have their origin in the period of 1050–1150 and not before." Harold J. Berman, *Law and Revolution* (Cambridge, Mass.: Harvard University Press, 1983), 4.

6. A. J. Conyers, *The Long Truce: How Toleration Made the World Safe for Power and Profit* (Dallas: Spence Publishing, 2001).

for hegemony on the chessboard of Europe. Government influence over religious institutions became the norm in northern Europe and England after the so-called "Wars of Religion," which were ostensibly ended by the Peace of Westphalia in 1648. The term "Wars of Religion" itself was part of an instrumentalized discourse to marginalize religion. It was clear in those wars that Protestant princes supported Catholic forces, and Catholic princes supported Protestant forces whenever dictated by *raison d'état*. Without resorting to a formal break with Rome à la Henry VIII, similarly motivated Gallican and Josephist policies, in France and Austria respectively, were no less effective at controlling national episcopates and marginalizing papal interference in political affairs.

The modern shift in authority, not just political but also moral and educational, away from church and toward state occurred in the context of aggressive realpolitik among state-builders. But it was also facilitated among educated elites whose thinking was increasingly molded by optimism concerning the progress of science, technology, and material civilization. A faith in progress per se, and in the perfectability of humanity, offered an alternative worldview to the theology of sin and redemption. The idea became widespread in the eighteenth-century Enlightenment that moral and political "sciences" would track the progress of natural science.[7] Whether drawing on idealistic, dualistic, or materialistic metaphysics, it became a commonplace among educated elites that a Newton of society, or a Newton of the mind, would appear and that the elimination of human conflict and suffering was just over the horizon—since, it was supposed, human misbehavior derived from competition over unscientifically managed material resources or from unscientific thinking.

On the same historical axis as the modern state's development of absolutist institutions with the support of a subservient religious bureaucracy—the Throne and Altar ideology from the Throne's point of view—there was a growing secularization of educated elites, who fell

---

7. See especially the essay of Marie-Jean-Antoine-Nicolas Caritat, Marquis de Condorcet, *Outlines of an Historical View of the Progress of the Human Mind: Being a Posthumous Work of the Late M. De Condorcet*. Translated from the French. (Philadelphia: M. Carey, 1796). Or, for example, Immanuel Kant's essays, "An Answer to the Question: What is Enlightenment?" (1784) and "To Perpetual Peace: A Philosophical Sketch" (1795), in Immanuel Kant, *Perpetual Peace and Other Essays on Politics, History and Moral Practice*, trans. Ted Humphrey (Indianapolis: Hackett Publishing, 1983).

more and more under the sway of rationalist philosophical assumptions. The takeoff of the European economic system, in all its dimensions, inspired and seemed to justify confidence in the unlimited powers of independent reason. A collision course was set between absolutist state institutions with their growing financial demands, and the interests of the rising capitalist classes, who grew increasingly hostile to government exactions and the arbitrary exercise of authority. Political revolution, occurring across Europe, varying from context to context, was inevitable in such conditions. After the worst excesses of the French Revolution, the effort of Napoleon to restore the Throne and Altar status quo ante by the Concordat of 1801 with Pius VII was bound to be of little avail.[8]

From the point of view of the Catholic Church, broadly speaking, there had been a failure of intellectual engagement with the tides of modern development, posing, as they did, such profound challenges. In the areas of greatest sociocultural dynamism, the minority status of the church (as in Great Britain), or its manipulation and persecution (as in France), explains much of this failure.

After the French revolutionary experiment in Cartesian government had run its course, leaving millions dead and the continental economy and society in shambles, there was a period during which Catholic thinkers had the freedom, and indeed felt the duty, to try to make sense of the infernal upheaval. Catholic Traditionalist thinkers at the time diagnosed the disaster quite differently than did Bonapartists, Jacobins, or classical Liberals. They identified Enlightenment abuse of reason and rejection of religious authority as the eye of the revolutionary storm, around which all else had spun out of control. Traditionalist thinkers became convinced on this account that only a revitalization of the faith of the people and submission to the authority of the pope— the base and summit of European order—could prevent the recurrence of the murderous anarchy of their times.[9]

---

8. Henri Daniel-Rops, *The Church in an Age of Revolution*, trans. John Warrington (London: J.M. Dent & Sons, Ltd., 1965), 54–58; and more generally, Frank J. Coppa, *The Papacy Confronts the Modern World* (Malabar, Fla.: Krieger Publishing, 2003), chaps. 1–3.

9. Owen Chadwick, *The Popes and European Revolution* (Oxford: Clarendon Press, 1981), chap. 5.

In the confused political arena following Napoleon's defeat, conservative Catholics were in no position to attempt a return to the prerevolutionary situation. Royalists in France and elsewhere were rarely sympathetic in any significant way to the losses in church prestige, property, and power that the revolution had wrought. The victorious powers of the Congress of Vienna were Protestant (English), Orthodox (Russian) and Josephist (Austro-Hungarian), and in defeated France, the Gallican heritage was still strong among the hierarchy (if not among the younger clergy, divided as they were on the basis of their varying social and political experiences under the imperial regime). Spain, backward developmentally, was in the process of losing its empire and becoming a less important player in Europe. Even though he was influenced by conservative Catholic political thought, Metternich, the chief architect of the Congress of Vienna, applied the Troppau Doctrine on legitimism and interventionism prudentially, in the religious as well as the political sphere.[10] Catholic political conservatives generally believed it unreasonable to try to undo the material losses incurred by the church, as they were more concerned with the spiritual-cultural legacy of Jacobinism as the main threat to European society.[11]

Traditionalists and Liberals in the Restorationist Period

With the defeat of the French revolutionary and Napoleonic enterprises, the church's first task was to find a way of recovering its autonomy in the wake of the widespread Throne and Altar arrangements that had characterized the Old Regime but that were no longer serving Throne or Altar well. The sociocultural and political impact of the 1789 revolution and the Napoleonic Empire was such that French ideological and political vicissitudes continued to largely dictate the rhythms of political life throughout

---

10. Bela Menczer, ed., *Catholic Political Thought, 1789–1848 Selected Texts* (London: Burns, Oates and Washbourne Ltd., 1953), 136–56. Also see Chadwick, *The Popes and European Revolution*, 536–38.

11. Cristina Cassina, "L'obsession interminable: La révolution française dans la littérature ultra-royaliste au début de la Restauration" [The unending obsession: The French Revolution in Ultraroyalist literature at the beginning of the Restoration], *Storia della storiografia* 27, no. 1 (1995): 17–38.

the whole of Europe for much of the nineteenth century. In the Restoration era, the political thinking of Pope Gregory XVI was dominated by a reliance on the bulwark of the temporal sword at a time when, with good reason, the "religious question" seemed of first importance. Only in due time was the church at liberty (and indeed was obliged to by the course of events) to reflect on how best to guide the social, charitable, cultural, and political work of what is referred to in nineteenth-century European historiography as the "Catholic Movement."

In the first half of the nineteenth century, after the restoration of the monarchies in 1815, debates among Catholic lay activists and academicians over issues of economy, society, and politics flourished, even more with the inception of the Orleanist dynasty in France after 1830. It was inevitable that in such a period of instability and paradigm interregnum, misunderstandings, missteps, and conflicts should occur among various influential Catholic groupings, and between these groupings and the church hierarchy. Certain crucial clarifications had been made by mid-century, de facto through force of circumstances—the Throne and Altar political paradigm of the Old Regime was no more revivable in the new reality than that of the Three Estates of the *Ancien régime* political-religious imagination (i.e., those who pray, those who fight, those who work the land). Conservative Catholic intellectual paradigms began to take on new life once detached from the Royalist cause, and over time provided an important lens through which CST came to be interpreted, *inter medium montium*, amidst classical liberal and socialist paradigms.

The great ideological divide that the church was called to address was roughly between laissez-faire liberalism and varieties of socialism. In the Restoration period, 1815 to 1830, an aristocratic, royalist, and conservative ideology continued to dominate much of continental politics, but the aristocratic cause suffered setbacks with revolutionary uprisings in 1820–21 (in Spain, Naples, and Piedmont), and then became increasingly sidelined after the European-wide revolutions of 1830. In intellectual, aesthetic, and spiritual terms, the wave of Romantic reaction against Enlightenment rationalistic excesses found expression in Catholic thought as well. The political parties that emerged from the French revolutionary era featured ideologies and regime preferences that ranged from Ultraroyalists and Legitimists,

Constitutional Monarchists, moderate Liberals and anticlerical Liberals, to Radical Republicans and Democrats, and by mid-century, with the growth of an industrial proletariat on the Continent, also Socialists and Communists became important political forces. Restoration-era Catholics were to be found across these political camps, with tendencies that ranged from conservative to laissez-faire liberal to socialist, largely conditioned by class affiliation—aristocratic, bourgeois, or working class. However, Radical Republicans and Socialists of the Jacobin tradition, who held an Enlightenment worldview of the atheist variety, were totally opposed to any cooperation with Catholics whatsoever.[12]

Catholic political ideas during this period, which played a considerable role in the development of modern CST, were related to political affiliation. A rather polemical primary categorization involved three groups: "liberal Catholics," "conservative" or "Ultramontane" Catholics, and "just plain Catholics," as Louis Veuillot put it.[13] But it is necessary to be clear—"Catholic Liberals," Catholics who happened to be Liberals in politics and economics (and might simultaneously be conservative and Ultramontane in their religious beliefs and ecclesiology) must be distinguished from "liberal Catholics" who held liberal, progressive ideas about the direction of modernity and the nature of ecclesial authority, ideas that were connected to the Enlightenment critique of religion. Self-identified liberal Catholics might refer to conservative Catholics as Ultramontanists, Zealots, or Intransigents, depending on the country and issues involved. Ultramontanists, Catholics who particularly emphasized the necessity of papal independence and leadership in the church, tended to be Royalists during the Restoration period (1815–1830) and supporters of reviving the alliance between Throne and Altar, albeit favoring papal supremacy.

One person dominated Catholic political-religious thought in the Restoration era: Joseph de Maistre.[14] His *Considérations sur la France*, published in 1796 while he was in exile in Lausanne, set forth an

---

12. Ralph Gibson, "Why Republicans and Catholics Couldn't Stand Each Other in the Nineteenth Century," in *Religion, Society and Politics in France Since 1789*, ed. Frank Tallett and Nicholas Atkin (London: Hambledon Press, 1991).
13. Louis Veuillot, *L'Illusion libérale* (Paris: Palmé, 1866), 5–10.
14. Gabriele De Rosa, *Storia del movimento cattolico in Italia* (Bari: Laterza, 1988), 1–16.

understanding of political developments as conforming to divine will.[15] Maistre, who spent the subsequent sixteen years of the Napoleonic period as the representative of King Victor Amadeus of Piedmont to the czar in St. Petersburg, elaborated his analysis of the chastisements being suffered by revolutionary Europe with undeniable style and persuasive force. He predicted the dehumanized dictatorships that the future held in store should there not be a return to the foundations of true order based on religion and pious monarchy.[16]

Maistre and other Traditionalists—including contemporaries Louis de Bonald and François-René de Chateaubriand—described the roots of the revolutionary conflagration in Europe as stemming from the moral decadence of both the ruling and popular classes, which in turn had its source in the rebellion of the spirit and intellect propagated by the philosophes.[17] The excesses of 1789 and the Terror were but the natural consequence of tearing down conventions and norms derived from church and society over centuries in favor of the tabula rasa of abstract reason. This was a thesis already presciently advanced before the Terror by Edmund Burke in *Reflections on the Revolution in France* (1790), which Maistre had read within a few months of its publication.[18] As opposed to Burke, arguably an orthodox Whig of Lockean sentiments,[19] Maistre had broad scientific, philosophical-epistemological, historical, and theological interests. For him, the horrors of the Revolution were, at a deep level, the manifestation of a providential and redemptive purpose.[20] Maistre's philosophical approach was unsystematic but, particularly in his *Essai sur le*

---

15. Joseph de Maistre, *Considerations on France*, trans. and ed. Richard A. Lebrun (Cambridge: Cambridge University Press, 1994), and see also his *Essai sur le principe générateur des constitutions politiques et des autres institutions humaines* (Paris: Société Typographique, 1814).
16. Joseph de Maistre, *Du pape* (Lyons: Chez Rusand, 1819); see Daniel-Rops, *The Church in an Age of Revolution*, 123–24.
17. Cassina, "L'obsession interminable," 34–35; Daniel-Rops, *The Church in an Age of Revolution*, 122–26.
18. Richard A. Lebrun, "Joseph de Maistre and Edmund Burke: A Comparison," in *Joseph de Maistre's Life, Thought, and Influence: Selected Studies*, ed. Richard A. Lebrun (Montreal: McGill-Queen's University Press, 2001), 153–72.
19. Frederick A. Dreyer, *Burke's Politics: A Study in Whig Orthodoxy* (Waterloo, Ontario: Wilfrid Laurier University Press, 1979), 68–83.
20. Cassina, "L'obsession interminable," 32–33.

Principe Générateur des Constitutions Politiques (1809, 1814) and *Soirées de Saint-Pétersbourg* (1821), incorporated elements of a sociological-political theory perceptibly influenced by Montesquieu, akin to the Burkean idea that constitutions develop as the result of historical conditions and precedents. Traditionalists like Maistre, Bonald, Chateaubriand, and others were not merely Romantic reactionaries. Informed by echoes of the medieval Scholastic view of human nature, they sought to understand the connections between culture, economy, society, and politics. They sought to diagnose the roiling trajectory of their times and to imagine possibilities for authentic progress.[21]

Traditionalists rejected that part of the Enlightenment and Encyclopedist heritage that they considered to have resulted from the *abuse* of reason. Their analysis traced the history of the concept of reason—the human faculty for judgment—from Descartes's shaky attempt to ground sure knowledge on the reasoning of the *cogito* to its withering under the wicked irony of Voltaire. Reason reified, whether in Rousseau's Romanticism or in Condorcet's Scientism, led inevitably, many conservative Catholics believed, to its diabolical instrumentalization in the hands of Robespierre or the Committee of Public Safety.

One of the most eloquent critics of the philosophe rebellion, who more forcefully than others cast blame on Martin Luther's defiance for giving birth to the long march of independent reason that culminated in the moral and material catastrophe of 1789, was Félicité de Lamennais. His ideological commitments changed radically over time from Traditionalist to democratic socialist, ending in a break with the Catholic Church. If there was a second voice to Maistre's in influence and renown in Restoration Catholic Europe, it was that of the Abbé Félicité de Lamennais. The emotional and aesthetic force of Chateaubriand's rehabilitation of Christianity in his *Génie du Christianisme* (1802) attracted the enthusiasm of a generation of disaffected Catholics, including young intellectuals like Lamennais. In his minor works before 1815, Lamennais argued that only a religious revival and regeneration of the church in France could counter the practical atheism of the times. His

---

21. Christopher Olaf Blum, *Critics of the Enlightenment: Readings in the French Counter-Revolutionary Tradition* (Wilmington, Del.: ISI Books, 2004), xv–xxxv.

major apologetical work, *Essay on Indifference in Matters of Religion* (1817), traced the genealogy of state toleration and religious indifference to Luther's elevation of private judgment, and it argued that hope for Europe could only be found in a restoration of church authority. Warmly received in the Vatican, Leo XII reportedly offered him the cardinalate, which he declined.

Still an ardent opponent of liberalism after the revolutions of 1820–21, by the late 1820's Lamennais came to believe that there was no hope of reforming the Royalist-Gallican political-religious alliance; that is, that the Throne and Altar arrangement was never going to operate in an Ultramontane direction no matter who was on the French throne. In a serious reversal of thinking, he gradually embraced the liberal Catholic cause of complete separation of church and state, perhaps inspired by developments in Belgium, where Ultramontanist ideas and liberal political reforms seemed a successful paradigm—but without considering the unique matrix of historical factors there versus those of France. Founding the journal *L'Avenir* in 1830 under the motto *"Dieu et Liberté,"* Lamennais gathered around himself powerful intellects such as Jean-Baptiste Henri-Dominique Lacordaire and Charles Forbes René de Montalembert. This group around *L'Avenir* believed that the best principles of the Revolution were nothing but the secular expression of evangelical ideals. Advocating freedom of speech, freedom of the press, freedom of association, freedom of education at all levels, separation of church and state, and universal suffrage, they believed the application of these liberal principles would lead to political stability but also to the purification and regeneration of the church and the advancement of a renewed Christian civilization.

Lamennais had been able to persuade Pius VIII to look benignly on the liberal revolution of 1830 in France so long as Louis-Philippe respected the religion of the people—or, read more cynically, maintained the bulwark of faith against social revolution.[22] The pope could consider the replacement of the Bourbon dynasty by Louis-Phillipe tolerable, barring hostility of the new regime to religious interests. But Lamennais was

---

22. Cf. Harry Hearder, *Italy in the Age of the Risorgimento, 1790–1870* (London: Longman, 1983), 283–85.

also personally voicing support for other Catholic populations in their struggles for religious freedom under non-Catholic sovereigns—the Irish (with O'Connell), the Poles, and the Belgians, for example—showing his tendency toward a subjective rights theory of rebellion that could not sit well with Rome. While Lamennais's Ultramontanism alienated the French hierarchy, at the same time his increasing liberalism ended up alienating even the sympathetic Pope Gregory XVI in 1832. *L'Avenir*'s open support for the Belgian, Irish, and Polish revolutions in 1830 and 1831 left the new pope with little choice but to condemn such liberalism, raised as it was to the level of a principle.[23] Despite his nearly paternal affection for Lamennais, Gregory was still the absolute monarch of a territorial state that no one in the church was yet contemplating relinquishing. Gregory could not tolerate advocacy of the rights of conscience or a free press as unqualified principles, and especially not a right of rebellion such as Lamennais was advocating.[24]

The church's response to Lamennais's subjective and democratic turn was symptomatic of the hierarchy's lack of a comprehensive theoretical and practical approach to the challenges that modernization posed to the faith and to the church. Catholic social and political thought in the period of the Restoration was complicated by the fact that existing side by side with currents of Romantic and Traditionalist religious thought (with its anti-rationalism bordering on fideism) and conservative political thought, there also continued a tradition of Enlightenment rationalist or "modernist" liberal Catholic thought that believed doctrinal accommodations to the changing conditions of culture and society were necessary. If these latter voices were little heard in the antirevolutionary, conservative, and Romantic atmosphere of the early Restoration, certainly sociocultural and political conditions changed with the revolutions of 1830 in France, Belgium, Italy, and elsewhere. The political standing of liberal Catholics began to gain strength. The Throne and Altar paradigm of political and religious order had lost much of its power to move hearts, even though

---

23. Henry Haag, "The Political Ideas of Belgian Catholics (1789–1914)," in *Church and Society: Catholic Social and Political Thought and Movements, 1789–1950*, ed. Joseph N. Moody (New York: Arts, Inc., 1953), 281–98.

24. E. E. Y. Hales, *Revolution and Papacy, 1769–1846* (New York: Doubleday & Company, 1960), 288–94.

European princes continued to invoke the rights and privileges of the old tradition where convenient. Yet there was hardly an adequate paradigm in the offing that was not laissez-faire liberal or socialist of one sort or another.

Under the bourgeois-dominated "July Monarchy" of Louis-Philippe (1830–1848), Ultramontane Catholics and Catholic Liberals rallied together to fight for religious freedom and private education. Some Catholics followed the eccentric spiritual-political path of Abbé Lamennais as he went from Ultramontane Royalist to Ultramontane Liberal, finally leaving the church as a democratic socialist. The revolutionary outbreaks of 1848 saw other alignments emerge, especially the fusionist, antirevolutionary "Party of Order" during the short-lived Second Republic in France (1848–51). The Party of Order included leading secular-minded Liberals and Conservatives, and also Catholics of both Liberal and Ultramontane sentiments. Their slogan, "Order, Property, Religion," signified their adherence to priorities that were problematic for Ultramontanists, who tended to reject factional allegiances, focused as they were on protecting the rights of the church.

The singularly effective polemicist Louis Veuillot was a potent and consistent example of an Ultramontane Catholic. The newspaper he edited, *L'Univers*, was in the forefront of the struggle for freedom of Catholic education from 1840 to 1850, and he minced no words in exposing what he saw as the atheistic and despotic program of the state monopoly in force beginning in 1789. Veuillot's sarcasm and brilliant exposés of his opponents' bad faith led him into frequent conflict with the directorship of the paper, which included some of the most prominent leaders of the liberal Catholic movement in France, including Montalembert, Lacordaire, De Coux, Guéranger, and Dupanloup. The cyclone around *L'Univers* was a microcosm of the complexity of lay and clerical political and religious opinion from 1830 to 1870. Veuillot had announced the arrival of a new, activist laity in his *De L'Action des Laïques dans la Question Religieuse* of 1843,[25] though the roots of changing lay Catholic opinion reached back to the early Restoration and into the late Empire. For Veuillot, wayward ecclesiastical authorities were

---

25. *De l'action des laïques dans la question religieuse* [On the action of the laity in the religious question] (Paris: Bureau de L'Univers, 1843).

not above criticism in the public square. Veuillot's engagement with church politics points to an important, objective turning point in modern thinking about both the church and the role of the faithful in society, a development in the history of what was then called the "religious question." The rise of mass production, mass communication, and the beginnings of mass culture fostered a totally new mass involvement of the Catholic laity, *qua* Catholics, in political, social, economic, cultural, political-religious, and even strictly religious issues.[26]

It was against this backdrop of tremendous turmoil—economic, social, political, and cultural—that Taparelli's engagement with the philosophy of Aquinas and of the later Scholastics began, developed, and shaped his natural law science of society. Taparelli's career as a central figure in the neo-Thomist revival grew from his first introduction to the Angelic Doctor in 1816, to his formalization of Scholastic philosophy as a basis for the restoration of Christian philosophy in the 1820s, to his fostering a circle of neo-Thomist scholars and protégés that gained momentum through the 1820s and 1830s, and then to his major neo-Thomist natural law treatise expounded in the 1840s and the practical divulgation of his work in the pages of the *Civiltà Cattolica* in the 1850s until his death in 1862. Aquinas's philosophy and theology had been instrumental at the Council of Trent at the beginning of the Catholic Reformation in the sixteenth century and his works were adopted as the foundation for Jesuit education. But from the seventeenth century onward, the Scholastics had generally been neglected and even fallen into disrepute, primarily in Protestant countries as was to be expected, but also in Catholic countries and in many Catholic universities and seminaries. Vestiges did persist, particularly in the area of natural law. The modern reversal of classical ideas about the nature of man and of political society can be said to have begun with Machiavelli and Hobbes, but some liberal ideas and arguments from Scholastic natural law reasoning had come down to eighteenth- and nineteenth-century intellectuals via inconsistent borrowings by major classical liberal thinkers. The thought of Adam Smith, for instance, displayed the influence of a genealogy that

---

26. Emile Poulat, *Église contre bourgeoisie: Introduction au devenir du catholicisme actuel* (Paris: Casterman, 1977).

led through Pufendorf and Grotius to Vitoria and other Hispanic Scholastics, reaching back to Aquinas.[27] The political thought of John Locke linked to Aquinas more directly, through Richard Hooker.[28] Outside of academic settings, where the idealist, dualist, or materialist rationalism of Descartes, Locke, Kant, or Hegel held sway, a range of eclectic intellectual figures found large audiences for their publications and lectures. Popular professors or public intellectuals like Victor Cousin and Vincenzo Gioberti (Lamennais was also a prime example), spoke to Catholics looking to reconcile their religion with their experiences of modernity. And there were others with more radical proposals, though not from dissimilar roots, for a religion *of* modernity, such as Auguste Comte, John Stuart Mill, and Karl Marx.

Eclecticism and Taparelli's "Conversion" to Scholastic Philosophy

Taparelli's philosophical turn to Scholasticism, which would heavily inform the development of modern CST, originated with reforms in Catholic higher education and the seminary training of priests—such reforms being a top priority, frequently reiterated, of all the nineteenth-century popes. The Collegio Romano seminary was returned to the Jesuits in 1824 by Pope Leo XII. The Society of Jesus was officially reestablished by Pius VII in 1814—it had been suppressed in 1773 ("forever extinguished"), by Pope Clement XIV under political pressure from the absolute monarchs of France, Spain, Portugal, and Naples. Taparelli was the first rector of the restored college, and he had already been introduced to Aquinas's philosophy as a Jesuit novice by Serafino Sordi in 1816.[29] Taparelli prepared a report in 1827 documenting what he saw as the intellectual confusion that prevailed at the Collegio Romano because of the abandonment of the

---

27. Alejandro A. Chafuen, *Faith and Liberty: The Economic Thought of the Late Scholastics* (Lanham, Md.: Lexington Books, 2003).

28. Peter Munz, *The Place of Hooker in the History of Thought* (London: Routledge & Kegan Paul, 1952).

29. Leonard E. Boyle, OP, "A Remembrance of Pope Leo XIII: The Encyclical *Aeterni Patris*," in *One Hundred Years of Thomism, Aeterni Patris and Afterwards: A Symposium*, ed. Victor B. Brezik, CSB, (Houston: Center for Thomistic Studies, 1981), 7–22.

Aristotelian-Thomistic philosophical system.[30] He argued for a return to the sound doctrines which had formed the basis of the Society since the first *Ratio Studiorum* promulgated in 1586. In particular, he proposed that in order to combat the corrosive influence of Cartesian universal doubt on intellectual and moral certainty, the course of study at the Collegio Romano be reoriented to return to the metaphysics of the Scholastics.[31]

Taparelli explained the origin of his ideas in the light of what he later, in the introduction to his magnum opus, termed the "scientific revolution" that had overturned "Lockean sensism" and opened the possibility for a new foundation for metaphysics. German "transcendental idealism" and Scottish common sense realism (as in Reid) had combined in the French cultural crucible to produce an eclectic, syncretistic school that enjoyed huge success among Catholics of the Restoration "eager to throw off the yoke of Locke and Condillac."[32] It was this success of the "eclectic" school, led by Victor Cousin, that stimulated the revival of Catholic metaphysical studies aimed at resolving conflicting claims over the relationship between natural reason and supernatural revelation, a question that was at the heart of a number of doctrinal and even political controversies.[33] Taparelli's more strictly theological concerns involved the triangular arguments in theology between Traditionalists, moderate Traditionalists (who accepted the post-Kantian metaphysics and the idea of the necessity of noumenal revelation, or "intuitionism," as respected theological science), and, eventually, the neoscholastics. These developments prompted Taparelli's "conversion" to Thomism in the early 1820s.[34]

---

30. "Osservazioni sugli Studii del Collegio Romano," 1827, Archivio della Civiltà Cattolica (hereafter ACC), file "Difesa della Scolastica," box not numbered, n. 20.

31. "Abbozzo del Progetto d'Ordinazione intorno agli Studii Supp," ACC, file 7b1, box 8, n. 3.

32. *Saggio*, p. 3.

33. Jean-René Derré, *Lamennais: Ses amis et le mouvement des idées a l'époque romantique* (Paris: Librairie C. Klincksieck, 1962).

34. Gerald McCool, *Nineteenth-Century Scholasticism: The Search for a Unitary Method* (New York: Fordham University Press, 1989), 25–36, 56–58. See also, generally, Amato Masnovo, *Il neo-tomismo in Italia* (Milan: Soc. Ed. Vita e Pensiero, 1923); Roger Aubert, *Aspects divers du néo-thomisme sous le pontificat de Léon XIII* (Rome: Ed. 5 Lune, 1961); Paolo Dezza, *Alle origini del neo-tomismo* (Milan: Fratelli Bocca, 1940); Luciano Malusa, *Neotomismo e intransigentismo cattolico* (Milan: Ist. Propaganda Libraria, 1986).

Taparelli's own account of this conversion in 1825 leaves no doubt about his motivation: metaphysical confusion was dangerous to sound theology and to morality.[35] Taparelli argued that the post-Cartesian abandonment of the hylomorphism of Aristotle and Aquinas came at a steep cultural and political price. He held that unlike the natural sciences, where differences of opinion have no effect on the actual course of nature, mistaken metaphysical assumptions have an inescapable bearing on the direction of individual wills, leading to disorder in society.[36] Taparelli identified the chief cultural-ideological problem for modernity as abstract reasoning run amok. Overcoming the confusion unleashed by Cartesian dualism was his immediate concern: "Philosophy in assigning the causes of the being and action of Man, must necessarily attribute them either to the soul alone or to the body alone, or to both to the extent that they are united. Cartesian philosophy attributes all of the bodily action to the body alone, animated action to the soul."[37]

Taparelli was unapologetic about his path to Aristotle and Aquinas through the teachings of the French eclectics. Other early indications of Taparelli's developing philosophical ideas were written in response to specific challenges; for example, in "Osservazioni sulla filosofia" (Observations on philosophy)[38] a polemical response from around 1829 to one of his Collegio Romano critics, and "Corso di filosofia moderna" (Course of modern philosophy),[39] probably from around 1832 when he was charged with teaching an elementary philosophy course at the Royal Convent of Lecce. These documents show again his central concern for promoting the concept of hylomorphism and his readiness to defend the inspiration for the eclectics' ideas, incomplete and potentially confusing as they might be, but which he believed could be harmonized with Catholic doctrine.

---

35. Pirri, *Carteggi del Padre Taparelli*, 712–18, esp. 717.
36. ACC, "Abbozzo del Progetto."
37. "La Filosofia nello assegnarci le cause dell'essere ed operazioni dell'Uomo, dee necessariamente attribuirle o all'anima sola o al corpo solo, o ad entrambi in quanto congiunte. La filosofia cartesiana attribuisce tutta l'azione corporea al corpo solo, l'azione animata all'anima." "Ai lettore di Filsofia cattolica, In che consiste essenzialmente quella che chiamasi Filosofia degli Scolastici," ACC, box 8, n. 4.
38. "Osservazioni sulla filosofia," ACC, box 8, n. 3.
39. "Corso di Filsofia moderna," ACC, box A9.

He understood that rebuilding Catholic moral philosophy, his chief concern, would be dependent on the work of many experts and would take time. Presumably from 1827, if not sooner, Taparelli formed a clandestine study circle on the works of Aquinas at the Collegio Romano. Vincenzo Gioacchino Pecci, the future Pope Leo XIII, was then a student at the Collegio and an assistant to Taparelli, and in 1828 he requested the complete works of Aquinas from his family's library.[40] Fifty years later, Leo XIII would issue *Aeterni Patris* (*On the Restoration of Christian Philosophy*, 1879), which he stated was concerned with "the restoration in Catholic schools of Christian philosophy according to the mind of St. Thomas Aquinas, the Angelic Doctor."[41]

The course of Taparelli's early advocacy of neo-Thomistic studies led to his transfer from Rome, first to Naples and then to Palermo. As rector of the seminary in Naples, he encouraged neo-Thomist scholars like the Sordi brothers and others, including his eventual protégé Matteo Liberatore. Domenico Sordi teaching Aquinas on natural law and kingship in Naples, however, made the absolute monarch of the Kingdom of the Two Sicilies nervous enough to call in the censors. It is not clear that the subsequent orders from Taparelli's superiors moving him again, which had the appearance of an effort to marginalize him, were signs of an opposition among some Jesuits (Suarezians or Cartesians), or an appeasement of the Bourbons, or mere administrative expediency—because apart from other considerations, Taparelli did not have a good record of practical management.[42] The result of his transfer in the late 1830s to Palermo, in any case, was felicitous viewed in retrospect.

Taparelli's *Saggio* was the fruit of his responsibilities at the Collegio Massimo in Palermo, where he was assigned to teach a course in natural law. It was Taparelli's opinion that none of the contemporary natural law textbooks were suitable; for example, those authored by popularizers like the Swiss Jean-Jacques Burlamaqui and the German Johann Gottlieb Heineccius. He spent the first year of the course refuting or heavily critiquing the works of the modern natural law theorists, including Grotius,

40. Jacquin, *Taparelli*, 57n152.
41. Boyle, "A Remembrance," 7n1.
42. Jacquin, *Taparelli*, 65–67.

Pufendorf, Hobbes, Locke, and Rousseau. After that year, he decided, at the urging of his superiors, to put together his own manual, which he published between 1840 and 1843. The time-constrained conditions under which the first edition of the *Saggio* was prepared were significantly different from Taparelli's next decade of study, during which he prepared subsequent Italian editions, directly oversaw the first French edition, and expanded and reorganized the definitive edition of 1855.[43] Some commentators have taken a brief note to a young seminarian, who had asked for some guidance in his studies, written in 1862, the last year of Taparelli's life, as a precise account of his intellectual development justifying a dismissive attitude toward his treatise, but this is a mistake. Such a judgment overlooks Taparelli's intellectual engagement in the Thomistic revival for some twenty years before the first edition of his *Saggio*, and it minimizes his studies and the quantity of his writings in the 1840s and 1850s (which exploded in the 1850s in the *Civiltà Cattolica*), including his revisions and updates to the *Saggio* in 1855. What is actually evident from this note is Taparelli's humble and gentle disposition—which, to be fair, would be hard to imagine from the often polemical tone of his published writings, but which is very clear in his personal correspondence. His description, then, of his reading prior to 1840 must be taken in context and with a large grain of salt:

> That little good that the *Saggio teoretico* might accomplish is not the fruit of either deep study nor of much reading. Up to age 50, I never dreamed (and my ill health was enough to dissuade me from it) of being either a professor or a writer. At that age, I was sent to Sicily to teach natural law, and handed that saddest Burlamacchi, quite dishonest as an adorer of the temporal power, who paid attention to nothing else than the interests of the government. Thus for that first year I did nothing else but confute Burlamacchi. The following year I protested to superiors that teaching in this manner was more betraying the young people than instructing them. And they responded that I should write my own course. Thus was born the *Saggio*, that in its form

43. *Saggio*, p. XV.

shows itself to be improvised ... without premeditated design, without symmetry of parts. ...

... As the theories emerged, the rock standard, to assure myself not to have been mistaken, was always to compare them with St. Thomas. ... Thus I came to recognize that this science finds itself already beautifully accomplished in the Scholastics, and particularly in St. Thomas, Suarez, Bellarmine, Vitoria, etc.[44]

Taparelli was persuaded that the science of natural law needed to be restructured from the ground up because of the historical developments that had divided the ethical and moral aspects of law from its strictly positive aspect—a division that had only served the interests of the temporal power. As a consequence of this split between ethics and law, Taparelli argued, temporal rulers no longer concerned themselves with issues of morality or with public or private virtue. The people reacted in kind, elevating private interests over public morality. In this way, Taparelli suggested, modern political theory about rights and obligations had become reduced, as a logical consequence and in practice, to the justification of sovereign will and brutish calculations of self-interest.[45]

Taparelli's answer to the ideological tendencies of the developing political, social, and economic sciences was to apply a method that integrated the philosophical realism of the Scholastics, including deductive reasoning from sound first principles, with modern empirical methods

---

44. Quel po' di bene che va facendo il *Sagio teorico* [sic] non è frutto nè di studi profondi, nè di molta lettura. Fino a cinquant'anni io non avea sognato mai (e bastava l'inferm salute a dissuadermelo) di essere nè professore, nè scrittore. Giunto a quell'età fui destinato in Sicilia a insegnare Diritto di natura, [sic] e postomi in mano quel tristissimo Burlamacchi malamente corretto da un adoratore del potere temporale, il quale a null'altro avea badato se non agli interessi del governo. Sicchè per quel primo anno altro non feci, che confutare Burlamacchi. L'anno seguente rimostrai ai superiori che insegnare in questo modo era piuttosto tradire i giovani che un istruirli. Ed essi risposero che scrivessi da me il mio corso. Così nacque il *Saggio*, che nella stessa sua forma si mostra improvvisato, ...senza disegno premeditato, senza simmetria di partizioni...." and,"... A misura poi che le teorie nascevano, la pietra di paragone, per assicurarmi di non avere sbagliato, era sempre di confrontarle con S. Tommaso. ...Così mi avvenne di riconoscere che questa scienza si trova già bella e fatta negli scolastici, e particolarmente in S. Tommaso, Suarez, Bellarmine, Vitoria, ecc. ...
Pirri, *Carteggi del Padre Taparelli*, CCCLXXII; cited in part in Jacquin, *Taparelli*, 168–69.
45. *Saggio*, §§ 9–10.

of observation and inductive reasoning for confirmation. Sound theoretical principles are applied prudentially to factual contexts, as thesis to hypothesis. He considered this move to be a return to the primordial unity of the sciences, including the human sciences.[46] His method was not at all a rejection of positive science, nor of empiricism and inductive reasoning, but a recognition that the operation of the scientific mind necessarily depends on the first science, that of Being considered in itself; otherwise, the empirical method risks conveying nothing more than an arbitrary distortion of humanity, an *ideology* of man and of state.[47]

---

46. *Saggio*, Note XXIII.

47. Heinrich Rommen affirms the significance of this turn by Taparelli, noting that he stood in the tradition of Aristotle and Aquinas, both of whom had stressed the value of observation and experience for sound natural law reasoning: "It was more than a gesture in conformity with the [scientific] spirit of the nineteenth century when Taparelli wished to construct his systematic exposition of the doctrine of natural law on the basis of experience. Indeed his labors were altogether in line with the whole tendency of the natural-law doctrine of the *philosophia perennis*." Heinrich A. Rommen, *The Natural Law: A Study in Legal and Social History and Philosophy*, rev. ed. (Carmel, Ind.: Liberty Fund, 1998), 193.

CHAPTER II

TAPARELLI AND THE REVIVAL OF SCHOLASTIC NATURAL LAW REASONING

TAPARELLI'S ROLE IN THE REVIVAL of the study of both Thomas Aquinas and the Scholastics generally is well-established among scholars. His development of a natural law science of society became a cornerstone of CST.

The Scholastic Revival: The Appeal of Thomism

To appreciate the appeal of Thomist thought to Taparelli, which began definitively with his time as rector of the Collegio Romano, and to his students and protégés facing the contemporary conflict of ideologies that challenged both Christian faith and institutional church, it is worth reviewing the relevant basic tenets of Aquinas's philosophy, both speculative and practical, at least in its outlines. This is necessarily a schematic portrayal of the pivotal points of that philosophy as appreciated by Taparelli in his own intellectual development.

Much of the elaboration of Aquinas's thought is to be found in his two great theological works, the *Summa Contra Gentiles* and the *Summa Theologiae*. Aquinas's responses to the disputes that regularly came up in the medieval university setting and his commentaries on works of Aristotle and on Boethius round out the major sources. Although there is certainly a systematic dimension to his thought, we cannot overlook the fact that in his works Aquinas was often attempting to respond to the intellectual and spiritual concerns of his day, and he did this within the context of the practical institutional considerations of the university, his religious order, and the church.[1] Resurrecting the details of the Thomist natural law system of morality was not Taparelli's goal, nor would it have been a reasonable goal since the detailed conclusions of a system founded in the concrete historical circumstances of thirteenth-century Europe would have required tremendous adaptations to both philosophical and historical developments that occurred after that time.

If the dramatic and terrible events of the French Revolution revealed the explosive potential of rapid economic, social, and political change, for many Catholic thinkers these events also revealed what they considered to be the natural consequences of disordered thinking and pointed to the need for a return to a sounder foundation for intellectual authority. One of Taparelli's chief contributions to this effort was to disentangle the political, social, and economic implications of the natural law as derived from Aquinas's writings from the Traditionalist ideological and philosophical circles in which they first obtained some purchase.

Metaphysics and Epistemology

Choosing where one should begin an analysis of Aquinas's moral philosophy and natural law in the *Summa Theologiae* presents a difficult challenge. One starting point, following Gilson's emphasis, might naturally be Aquinas's metaphysics of being, his most profound and unique contribution to the history of philosophy. Taparelli follows this itinerary because he saw that the unity of, and relations between, the sciences depends on a grasp of being as being, if the study of beings of this or that sort is to be coherent.

Being, for Aquinas, is the first object known to the mind or intellect (*primum notum*) and is known immediately in itself (*per se notum*),

---

1. See Pasquale Porro, *Thomas Aquinas: A Historical and Philosophical Profile*, trans. Joseph G. Trabbic and Roger W. Nutt (Washington, D. C.: The Catholic University of America Press, 2016); Jean-Pierre Torrell, *St. Thomas Aquinas: The Person and His Work*, trans. Robert Royal (Washington, D. C.: The Catholic University of America Press, 1996); Marie-Dominique Chenu, *Toward Understanding Saint Thomas*, trans. A.-M. Landry and D. Hughes (Chicago: Henry Regnery Company, 1963). See also, generally, three books authored by Etienne Gilson: *Reason and Revelation in the Middle Ages*, rev. ed. (1938; repr., New York: Scribners, 1966); *The Spirit of Thomism* (New York: P. J. Kenedy & Sons, 1964); and *Thomist Realism and the Critique of Knowledge*, trans. Mark A. Wauck (San Francisco: Ignatius Press, 1986).

making it an evidence knowable beyond possibility of error or doubt.[2] The existence of individual beings distinct from each other is the first step, so to speak, of the intellect and in the mind leads seamlessly to formation of concepts and the ability to distinguish objects; that is, "judgment." Moreover, Aquinas's (and Taparelli's) absolute certainty about the unity of truth adds confidence to our ability to extend evidence across the whole range of human experience. There can be no conflict between faith, which takes God as the author of revelation, and reason, which in Aquinas has God as the creator of the universe and of the human intellect.[3] Aquinas thus sees reason and faith as independent yet harmonious categories: his system allows for a faith that can be complemented—through an open-ended pursuit of experimental knowledge—by reason, and a reason that can be complemented—guided ethically in the objectives and means it sets for itself—by faith. Clarifying the relationship between revealed truth and the truth available to natural reason, a perennial challenge in Judeo-Christian thought, was at the heart of Aquinas's project. The resolution of this presumed conflict is another reason for Aquinas's appeal in post-revolutionary Europe, albeit also a source of confusion and hostility (no less than in his medieval setting) between Traditionalists, Scholastics, and Rationalists.

Aquinas agrees with Aristotle that the ultimate goal of human will and of human perfection is happiness. He holds that we can know this by means of reason, but he sees the content of revelation as adding the possibility of a higher, more complete happiness than is available to us in nature. To achieve this happiness, then, we need revelation to show us the way, as a necessary supplement to the human sciences, as Aquinas points out at the very beginning of the *Summa Theologiae*.[4] This consideration forms, together with the treatment of the science of God, the science of nature, and the science of man making up the whole of the First Part, the

---

2. John F. Wippel, "Metaphysics," in *The Cambridge Companion to Aquinas*, ed. Norman Kretzmann and Eleonore Stump (Cambridge: Cambridge University Press, 1996), 85–126, discussing Thomas Aquinas, *Quaestiones Disputatae: De Veritate*, q. 1, a. 1; Thomas Aquinas, *The Summa Theologica* (New York: Benziger Brothers, 1947–48), I-II, q. 94, a. 2 (hereafter cited as *ST*).
3. Thomas Aquinas, *Summa Contra Gentiles, Book I: God*, trans. Anton C. Pegis (New York: Hanover House, 1955–57), I, 7 (hereafter cited as *SCG*).
4. *ST*, I-I, q. 1.

comprehensive foundation for the rest of Aquinas's theological and philosophical analysis. Trying to understand Aquinas's political ideas, or his natural law or moral philosophy, without this understanding of the relationship in Aquinas between revelation and reason has led to differing conclusions respecting Aquinas's intentions and coherence.[5] However, for our purposes, it is enough to recognize that for Aquinas the faith of believers supplements natural knowledge on relatively well-defined but crucial points, but at the same time can never actually conflict with natural knowledge. The relevance of any natural law social theory aimed at human flourishing in a pluralistic society is obviously a point of contention. For Taparelli, the common ground of natural reason was sufficient in any actual historical circumstance of society or government for facilitating personal and social behavior toward the common, limited goods of this world; namely, the protection of life, liberty, and the pursuit of happiness among individuals and in their multiple intermediary associations. This is the background to Taparelli's definition of social justice.

Aquinas sees the whole of reality as hierarchically ordered. Everything that exists depends on God, who is pure being or existence (*ipsum esse*).[6] God is pure being because in him essence and existence are the same.[7] In other words, being or existence is just *what God is*. All other beings ultimately derive their being from him. Whereas God *is* being, all other beings share or participate in being. Since being does not belong to the essence of the beings that have their being from God, Aquinas understands there to be a real distinction between their being and their essence.[8] Although we can attribute being to God and to the beings that

---

5. Russell Hittinger makes the point that the second part of the *Summa Theologiae* beginning at question 55, in which Aquinas discusses the virtues, emphasizes an Aristotelian ethics of virtue, and that the section on law, beginning with question 94, where Aquinas derives the first ethical precept from the first principle of practical reason, leads one to a "preceptive" ethics of a more modern or Kantian sort. Russell Hittinger, "Recovery of Natural Law and the 'Common Morality,'" *This World* 18 (Summer 1987), 62–74; Russell Hittinger, *A Critique of the New Natural Law Theory*, rev. ed. (1988; repr., South Bend, Ind.: University of Notre Dame Press, 1989).

6. *De Ente et Essentia*, trans. Robert T. Miller, (New York: Fordham University, Medieval Sourcebook Online, 1997), III, follows the Leonine Edition of Aquinas's works, *Sancti Thomae de Aquino, Opera Omnia*, vol. 43 (Rome: Dominican Friars, 1976), 368–81.

7. Ibid.

8. Ibid.

depend on him because they possess being in different ways, this attribution must be regarded as analogical.⁹

With respect to essences, it is worth pointing out that neither Aristotle nor Aquinas ever suggested that the essences of things can be known directly and in themselves, but a certain knowledge can be had of essences (if always and only indirectly) by their operations, sensible qualities, and their effects, through the power of reason.¹⁰ Faith for Aquinas and for believers does indeed offer additional knowledge of some things, primarily of God and other assertedly supernatural realities.¹¹

The instrument of knowledge with which Aquinas builds his intellectual cathedral is, of course, logic. But logic for him is much more than merely an instrument of knowledge; it is the objective part of his theory of knowledge, or, more comprehensively, the basis of his epistemology. Logic rules over judgment and represents the discursive activity of intellect. All knowledge starts from logic, beginning with the principle of non-contradiction.

Aquinas maintains the crucial Aristotelian distinction between the two chief rational activities of the mind: the speculative, aimed at truth, and the practical, aimed at the good achievable by action.¹² Speculative reason deals with abstractions and concepts, including number and forms. Practical reason concerns the pursuit of the good and the ends of the activities of rational creatures under concrete and historical circumstances. The importance of this distinction for Taparelli's natural law social science cannot be overstated.

Aquinas follows Aristotle in assuming that the intellect possesses no innate ideas, that it is a tabula rasa, and that all knowledge comes from experience: *"nihil est in intellectu quod non prius fuerit in sensu."*¹³ Locke did not discover this axiom of human psychology. Yet the first and most

---

9. *ST*, I, q. 13, a. 5.
10. Thomas Aquinas, *Quaestiones Disputatae: De Veritate, Questions 1–9*, trans. Robert W. Mulligan, SJ (Chicago: Henry Regnery, 1952), q. 1, a. 10. See also W. Norris Clarke, "Action as the Self-Revelation of Being: A Central Theme in the Thought of St. Thomas," chap. 3 in *Explorations in Metaphysics* (South Bend, Ind.: University of Notre Dame Press, 1994), 45–64.
11. *SCG*, I, 3.
12. *ST*, I, q. 79, a. 11.
13. Thomas Aquinas, *De Veritate*, q. 2, a. 3, arg. 19.

fundamental judgments are of a sort that puts them beyond doubt: that beings exist and act is derived immediately from experience, but so are the principles of non-contradiction and related axioms.[14] The further away from these first principles and from the "authority of the senses" that the deductions of judgment take one, the greater the possibility of different conclusions in different contexts and the risk of error.[15] This is a crucial aspect of the Thomist system—it leaves conclusions, especially practical ones, open to reevaluation upon the acquisition of new experience. An important point, therefore, that will become relevant in the discussion of natural law and its applications in Taparelli's theory of human action—the difference between abstract principles and concrete de facto circumstances that require an evaluation of conflicting duties and rights—is that evaluations in the practical and moral spheres inevitably involve the exercise of prudence.[16] The Scholastic system is, for all of its hierarchies and structure, an open-ended project dictated by the nature of man's inevitably progressive intellectual apprehension of the world, tied to variations in and expansions of societies and cultures; this results in the impossibility of any definitive grasp on the underpinnings of the whole of nature, precisely because of our complete, but finite, immersion in it. Taparelli, like Aquinas and like Aristotle, considers all evidence from any source whatsoever as subject to being examined for its truth content, logically and intersubjectively considered, and for its psychological weight in leading the will to action. And yet, unlike Aristotle, for Aquinas and Taparelli, despite their genuine enthusiasm for the intellectual and spiritual heights it is possible to attain by philosophy, the knowledge provided by faith remains the ultimate source for sure access to transcendent truths, from which science and even life itself can derive meaning and purpose.[17]

Aquinas accepts Aristotle's philosophical anthropology with its famous analysis of human nature in the *Nichomachean Ethics*, which

14. *ST*, I-II, q. 94, a. 2.
15. *ST*, I-II, q. 94, a. 4, and also q. 97 on judgments concerning human laws.
16. Charles O'Neil, "Prudence the Incommunicable Wisdom," in *Essays in Thomism*, ed. Robert Brennan (New York: Sheed & Ward, 1942), 85–203.
17. *ST*, I, q. 1, a. 6, ad. 2.

ranks intellectual contemplation as man's highest function, and contemplation of God as the intellect's highest object and the source of ultimate human happiness.[18] Aquinas shares fully the assumption of both Plato and Aristotle that nature can be understood from its operation.[19] Happiness is in this sense the fulfillment of the potentiality of one's essential nature. It is the apprehension of this end of human activity by the pagan philosophers that draws the special admiration of Aquinas and the other Christian philosophers, who are willing to see classical thought as a distinct kind of revelation among the Greeks that prepared them for the eventual acceptance of faith, a *praeparatio evangelica*.

Psychology and Anthropology

In Aquinas's expansion of Aristotle's psychology and anthropology, we find the incipient elements for the development of his moral philosophy, theory of natural law, and sociopolitical thought. Aquinas accepts Aristotle's hylomorphic conception of nature; that is, that material objects are the result of both material and formal causes. This doctrine eliminates the Platonic tendency toward dualistic theories, apparent even in Augustine, which has led historically to the various types of gnostic extremism, including that of Albigensianism in Aquinas's day. Descartes revives a dualistic view of the human person in conceiving of the mind and body as distinct substances—*res cogitans* and *res extensa*. But for Aquinas, the soul—the animating, vital factor of all living things, Aristotle's *psyche*—is the formal cause of a human person while the body is the material cause. The human person is, therefore, a unique and indivisible unity.[20]

In the hierarchy of souls, from vegetative to sensitive to rational, the hylomorphic theory posits a unitary substance created by the specific union of souls, as form, to bodies, as matter; Aquinas explicitly rejects

---

18. *ST*, I-II, q. 3, a. 8. Aristotle, *Nicomachean Ethics*, trans. David Ross, ed. Leslie Brown (Oxford: Oxford University Press, 2009), Book X (hereafter cited as *NE*).

19. *Questiones Disputatae: De Potentia Dei*, trans. English Dominican Fathers, rev. ed. (1932; repr., Westminster, Maryland: Newman Press, 1952) q. 2, a. 1. See also W. Norris Clarke, "Action as the Self-Revelation of Being," 45–64.

20. *ST*, I, q. 75, a. 4.

in the *Contra Gentiles* the Platonic notion that the soul is like a pilot of a craft or that a person's entire identity is summed up in his soul.[21] Thus, sensation and all the subsequent operations of the intellect and the will are operations of the entire psychophysical organism.

But while the human soul is in a sense joined to the body, it is clear to Aquinas that it also has capacities that transcend matter. Aquinas sees, for example, the acts of the intellect and the will as being performed without any bodily organ.[22] He also holds that the human soul is immortal and that it does not cease to exist when the body is corrupted.[23] Personal immortality is of course a crucial article of the Christian faith and also is intimately connected to the arguments for free will and responsibility that are the underpinnings of Catholic moral theology and social teaching.

Aquinas holds that human beings are, to some extent, free creatures; neither God's foreknowledge nor any created thing can force our choices. Although God knows everything we will do in the future, this knowledge no more forces our choice to do what we do than does our seeing Socrates sit down force his choice to have done so.[24] And because every created good is finite (that is, limited), none can attract our will to such an extent that we cannot resist its power.[25] Were we to see God in himself, of course, we could not resist him since he is pure goodness.[26] But that would be the beatific vision and, while it is our ultimate end, it is not something we can expect in this life.[27] All the other goods we seek are intermediate ends.[28]

---

21. *SCG, Book II: Creation*, trans. James F. Anderson (New York: Hanover House, 1955–57), II, 57.
22. *ST*, I, q. 75, a. 2; q. 77, a. 5.
23. *ST*, I, q. 75, a. 6.
24. Thomas Aquinas, *Peri Hermeneias* [Commentary on Aristotle's "On Interpretation"], trans. Jean T. Oesterle (Milwaukee: Marquette University Press, 1962), I, 21.
25. Thomas Aquinas, *De Malo*, trans. Richard Regan (New York: Oxford University Press, 2003), q. 6; *ST*, I, q. 105, a. 4. See Taparelli in the *Saggio* on the will, §§29–46, on intellect, reason, and free will, §§47–76, on principles of morality, §§77–102, and on practical reason and conscience, §§103–23.
26. *ST*, I, q. 82, a. 2.
27. *ST*, I-II, q. 5, a. 3.
28. *ST*, I, q. 103, a. 2.

Our choice between those particular goods, as intermediate ends, belongs to the task of moral philosophy conceived as the science of ends and means appropriate to human fulfillment.[29] Taparelli concludes that because no intellectual apprehension of the infinite good that would bind our wills is possible in this world, we are "free," at least to the extent of our impeded perception of the infinite good.

For Aristotle this science of rationally ordering actions to their ends is equivalent to ethics, but he has in mind ultimate ends—those ends that would inform one's choice of all the intermediate ends. In his eyes, intellect is at the core of man's essence. The fulfillment of intellect's potential, its ultimate end, following his reasoning in the *Nicomachean Ethics*, is the contemplation of God—to be striven after with all possible effort. Aristotle allows that the contemplative life is the best and happiest, but too lofty a goal for most because of our human, "composite nature," in view of which our next-best pursuit must be a life of practical virtue.[30]

Aquinas agrees with Aristotle concerning the limitations of the good and of the happiness attainable in this life. Our limited knowledge of

---

29. Ralph McInerny distinguishes this view of moral philosophy from the complementary science of principles and their application that characterizes the approach of the natural law. McInerny, *Ethica Thomistica* (Washington, D. C.: The Catholic University of America Press, 1997), 35, 99–102.

30. But such a life would be too high for man; for it is not in so far as he is man that he will live so, but in so far as something divine is present in him; and by so much as this is superior to our composite nature is its activity superior to that which is the exercise of the other kind of virtue. If reason is divine, then, in comparison with man, the life according to it is divine in comparison with human life. But we must not follow those who advise us, being men, to think of human things, and, being mortal, of mortal things, but must, so far as we can, make ourselves immortal, and strain every nerve to live in accordance with the best thing in us; for even if it be small in bulk, much more does it in power and worth surpass everything.
NE, X, 7.

Also,

But in a secondary degree the life in accordance with the other kind of virtue is happy; for the activities in accordance with this befit our human estate. Just and brave acts, and other virtuous acts, we do in relation to each other, observing our respective duties with regard to contracts and services and all manner of actions and with regard to passions; and all of these seem to be typically human. Some of them seem even to arise from the body, and virtue of character to be in many ways bound up with the passions. Practical wisdom, too, is linked to virtue of character, and this to practical wisdom, since the principles of practical wisdom are in accordance with the moral virtues and rightness in morals is in accordance with practical wisdom. Being connected with the passions also, the moral virtues must belong to our composite nature; and the virtues of our composite nature are human; so, therefore, are the life and the happiness which correspond to these.
NE, X, 8.

God in this life is what, in the end, makes the happiness we can now attain limited.[31] Philosophy can only point us in the direction of this limited happiness;[32] thus, if we are to attain perfect happiness, moral philosophy needs to be supplemented by guidance from revelation.[33] By employing these realist conceptions of human nature and human happiness, Taparelli sought to restore the ethical dimension to the sciences of society, politics, and economy that had been rejected by the modern theorists in pursuit of an elusive scientific objectivity. This involved considering what is required for the flourishing of a composite human nature, rescued from the one-dimensional man posited by the naturalists or rationalistic materialists.

Natural Law and Politics

The main texts of Aquinas dealing with the nature of law and natural law, and related applications of those ideas to politics, are those parts of the *Summa Theologiae* that have come to be known as the "Treatise on Law"[34] as well as the *De Regimine Principum (On Kingship)*, dedicated to the king of Cyprus in 1265.[35] The title of this section of the *Summa* can be misleading, implying a more complete analysis of law than Aquinas actually sets out to accomplish within the context of his overarching theological purpose. Aquinas begins his Treatise on Law in the *Summa Theologiae* with a definition of law in Question 90:[36]

> We can now gather from the preceding four articles the definition of a law which is nothing other than a certain dictate of reason for the Common Good, made by him who has the care of the community and promulgated.[37]

31. SCG, *Book III: Providence*, trans. Vernon J. Bourke (New York: Hanover House, 1955–57), III, 48.
32. SCG, III, 39, 63.
33. ST, I, q. 1, a. 1.
34. ST, I-II, qq. 90–97, 105.
35. Also known as *De Regno*, Aquinas is the author of only the first part of this manuscript, which he did not finish after the king's death in 1267, but which was finished by a later Dominican Scholastic, Ptolemy of Lucca (d. 1327). The citations herein are to R. W. Dyson, trans. and ed., *Aquinas: Political Writings* (Cambridge: Cambridge University Press, 2004) 5–52.
36. The following quotations from the Treatise on Law are from R. J. Henle, SJ, trans. and ed., *Saint Thomas Aquinas, The Treatise on Law: Summa Theologiae, I-II, QQ. 90–97* (South Bend, Ind.: Notre Dame University Press, 1993).
37. ST, I-II, q. 90, a. 4, in Henle, *Treatise on Law*, 145.

And of the eternal law, which amounts to the law of physics:

> Now it is clear that, granted that the world is governed by Divine providence, as was established in the First Part (q. 22, aa. 1 and 2), that the whole community of the universe is governed by Divine Reason. And, therefore, the very idea of the governance of things as it exists in God has the nature of a law.[38]

From this flows the idea of natural law, defined in I-II, q. 91, a. 2, not merely as a different kind of law but as derived from man's rational participation by design in the eternal law. The natural law has no independent dictates other than as derived from observations of the norms of the eternal arrangement of things as stamped on us and on the rest of nature. However, as rational creatures, human beings have a unique position of responsibility in God's plan, along with the accompanying means to fulfill it.

> Compared to others, the rational creature is subject to Divine Providence in a more excellent way, inasmuch as it participates in Divine Providence by providing for itself and others. Hence, it participates in the eternal plan through which it has a natural inclination to its due act and end. And this participation in the Eternal Law by the rational creature is called the Natural Law. Hence, after the Psalmist had said (Ps. IV, 6), "Offer up a sacrifice of justice" he adds, as though responding to some who asked what the works of justice are, "Many say, who shows us good things?" He answers this question by saying, "The light of your countenance, Lord, is signed upon us," as though the light of natural reason, by which we discern what is good and evil—which pertains to the Natural Law—is nothing other than an impression in us of the divine light.[39]

The first principles of the natural law hold for Aquinas the same function with respect to practical reason in its resolution of specific issues

---

38. *ST*, I-II, q. 91, a. 1, in Henle, *Treatise on Law*, 154.
39. *ST*, I-II, q. 91, a. 2, in Henle, *Treatise on Law*, 159–60. Cf. Taparelli on the character of this participation, *Saggio*, §§7–11.

in actual circumstances as the first principles of demonstration do with respect to speculative reason. Speculative reason proceeds from naturally known, indemonstrable principles to the conclusions of the various sciences, which are not innate in us but are acquired by the effort of our reason. In the same way, human practical reason must proceed from the precepts of the natural law as from certain common and indemonstrable principles to other more particular determinations.[40]

Aquinas does not limit the range of virtuous conduct to what can be deduced from the natural law, and here, as in other aspects of his philosophy, we see his openness to historical change and to progressive insight into the human condition. Apart from those good acts that are related to man's highest end, which would be part of the natural law, there are other practices to be honored that are the result of historically acquired cultural inclinations, customs, and positive law, which are not originally required by man's essence: "For many things are done in accordance with virtue to which nature does not at first incline men but have been discovered by the investigation of reason as helpful to man for living well."[41]

As he develops further in Question 94, articles 5 and 6 on natural law, there are primary precepts having "very universal" validity and secondary precepts deduced from the primary ones in the light of particular circumstances. In article 4, following Aquinas's reasoning, clearly there is a range of secondary precepts from the logically "closest" of universal conclusions obvious to all to the most distant conclusions, which pertain to highly contingent circumstances and are less certain, either in correctness or in apprehension. "The more we descend to details, the greater the chance of error.... But with reference to the particular conclusions of Practical Reason, neither is the truth the same for all nor is it equally known even to those for whom it is the same."[42] This is why prudence and not pure logic is the operative mode of reasoning in the application of the natural law to specific cases.

Taparelli sought to clarify the relationship between abstract reasoning and practical reasoning about ethical judgment that had become problematized in modern thought. The former is governed

---

40. *ST*, I-II, q. 94, a. 2, in Henle, *Treatise on Law*, 245–50.
41. *ST*, I-II, q. 94, a. 3, in Henle, *Treatise on Law*, 255.
42. *ST*, I-II, q. 94, a. 4, in Henle, *Treatise on Law*, 261.

strictly by logic, and it works upon concepts and derived principles (aimed at truth), while the latter (aimed at the good), being based on concrete historical circumstances or facts, also involves prudence. This is a key dimension of Taparelli's methodology of realist social science "based on fact." A good example of this methodological distinction is found in comparison with Aquinas's consideration of the right of private property as an addition to the natural law, which evolved out of an original community of goods as a result of the inventiveness of reason (i.e., primarily for encouraging the productivity of property and avoiding conflicts over title). Private ownership for Aquinas is legitimate for pragmatic reasons, and yet as it is a useful development in the positive law, it remains subject to the regulation by positive law.[43] Taparelli adopted a different argument, noting that the abstract natural law right of universal dominion, as a right to the means of subsistence, only ever existed in historical reality in factual, concrete relations of property holding. Thus the natural law of property has always carried with it in practice a right of personal dominion, with different possible forms under which some have always exercised the right on behalf of others. Abstract reasoning stipulates that property holding be for the benefit of all, supplying the material needs of all. This distinction of Taparelli's (which also varies from the position of the late Scholastics and from Locke[44]) implies various consequences

---

43. *ST*, II-II, q. 66, a. 2.

44. In the "Second Treatise of Government," in *Locke: Political Writings*, ed. David Wooten (Indianapolis: Hackett Publishing Company, 1993), 273–74, from chap. 5, "Of Property," §§ 25–27, Locke advances some arguments that seem similar to those of Taparelli on the original universal destination of goods, but as to the right of property, Locke's moral argument still comes down to the commixture of alleged "property" in one's body through labor with natural resources, so long as at this origin of title in property there remains "enough and as good left in common for others." Locke argues, "[t]hough the earth and all inferior creatures be common to all men, yet every man has a property in his own person. ... [w]hatsoever, then, he removes out of the state that nature hath provided and left it in, he hath mixed his labor with, and joined to it something that is his own, and thereby makes it his property" (ibid., chap. 5, §27). This is an odd conclusion in any case, since Locke previously says explicitly that we do not own ourselves, but are the property of our creator: "For men being all the workmanship of one omnipotent and infinitely wise Maker; all the servants of one sovereign Master, sent into the world by His order and about His business; they are His property...." (ibid., chap. 1, §6). In any case, Taparelli's view is that property rights are concretely necessary conventional determinations (personal in places, communal in others) of the abstract right to the means of sustaining life. Property holding remains subject to conflicts of rights and prudential determinations concerning the common good properly understood. *Saggio*, §§398–420.

for the kind of positive law regulations that might be just—as will be discussed.

Aquinas's application of natural law principles to human action is hierarchical, based on the order of the "good" that practical reason apprehends from our various natural inclinations.

> Therefore, to the order of natural inclinations there corresponds the precepts of the Natural Law. For, first of all, there is in man an inclination to the good according to the nature which he shares with all substances, namely, inasmuch as all substances desire the conservation of their own existence according to its nature, and in accord with this inclination, all those things by which the life of man is preserved and the opposite impeded belong to the Natural Law.
>
> Secondly, there are in man certain special things according to the nature which he shares with the other animals, and, according to this, those things which nature teaches all animals are said to belong to the Natural Law such as intercourse between male and female, the education of children and the like.
>
> In a third way, there is in man an inclination to good according to the nature of reason which is proper to him, as man has a natural inclination to know the truth about God, and to live in society and, in accord with this inclination all those things which relate to it belong to the Natural Law, namely, that a man avoid ignorance and that he should not offend others with whom he ought to live and similar things which relate to this inclination.[45]

Aquinas took the social component of man's nature as fundamental, following in this Aristotle's description of man as a creature of the polis, and for this reason he argues that human civil law, derived as particular determinations from the natural law (not as "conclusions from principles"), must be ordered to the common good of the particular society.[46] However, for Aquinas the natural law concerning society and politics also has supernatural implications revealed in the divine law, which in this

---

45. *ST*, I-II, q. 94, a. 2., in Henle, *Treatise on Law*, 250.
46. *ST*, I-II, q. 95, a. 4., citing to Aristotle's *Politics*, I, in Henle, *Treatise on Law*, 301–2.

case are, typically, directly parallel to it: the highest law of scripture is to love God, and the second is to love your neighbor. On this basis, Aquinas elaborates his ideas on governance and expands on Aristotle's analysis in the *Politics* and the *Ethics*.

By adding a supernatural dimension to an evaluation of the social good, Aquinas does not thereby denigrate the material preconditions for the life of virtue, either for the individual or for society. As Aquinas elaborates in his extended treatment in *De Regimine Principum*, the king's duties are first to provide peace, secondly to promote virtue, and thirdly to see "there be a plentiful supply of those things necessary to living well."[47]

When a king fails to serve the common good in any of the fundamentals of peace, virtue, and prosperity, and instead serves his own private good, his subjects have certain rights, in the abstract, to depose him. In the *De Regimine Principum*, addressed as it was to a king, it is understandable that Aquinas underscores that any such rebellion should take place through public channels instead of through the private judgment of individuals. Yet in the *Summa Theologiae* and in his *Commentary* on Peter Lombard's *Sentences*, Aquinas does not condemn the overthrow of tyrants, nor even their assassination in some cases.

> The overthrow of [tyrannical] government does not have the character of sedition—unless perhaps it produces such disorder that the society under the tyrant suffers greater harm from the resulting disturbance than from the tyrant's rule. Rather it is the tyrant who is guilty of sedition because he spreads discord and division among the people under him so as to control them more easily.[48]

As with all the applications of the natural law in practice, the right to rebellion—or as Aquinas analyzes the relevant case, the right to restore order in the face of a tyrant's seditious disorder—requires the exercise of prudence and weighing the risks of greater injustice, which is to say the competing rights of others and of the whole community to order. Such prudential analysis involving the weighing of conflicting rights is seen

47. *On Kingship*, Book I, chap. XVI, in Dyson, *Aquinas*, 44.
48. *ST*, II-II, q. 42.

also in the application of Aquinas's well-known theories on the possibility of "just war" when right cause, right authority, and right intention (and relevant means) are present.[49]

As for the best forms of government in light of the natural law, Aquinas follows Aristotle in all the essential details—among just governments, monarchy is obviously the best (at a minimum, in terms of efficiency); but among unjust governments, it would be the worst (for the same reason), while a mixed constitutional form would be the best of the less good forms (the best of the worst, where, as can be imagined in particular cases, systemic inefficiency is a benefit): "Tyranny is more harmful than oligarchy, and oligarchy than democracy....Among the forms of unjust rule, therefore, democracy is the most tolerable and tyranny is the worst."[50] Aquinas argues in favor of the merits of republican forms of government insofar as the practice of individual virtue may in some circumstances be enhanced by the citizens' sense of participation and responsibility, as Aquinas took to be the case for the Roman Republic before the onset of the civil wars. It is the greater frequency with which republics fall into discord and even tyranny, as set forth in theoretical considerations and as seen from historical observation, that leads Aquinas to conclude that government by one person is preferable to government by many, although there are dangers in both.[51] Aquinas makes the case for Aristotle's "mixed polity" in the *Summa Theologiae*.

> Two points are to be observed concerning the right ordering of rulers in a state or nation. One is that all should take some share in the government: for this form of constitution ensures peace among the people, commends itself to all, and is most enduring, as stated in Polit. ii, 6. The other point is to be observed in respect of the kinds of government, or the different ways in which the constitutions are established. For whereas these differ in kind, as the Philosopher states (Polit. iii, 5), nevertheless the first place is held by the "kingdom," where the power of government is vested in one;

---

49. *ST*, II-II, q. 40, a. 1.
50. *On Kingship*, Book I, chap. IV, in Dyson, *Aquinas*, 11–13.
51. *On Kingship*, Book I, chaps. V-VII, in Dyson, *Aquinas*, 15–21

and "aristocracy," which signifies government by the best, where the power of government is vested in a few. Accordingly, the best form of government is in a state or kingdom, where one is given the power to preside over all; while under him are others having governing powers: and yet a government of this kind is shared by all, both because all are eligible to govern, and because the rules are chosen by all. For this is the best form of polity, being partly kingdom, since there is one at the head of all; partly aristocracy, in so far as a number of persons are set in authority; partly democracy, i.e. government by the people, in so far as the rulers can be chosen from the people, and the people have the right to choose their rulers.[52]

In conclusion, one of the important insights of Thomism as a system and animating outlook is its ability to account for the subjective and prudential aspects of practical, rational activity.[53] Taparelli's attraction to the philosophy of man and society in Aristotle and Aquinas was a response to the confusion that he saw from the conflation of speculative and practical reasoning in both idealist and materialist rationalistic camps. He enthusiastically embraced the reasoning of Aquinas on human nature, and on the limited purpose of government for facilitating the pursuit of human happiness, as he opposed the reductionist anthropological views of laissez-faire liberals and statist socialists alike. He saw in the natural law and in Aquinas's thinking about virtue a holistic framework for addressing the conflicts of modernity—what remained to be elaborated were the historical and social scientific applications implicit in natural law ethics.

Metaphysics and Methodology in the *Saggio teoretico*

Reading the Saggio

The *Saggio* is divided into seven *Dissertazioni* (which I translate as "books") that are intended to proceed from the most fundamental principles to general conclusions and then to specific applications. The first book, a metaphysical and anthropological inquiry into first principles,

52. *ST*, I-II, q. 105.
53. *ST*, II-II, q. 50.

concerns the nature of man, of human agency, and of individual moral action. The second considers the concept of society as an outgrowth of human nature and agency. These first two books together comprise, as Taparelli explains in his abridged manual on natural law (the *Corso elementare*), his philosophy of individual moral conduct, or ethics.

The third book concerns the necessary theoretical and actual historical conditions for the formation of society as the foundation of natural rights. Here is where he most strongly takes issue with the modern natural law and natural rights schools of thought based on abstracted and reductionist views of the human person, and with the abstract fictions of the "state of nature." The fourth considers the natural law basis of positive lawmaking in society in terms of its ends—that is, for the perfecting of human felicity—and discusses the intermediary associations that persons necessarily form in the pursuit thereof. The fifth book considers the forms of political authority resulting organically from the associative nature of individuals. Thus the third, fourth, and fifth books constitute Taparelli's natural law sociology and science of politics, based on his anthropological and metaphysical premises.[54]

The sixth book considers the relationship between human societies; that is, his natural law conception of hypotactical society in the context of global integration, including questions of war and of global governance. The seventh deals with his realist, natural law social theory applied to special considerations, including "Christian society," "domestic society," and the question of social progress (moral and material) in general. The last two books are worthy of an extended evaluation in subsequent research beyond this brief introduction to Taparelli's realist social theory. Finally, there is a summary "Reasoned Epilogue" ("Epilogo ragionato") in the form of an outline of the argument in each part of the whole work.[55] He published a condensed version of the *Saggio* in 1845, the *Corso elementare di natural diritto ad uso delle scuole* (Elementary course of natural

---

54. *Saggio*, §§10–11.
55. The Epilogo Ragionato was published as a separate manual of natural law. The *Sintesi di diritto naturale* [Synthesis of natural law] (Bologna: Zanichelli, 1940) came out in the first years of World War II based on Pius XI's repeated praise for Taparelli's work and on Pius XII's hopes for the postwar emergence of an international order based on natural law and respect for human rights. See, *Sintesi di diritto naturale*, vi.

law for use in schools) that also underwent expansions and corrections in subsequent editions.[56]

It is important to keep in mind that Taparelli originally assembled his treatise while he was teaching his course in Palermo, and readers can appreciate a certain unevenness in the work. Taparelli continued his studies in modern social, political, and economic thought over the decade after the treatise's original publication. He brought out a revision in French and spent several years writing about the subjects covered in the *Saggio* for *Civiltà Cattolica*, before the definitive, revised, and enlarged version came out in 1855.

The organization of the work, even in the definitive 1855 edition, is still uneven in parts. It was expanded and revised between 1843 and 1855, with detailed excurses added as "Notes" and a large number of cross-references, moderating the somewhat heavily syllogistic form. Taparelli's sympathetic biographer, Robert Jacquin, describes the tone and argumentation in the work as making a sustained reading difficult, and he suggests that Taparelli's fault lies in his "failure to have pity" on his readers.[57] Jacquin also criticizes Taparelli for sometimes rushing over subtle arguments or lacking precision in his definitions of complex ideas. But this criticism misses the point that Taparelli's work, in his *Saggio* and especially in his *Civiltà Cattolica* articles, was part of an engaged intellectual project in a revolutionary era, an age of contested ideologies and competing paradigms of social order and progress—there was nothing dispassionate about his intellectual pursuits or narrow about his interests.[58] He is exactly the sort of nontraditional, intellectual iconoclast who shapes scientific revolutions, a phenomenon described by Thomas Kuhn. At any rate, once one enters into an appreciation of Taparelli's conceptualization of the main problems, and

---

56. Luigi Taparelli, *Corso elementare di natural diritto ad uso delle scuole* (Napoli: Tipografia all'Insegna del Diogene, 1845). A third edition was published in 1851, *Corso elementare di natural diritto, opera del padre Luigi Taparelli della Compagnia di Gesùm adotata per testo presso la R. Università degli Studii in Modena*, which was "enlarged with many new additions and corrections by the Author" (Modena: Carlo Vincenzi, 1851), and a sixth edition appeared in 1860, again "with new additions by the author" (Napoli: Boutteaux e Aubry, 1860).

57. Jacquin, *Taparelli*, 158.

58. Among other interests, we can recall his invention of the *violicembolo*, renamed the "symphonium" after the suggestion of an appreciative Franz Liszt. Cf. Charles Macksey, "Aloysius Taparelli," in *The Catholic Encyclopedia*, vol. 14 (New York: Robert Appleton Company, 1912).

of the methodology he employs toward their solution, a more sympathetic appreciation for the insights contained in the work can emerge from underneath criticisms of tone and style.

Two Philosophies

Taparelli's objective in the *Saggio* was to elaborate a normative social theory and social science based on natural reason.[59] However, he saw an unbridgeable gulf between Scholastic, or more generically, "Catholic" philosophy, and the "heterodox" philosophy of his time based on "independence of reason." In an article in the *Civiltà Cattolica* in 1853, "Di due filosofie,"[60] he lays out his main contentions on the fundamental contrast between the Catholic and heterodox philosophical positions and between their different social consequences, similar to what he did in his introduction to the *Saggio*, but in the article he also pointed out the differences in their methods, a subject that particularly concerns us here. In this regard, he stated that

> We will demonstrate therefore that the philosophy of the Scholastics, as *demonstrative*, can be contrasted with modern philosophy, as *inquisitive*, in regards to four aspects: namely,
>
> 1. The former proceeded from certainty, the latter from doubt;
> 2. The *proper* scope of the former was evidence, of the latter certainty;
> 3. The former in ascertaining its judgments relied on any rational element whatsoever, the latter accepts only one, ratiocination.[61]

59. *Saggio*, p. 5.
60. *Civiltà Cattolica*, ser. II, vol. 1 (1853): 369–80, 481–506, 626–47 (hereafter cited as CC). See also "Dell'armonia filosofica," CC, ser. II, vol. 2 (1853): 128–44, 253–73, 378–99, which together with "Di due filosofie" appear to be a reworking of Taparelli's unpublished essay titled "Tradizionalismo." The "Tradizionalismo" article was rejected either by the *Civiltà Cattolica* editorial board or by the Papal Curia (secretary of state), which had direct editorial oversight of the Jesuit journal. Reworking the article to expunge criticism of the Traditionalist position suggests that efforts were expended not to alienate those theologically right-leaning Catholics even though intellectually the journal had completely embraced Taparelli's neoscholastic orientation. See generally, Francesco Dante, *Storia della 'Civiltà Cattolica' (1850–1891): Il laboratorio del Papa* (Roma: Edizioni Studium, 1990).
61. Mostreremo dunque che la filosofia degli Scolastici può come *dimostrativa* contrapporsi alla moderna *inquisitiva* per quattro sue proprietà: vale a dire perchè,
  1° Quella moveva dal certo, questa dal dubbio:

4. The former produced in souls a disposition that was catholic, social, and practical, the latter a disposition that is heterodox, antisocial, and impractical.

Thus, for Taparelli, the superior characteristics of the Scholastic approach are found in its beginning from knowledge of the immediate certainties of the Aristotelian-Thomist system, including, for instance, existence and the first principles of logic. The apprehension of being, and subsequently of abstract concepts and universals, is, in Taparelli's understanding of Aquinas, not an act of faith, but of natural reason, which occurs spontaneously as long as neither the senses nor the intellect are handicapped by some illness or "sophism."[62] The role of revelation is to function only as a certain kind of advantage for Christian believers who are free to use its certainties as points of departure, but more importantly, revelation is an example of the kind of method by which "evident" knowledge (even revealed "evident" knowledge for Christians) can find additional confirmation by rational demonstration. Thus the Scholastic method (whether supplemented by revelation or not) moves from certainty toward evidence and rational confirmation, lending confidence and practical energy to the philosophizing person, whereas Cartesian rationalism moves from universal doubt seeking a certainty or foundation that is ever out of reach, absent a certain ontological legerdemain. The social consequences of the heterodox philosophy for Taparelli were pride and rashness, uncertainty among the educated, and the presumptuousness of the ignorant.

Taparelli's understanding of Scholastic natural law reasoning reveals an interesting parallel to the characteristic methods of the modern sciences in that they both involve a combination of deduction and induction; hypotheses based on normal (that is, established) paradigms; and experimentation. Thomas Kuhn showed that normal science takes place

---

2° *Proprio* scopo di quella era l'evidenza, di questa la certezza;
3° Quella per accertare nelle sue sentenze invocava a sostegno qualsivoglia elemento ragionevole, questa ne accetta un solo, il raziocinio:
4° Quella produceva negli animi una disposizione cattolica, sociale, pratica, questa una disposizione eterodossa, antisociale, impraticabile.
Taparelli, "Di due Filosofie," 378.
62. Taparelli, "Di due Filosofie," 484.

within a given scientific paradigm or community of discourse by means of accepted axioms and facts, and it thus never operates in a metaphysical or epistemological vacuum. Therefore, the original points of departure for Taparelli—immediate, connatural knowledge and commonly held ideas, including those ideas found in the sciences, history, and revelation—are not required to pass the Cartesian bar of universal doubt before they can be considered for their evidentiary value. Once confirmed via rational demonstration based on evidence, these have a rational value that can lead to further elaboration and application in further scientific inquiry.[63] Taparelli takes from Aquinas that "facts" of revelation, history, commonly held ideas, scholarly ideas, and a myriad of other "facts" can all function in the dialectical role of points of departure and/or sources of confirmation of some prior point of departure, and subsequently as further points of departure, leading to elaboration and confirmation of judgment in the exercise of practical reason. By functioning in this way, these other "facts" gain in certainty during the inquiry, tying distant conclusions with greater or lesser confidence to the certainty provided by the first principles.[64] Thus Taparelli argues that his method, characterized by a correct understanding of human nature, is the only proper approach to practical reasoning concerning law and policy, belonging, as they should, to the category of practical and moral judgment.[65]

Taparelli thus addressed what he saw as the fundamental problem in the rationalistic search for objective knowledge in the human sciences as they were developing within nineteenth-century rationalist schools of thought.[66] Taparelli's reaction to the positivistic tendency of rationalistic thought led him to appreciate the eclectic school of Cousin, with its historicist emphasis that could make sense of the history of intellectual development as a history of partial and complementary insights. For Taparelli, the return to an Aristotelian and Thomist science and metaphysics is simply a return to a balanced view that had been lost in the Reformation and Enlightenment struggles between subjectivist and

63. *Saggio*, p. 5.
64. *ST*, I-II, q. 94, a. 4.
65. *Saggio*, pp. 5–8.
66. See Friedrich Hayek, *The Counter-Revolution of Science*, rev. ed. (1952; repr., Indianapolis: Liberty Fund, 1979), especially chap. 12.

objectivist paradigms, but which, and this is the essential point, could be resolved by an empirical science of human action based on a restored understanding of composite human nature and human needs, allied with an appreciation of the articulation of abstract moral principles in hylomorphic, concrete reality.

Therefore, Taparelli uses the term "facts" in two different senses: 1) referring to the broad range of data taken as starting points of abstract practical reasoning and accumulated as evidence in the pursuit of psychological conviction and moral obligation; and 2) referring to the actual concrete historical contexts within which the abstract conclusions of practical reason actually operate. This latter usage is the crucial one, and it is the basis for his thesis-and-hypothesis form of prudential reasoning about ethics and politics, as a matter of social scientific research and policy.

Dialectic of Theory and Fact

In his biography of Taparelli, Jacquin conceives the methodological function of *appoggiato sul fatto* (based on fact) too narrowly, and even with a certain disdain. He makes the argument that Taparelli's use of the word *fatto* is misleading if one were to take the translated title of his work—the "Theoretical Treatise of Natural Right Based on Fact"—to imply "facts" of the sort understood by modern experimental science.[67] Taparelli was influenced in his thinking about the role of historical and other structural facts by his appreciation of Montesquieu and early interest in Victor Cousin, and then by Maistre, among other Traditionalists. Jacquin seems to consider Taparelli's effort to base his theorizing on facts as an attempt to appear scientific, viewing the spirit of his broad philosophical project as being somewhat quaint.[68] Jacquin describes Taparelli's use of facts as consisting of scattered examples, not based on empirical research like modern sociologists, but only on anecdotal evidence confirming his theories arrived at deductively from metaphysical truths. According to Jacquin,

---

67. Jacquin, *Taparelli*, 169–70.
68. Jacquin, *Taparelli*, 170–72. It is no surprise that English-speaking commentators who read Jacquin in French, but not Taparelli directly in Italian, at least not in any sustained manner, could come away with a dismissive or highly critical assessment of the *Saggio*.

Taparelli "fertilized" those metaphysical truths with facts to give them practical significance.[69] Jacquin focuses too much on Taparelli's reference to facts based on common sense as starting points of practical reasoning, and in so doing he largely misses how the theoretical part of the treatise, on the nature and operation of man and society, is based on the facts of their material instantiation: this distinction, largely between speculative and practical reasoning, is the foundation for Taparelli's normative social science. His methodology proceeds from sound metaphysical principles, arrived at by reason and evidence, to a theoretical truth (or "thesis") that carries universal validity, and which can be verified by, among other ways, by extrapolating from the various concrete historical arrangements in which the thesis has manifested itself (these concrete arrangments being the "hypothesis"). Confirmed in this way, the thesis, as a principle or conclusion of natural law, can then be applied prudentially to judge particular concrete historical contexts, hypothetically.

Taparelli uses the terms "facts" and "common sense" in both their Aristotelian and Thomist meanings, citing also Reid. For the data of common sense he prefers the term *"idee comunissime"* (most-commonly held ideas) and for the faculty of common sense, he refers to a *"senso intimo"* (intimate sense), which, by forming an image of the objective world is the source of the relative truth value of perceptions and judgments.[70]

Taparelli makes two main methodological uses of "facts": first, following Aristotle, the abstract reasoning of natural law must be derived from and, importantly, confirmed by facts.[71] The facts may thus require the investigator to recognize the need for a revision in the reasoning. The facts of life and reality are the beginning and the end of practical reasoning

---

69. Jacquin, *Taparelli*, 170–71.

70. Jacquin, *Taparelli*, chap. VII, nn 66, 70. Jacquin rejects the link between Taparelli's ideas and his usage of the language of Cousin and Reid, yet Taparelli explicitly states that he is using language forms and common sense in the way Reid does, as representations produced by a faculty of mind, which is the *"intimo senso"* in the *Saggio*, Note VI. Cf. Gilson, *Thomist Realism*, chap. 1, esp. 36–44.

71. The opinions of the wise seem, then, to harmonize with our arguments. But while even such things carry some conviction, the truth in practical matters is discerned from the facts of life; for these are the decisive factor. We must therefore survey what we have already said, bringing it to the test of the facts of life, and if it harmonizes with the facts we must accept it, but if it clashes with them we must suppose it to be mere theory.
NE, X, 8.

about the good. This includes an appreciation of the potential evidentiary value of common ideas. But, much more significantly, and at the heart of his realist social theory, Taparelli also insists that in practical, natural law reasoning about the good, the abstract natural right (deduced first from observed facts), is always embodied in concrete historical facts and never exists only abstractly except as a concept used in speculation—certainly not in the realm of scientific (social scientific) application to real life. Universals exist only as concepts in the created order, as abstractions in the mind, while in the actual, historical world they exist in specific, variable, concrete arrangements. Taparelli considered that only a return to a hylomorphic understanding of man's essential nature, and of truth and reality generally, offered a way out of what he saw as the dangerous ideologies of rationalistic materialists and idealists. Taparelli takes Aristotelian eudaemonia ethics (human flourishing as the goal and standard of right acting), adds the inviolable dignity of the human person, elaborates the complex character of sociological relations, and combines these with natural rights reasoning, to yield a conception of subjective rights that morally oblige us in conscience. He considered that the only sufficiently compelling moral reasoning is one in which right and wrong are clearly knowable, at least in principle, with respect to some perfective end. For him, deontological ethics were mere ideology and end in a labyrinth of speculation.[72] Such reasoning tends toward debatable rules that carry dubious moral weight (or psychological conviction). In contrast, Taparelli's approach to natural rights takes into account de facto contexts and carries psychological weight and moral obligation, even in a pluralistic political community, with

72. *Saggio*, §§1–28. Taparelli rejects Kant's subjectivism explicitly:
Chi volesse col Kant mettere in dubbio se l'intelletto tenda al vero obbiettivo, faria lo stesso che se ne mettesse in dubbio ogni tendenza al vero: giacchè il vero è la conformità del nostro giudizio con gli obbietti. Il kantismo è dunque l'abolizione della filosofia. Quando si giunge a dire 'l'entendement ne tire pas ses lois de la nature, c'est lui qui donne des lois à la nature,' (quoting from Villers, *Philosophie de Kant*) allora l'idealismo è compiuto, nè si può più sperar filosofia che spieghi nature: ogni filosofia è ridotta a spiegar l'io. [Who would wish, with Kant, to put into doubt whether the intellect tends toward its true object, acts the same as if to put in doubt every tendency to the true: since the true is the conformity of our judgment with objects. Kantianism is therefore the abolition of philosophy. When one adds to that to say 'the understanding does not draw its laws from nature, it is the understanding that gives its laws to nature' (citing Villers, *Philosophy of Kant*) then idealism is complete, neither can one anymore hope that philosophy will explain nature: every philosophy is reduced to explaining the I.] *Saggio*, Note XXVI.

regard to the limited ends of natural and social felicity—at least among persons capable of right reasoning.[73] The possibility of mistaken judgment about the actual correspondence of a desired temporal end with its perfective quality contains within itself the concept of goodness and "ought," without reference to controversial ultimate ends or the ultimate good—so long as inalienable human rights are protected and, in a just society, their exercise facilitated.

Application

Examining the implications of Taparelli's method, we arrive at his fundamentally important treatment of social organization and the just or unjust policies of governments. Taparelli begins with an analysis of the theoretical principles of society in general, its mode of being and the operation of its unitive authority, then he considers the varieties of concrete societies in order to identify their specific differences and to establish theoretically the differences among the kinds of these societies, including differing governmental regime forms—and only then is he in a position to evaluate principles of right as a matter of practical reason in the social context. The method is both inductive and deductive, arriving at "universal" laws of social behavior from actual historical situations—which can then be applied back to these actual situations for an analysis, in an ethico-critical mode, of their relevant contingencies and accidental factors as these relate to the natural law and to the moral norms having thus been discovered, as he writes:

> With the accurate analysis that we have given of the *two social elements in the abstract and in the concrete*, of the two social persons, *superior* [the actual person or persons exercising authority] and *subject*, and of the idea of *sovereignty* consisting in an *independent superiority*, we now seem *to have put ourselves in the position to consider without great difficulty* the progress of society in fact, and

---

73. McInerny, *Ethica Thomistica*, 35–38, 48–55. For which further reason the so-called naturalistic fallacy does not apply to eudaemonia ethics in general, or to Taparelli's natural law version specifically: that the end of human action is happiness is universally incontestable, and its attainment or satisfaction is empirically testable.

to understand its most universal laws. To this therefore I invite my reader, praying now more than ever it be remembered that the philosopher is the *interpreter* of nature, not quite its *inventor*; I do not enter therefore into my room to imagine to myself that which never was, but I invite [the reader] to stroll with me around the world meditating upon that which is, and making application to it there of the principles that analysis reveals to us.... This variety is the great fact in respect of which I seek to identify the essential differences and the *real* causes; I ask myself which are the essential varieties of *forms in Government*, and *From where must they have had to sprout by natural law?*, and how in the same essential form so many singular differences are seen? And this I seek as a philosopher, not quite as an historian; the philosopher contemplates them, separates out the purely individual circumstances, and coordinates them in a rational system. But, to coordinate them, to reason from them, one must always ground oneself on fact.[74]

As a philosopher of natural law and of the human sciences, Taparelli thus operates in a theoretical mode distinct from the analytical research of the historian or ethnologist, though he draws on those sciences, among others. Proceeding from the obvious fact of the variety of concrete factors determining social relations between abstractly conceived social persons (in particular, between governed and governors) in any given independent society (state), it is then his object to deduce general laws from the process of reflecting on singular variations occasioned by accidental

74. Coll'analisi accurata che abbiam dato dei *due elementi sociali dell'astratto cioè e del concreto*, delle due personne sociali *superiore e suddito*, e della idea di *sovranità* consistente in una *superiorità indipendente*, ci sembra ormai *esserci posti in istato di potere senze gran difficoltà riguardare i progressi della società nel fatto naturale* (i.e. the historical record), *comprenderne le leggi più universali.* A questo dunque invito il mio lettore, pregandolo adesso più che mai a ricordarsi che filosofo è l'*interprete* di natura, non già l'*inventore*; non entro dunque nel mio gabinetto per immaginarmi ciò che mai fu, ma lo invito a passeggiare pel mondo meditando sopra ciò che è, e facendovi l'applicazione de' principii che l'analisi ci rivelò....Questa varietà è il gran fatto di cui vo cercando le differenze essenziali e le cause *reali*; domando a me stesso quali sieno le *essenziali* varietà di *forme nel Governo*, e *d'onde abbian dovuto spuntare per legge naturale?* e come nelle stesse forme essenziali tante si osservino differenze singolari? ma lo cerco da filosofo, non già da storico; il filosofo li contempla, ne scevera tutte le circostanze puramente individuali, e li coordina in un sistema razionale. Ma per coordinarli, per ragionarne, sempre si dee fondare sul fatto. *Saggio*, §504. See generally, "Explication of Society: Its Forms," Book. II, chap. 9.

circumstances—this is the step that takes Taparelli beyond the positivistic classification of regimes by Montesquieu—and thus he finds the natural law criteria for diagnosing social ills and prescribing remedies.

Taparelli's conception of the influence of concrete historical factors on the articulation of the natural laws of man and society is surely influenced by the ideas of Montesquieu, whom he recognizes as a forerunner in sociological method, however misguided in first principles he was and however erroneous his resulting conclusions. In good Scholastic fashion, Taparelli looked to discover any aspect of a theory that might be true, or in which way some conclusion might be true, along the way explaining theoretical and logical errors. His efforts to situate his theories within the broader intellectual field resulted in significant additions to the 1855 edition of the *Saggio*, which contains lengthy additional remarks on thinkers he either excoriates, like the social contract theorists, or admires—for aspects either of their method or their conclusions—all the while exposing the logical and practical implications of the lapses in coherence of those writers he criticizes. His respect for the work of Montesquieu, whom he occasionally cites as a supporting authority, is significant.

> We must recognize that the *Spirit of the Laws* was a transition from the abstract to the concrete; . . .if his mind, corrupted with republican doctrines, had not perverted the ideas suggested to him by his genius; his thinking to search in the *individuality* of every people the base of the *individuality* of its laws would have merited him recognition for the cause of political philosophy. But he fell into the reigning pure empiricism, and instead of recognizing in individual conditions *a fact that determines* the universal and immutable laws of nature, it appeared *at times* (even though he contradicts himself elsewhere) that he wanted to bury in this material element both human liberty, as well as virtue and justice, deducing from such elements all morality, or at least submitting this to them.[75]

75. Dobbiam riconoscere che lo Spirito delle leggi fu una transizione del dritto sociale dall'astratto al concreto; e se l'empietà allora regnante non avesse strappato all'A. degl'incensi ch'egli abbominò morendo; se la sua mente, falsata da dottrine repubblicane, non avesse pervertite le idee suggeritegli dal suo ingegno; il pensiero di ricercare nelle individualità di ogni popolo la base della individualità di sue leggi avrebbe potuto meritargli riconoscenza per parte della

Raymond Aron identified the emergence of the sociological mind-set in the process whereby the concept of society assumes the central role that politics had held since Aristotle. For Aron, the most fruitful approaches to a science of the social hold in tension the two conceptions of science described here, the one claiming objective knowledge of generalities, the other an understanding of specific social phenomena. Aron asserts that differences in emphasis in the various kinds of social scientific knowledge respecting the part and the whole that are thereby conceivable define the major schools of sociological thought, and indeed, for him the study of the relationship of the part to the whole is the very essence of sociology.[76] It can be argued that Taparelli had rediscovered the sociological thrust of Aristotle's politics, a thrust that Aquinas was aware of when he intentionally translated Aristotle's definition of man—a "political animal"—as a "political and social animal" in his treatise *On Kingship*, having understood that the significance of the polis goes well beyond its political form.

> But man is by nature a political and social animal. Even more than other animals he lives in groups. This is demonstrated by the requirements of his nature. Nature has given other animals food, furry covering, teeth, and horns and claws—or at least speed of flight—as means to defend themselves. Man however, is given none of these by nature. Instead he has been given the use of his reason to secure all these things by the work of his hands. But a man cannot secure all these by himself, for a man cannot adequately provide for his life by himself. Therefore it is natural for man to live in association with his fellows.[77]

---

filosofia politica. Ma egli precipitò nel puro empirismo allora regnante, e invece di ravvisare nelle condizioni individuali un fatto determinante le leggi universali ed immutabili di natura, parve talora (benchè altrove si contraddica) voler seppellire in questo materiale elemento e la umana libertà e la virtù e la giustizia, deducendo da tali elementi ogni moralità, o almeno assoggettandola ad essi."
Saggio, Note LXV, 3. Taparelli is referring to, for example, Book 4 of *The Spirit of the Laws*, "De l'éducation."

76. Raymond Aron, *Montesquieu*, 9–10.

77. *On Kingship*, Book. I, chap. I, in Dyson, *Aquinas*, 5–8. Also *ST*, I-II, q. 72, a. 4; *Peri Hermeneias*, I, 2. For Aristotle on man as a "zöon politikon," see *NE*, I, 5:1097b 11; IX, 9:1169b 18; Aristotle, *Politics*, trans. Ernest Barker, ed. R. F. Stalley, rev. ed (1998, reissue, Oxford: Oxford University Press, 2009), I, 2:1253a 3. But it must be underlined that to say that man is "an animal of the polis" included even for Aristotle a broader conception of political life that

It is from man's personal dignity as an intellectual and rational creature, and also as an ineluctably social creature—materially at the very least—that Taparelli takes his point of departure. He rejected, therefore, what he believed to be Montesquieu's reduction of the sociological method to a materialistic determinism. Similarly was Taparelli motivated by the incomplete or distorted conceptions of human nature—personal, social, and political—that he found in Bentham, Hobbes, and Locke, for instance. He looked to reintegrate the philosophical realism of the Scholastics with the scientific method of observation and inductive reasoning, a return, as it were, to the basic unity of the sciences.

> The supreme principle of every science, properly speaking, is found in metaphysics, because every science studies the being of some thing, and being is the proper object of metaphysics.[78]

Taparelli's desire to reestablish the human sciences as they were developing in his day on the metaphysical foundation of Aristotelian and Thomist realism was not at all a rejection of positive science, nor of empiricism and inductive reasoning, but a recognition that the operation of the scientific mind necessarily depends on the first science and self-critical reflection; otherwise, the positivistic tendencies of the empirical sciences meets no defense against ideology or false consciousness.

Taparelli spent most of the last two decades of his life working on developing the essential points in his work and presenting them in more accessible forms. Thus, as early as 1843 he produced his *Corso elementare*, and in 1854 he compiled his articles on political theory that had appeared in the *Civiltà Cattolica* as the *Esame critico*, achieving some of his greatest popular attention (and liberal opprobrium). The revised and expanded edition of the *Saggio* came out in 1855. His articles in the *Civiltà Cattolica* from its founding in 1850 until his death in 1862

---

embraces economic, family, social, and cultural relationships.
78. "Il supremo principio di ogni scienza, a parlar propriamente si ritrova nella metafisica, perchè ogni scienza studia l'essere di qualche cosa, e l'essere è il proprio obbietto della metafisica." *Saggio*, Note XXIII.

and his other writings before and after 1850 number in the hundreds.⁷⁹ Lastly, he intended that his work on economic theory, begun in a series of articles appearing in *Civiltà Cattolica*, should be issued in a separate work by his colleague and protégé, Mateo Liberatore SJ, but it was not. By the time of his death in 1862, Taparelli's legacy had already been largely set in stone. Among liberal Catholics and Catholic Liberals, he was misunderstood to say the very least and given an unsympathetic and distorted reading in the heat of intense ideological and political contention. The Catholic Movement itself was divided by liberal and conservative political views. However, with the ascension of his neo-Thomist protégés in the Roman curia, especially of Vincenzo Gioacchino Pecci to the papacy as Leo XIII, Taparelli's realist natural law science of society came to provide the paradigm and methodology for the emergence of modern CST.

Taparelli and the Development of Modern Catholic Social Teaching

Pius IX and Civiltà Cattolica

Pius IX's exile, together with the revolutions of 1848 and the brief establishment of a Roman republic, convinced the pope of the dangers of a revolutionary tide—even though the revolutions of 1848 generally featured no antireligious animus.⁸⁰ Before his safe return to Rome (which occurred after the forces of Mazzini and Garibaldi were displaced by French troops), Pius IX contemplated launching some sort of journalistic research initiative. It was decided that a journal with serious intellectual credentials should be established, and the pope turned to the Jesuits and to Fr. Taparelli in particular, along with two of his protégés, Carlo Maria Curci and Matteo Liberatore.⁸¹ The younger, energetic Fr. Curci

---

79. A comprehensive list of Taparelli's works appears in Pirri, *Carteggi del Padre Taparelli*, 31–55. Taparelli's vast corpus, including a couple hundred book reviews, should have been a warning to those commentators on Taparelli not to take literally his humble assertion, in one place, that his work was not based on much reading.
80. William R. Collins, *Catholicism and the Second French Republic, 1848–52* (New York: Columbia University, 1923), chaps. 1–3.
81. Roger Aubert, *Le Pontificat de Pie IX (1846–1878)* (Paris: Bloud et Gay, 1952), 39, 53.

successfully argued that the journal should be of broad appeal in order to address the forces of secularism and popular journalism on their own terrain, and he was tasked with directing the enterprise.[82] *Civiltà Cattolica* was born in 1850 with an aggressive mandate and quickly became identified as the spearhead of Catholic intransigence and the "think tank" of the Vatican, under direction of a special Jesuit *Collegio degli Scrittori della Civiltà Cattolica* and with ultimate editorial control by the Papal Secretary of State.[83] The founding of this journal is particularly noteworthy for our purposes in that it was Matteo Liberatore who wrote the first draft and, with Cardinal Zigliara, was co-editor of the final draft of *Rerum Novarum*.[84]

Sympathetic to the liberalization of political and economic institutions, Pius IX was aware that some level of systematic understanding of the political forces and ideologies in upheaval was sorely required. The Church hierarchy needed to have a voice in the public square, with editorial approval reserved to the Curia itself. Up to that point, the main Catholic response to the upheavals had included an expansion of traditional charitable undertakings along with isolated episcopal calls for more charity and less capitalist greed. But this ad hoc approach found itself, especially after 1848, caught in an ideological no-man's land between socialists, who characterized the evangelical approach as reactionary, and laissez-faire capitalists who charged the activists carrying out this work with fanning the flames of revolution.[85] Closer to home in Italy, the "social

---

82. Carlo Maria Curci, "Il giornalismo moderno ed il nostro programma," CC, ser. I, vol. 1 (1850): 8–24. See, Giandomenico Mucci, *Carlo Maria Curci: Fondatore della Civiltà Cattolica* (Rome: Edizioni Studium, 1988), 13–14.

83. See generally, Francesco Dante, "La nascita e i primi anni della *Civiltà*," chap. 3 in *Storia della 'Civiltà Cattolica*,' 57–85. Pope Leo XIII reaffirmed Pius IX's unique establishment of papal authority over the journal in 1889, against the efforts of the Society of Jesus to assert the right of the Roman province to control the *collegio*; the Society controlled every other Jesuit college. Gabriele De Rosa, "Le Origini della 'Civiltà Cattolica,'" in *Civiltà Cattolica (1850–1945)* (Naples: Landi, 1971), 93.

84. Giovanni Antonazzi and Gabriele De Rosa, eds., *L'Encyclica* Rerum Novarum *e il suo tempo* (Roma: Edizioni di Storia e Letteratura, 1991), 63–74; see also, De Rosa, "Le Origini della 'Civiltà Cattolica,'" 94–98, in which De Rosa demonstrates the parallels between Liberatore's articles on the Christian view of economics which appeared in *Civiltà Cattolica* in 1887 and the text of *Rerum Novarum*. Also on this connection, see Francesco Dante, "Mateo Liberatore protagonista del 'Rerum Novarum,'" chap. 4 in *Storia della 'Civiltà Cattolica*,' 87–125.

85. See the articles by Paul Droulers, SJ, "Des *évêques* parlent de la question ouvrière en France avant 1848,'" "L'épiscopat devant la question ouvrière en France sous la Monarchie de Juillet," and

question" was less pressing than the "Roman question;" that is, the heated debate over reforms necessary in the Papal States, the constitutional form that an eventually united Italy would take, and the final place of the papacy within it. It was precisely the complexity and urgency of these critical situations that led Taparelli as early as 1847 to implore the Jesuit superior general to launch the kind of journal that the *Civiltà Cattolica* became in 1850, a journal that could engage heterodox ideologues—laissez-faire liberal or socialist—from the foundation of neoscholastic natural law.[86] The Jesuits, widely accused of political intrigue historically, had been reluctant to openly enter the fray between secularist liberalism and socialism in the defense of Catholic values, but the traumatic events of 1848 persuaded Pius IX to endorse the idea of the journal.

Pius IX established a neo-Thomist bastion at the *Civiltà Cattolica*.[87] Curci and Liberatore wasted no time implementing the journal's project of taking on both the laissez-faire liberal and socialist ideological paradigms. In the first issue, Curci outlined the Traditionalist critique of revolutionary socialism as being the direct by-product of the elevation of "independent reason," material self-interest, and the rejection of man's supernatural destiny.[88] Liberatore led with a Taparellian defense of the personalist raison d'être of society and civil government, which holds that the state exists only as a means for guaranteeing the peaceful enjoyment of one's proper rights, not as end in itself.

Taparelli, on the occasion of Pius IX's *motu proprio* reestablishing traditional professional associations in 1852, offered a sustained analysis of the new kind of economic and cultural worker associations, grounded in the natural law of society, that were needed as a countervailing force against the weight of contemporary economic forces.[89] Taparelli had already developed in his *Saggio* a natural law theory of society based on

---

"La presse et la mandements sociaux d'evêques français avant 1848," collected in Paul Droulers, SJ, *Cattolicesimo sociale nei secoli XIX e XX: Saggi di storia e sociologia* (Rome: Edizioni di storia e letturatura, 1982).

86. Aubert, *Pie IX*, 39. See also, generally, on papal politics and government of the era, Giacomo Martina, SJ, *Pio IX (1851–1866)* (Rome: Editrice Pontificia Università Gregoriana, 1986).

87. Paul Droulers, SJ, "Question sociale, état, église dans la *Civiltà Cattolica* à ses débuts," in *Cattolicesimo sociale*, 95–122.

88. Carlo Maria Curci, "Il Socialismo plebeo ed il volterianismo borghese," CC, ser. I, vol. 1 (1850): 613–42.

89. Luigi Taparelli, "I corpi d'arte e le associazioni moderne d'operai," CC, ser. I, vol. 10 (1852): 225–36, 368–80.

various levels of human association from the family to the state, all governed by principles of subsidiarity and social justice. While he was in Palermo during the revolutionary outbreak of 1848, Taparelli argued for religious liberty based on the right of association.[90] Taparelli demonstrated in practice the principle of political "indifference" and the prudential need to combine concerns for charity and virtue in light of the actual reality on the ground, as he personally rendered food and medical aid to the revolutionaries. He propounded the argument, repugnant in other fact situations, that the Church is, like the revolutionaries' groupings themselves, an association that "asks only for liberty," and maintained that "right, violated in one case, is violated in all."

Fr. Droulers sees in *Civiltà Cattolica*, already in the early 1850's, the grounding for *Rerum Novarum*.[91] Even in these early stages, the journal offered an equally pungent critique of the materialism of laissez-faire capitalism and of a collectivist socialism that treated persons as ciphers. The remedies *Civiltà Cattolica* proposed were restoration of Christian values in the culture and economy; regard for the natural law of society and politics, including specifically limited intervention by the state to assure the protection of the rights of all, but especially of the weakest; and lastly, the promotion of professional associations founded in natural law to facilitate the organic, harmonious development of society.[92]

Pius IX cleared the ideological decks for this work with his promulgation in 1864 of the encyclical *Quanta Cura* with its "Syllabus of Errors." He plainly set out the theological-cultural context of the modern crisis, and he provided a list in one place of condemned or misleading ideological propositions. The voice, arguments, and conclusions directly echo Taparelli, from the *Saggio* to the *Esame Critico* to his *Civiltà Cattolica* essays treating one or another aspect of the "heterodox spirit."

> Since Religion has been excluded from Civil Society, and the doctrine and authority of divine Revelation, or the true and germane notion of justice and human right have been obscured and lost, and material or brute force substituted in the place of true justice

---

90. Luigi Taparelli, "Sulla libertà di associazione," addressed "To the Sicilians," in Gabriele De Rosa, *I Gesuiti in Sicilia e la Rivoluzione del '48* (Roma: Edizioni di Storia e Letteratura, 1963), 211–45.
91. Paul Droulers, SJ, "Question sociale," in *Cattolicesimo sociale*, 95–122.
92. De Rosa, "Le Origini," 146.

and legitimate right, it is easy to perceive why some persons, forgetting and trampling upon the most certain principles of sound reason, dare cry out together "that the will of the people, manifested by what they call public opinion, or in any other way, constitutes the supreme law, independent of all divine and human right, and that, in the political order, accomplished facts, by the mere fact of having been accomplished, have the force of right." But who does not see and plainly understand, that the Society of man, freed from the bonds of Religion and of true justice, can certainly have no other purpose than the effort to obtain and accumulate wealth, and that in its actions it follows no other law than that of uncurbed cupidity?[93]

With the Syllabus, with its absolutely baneful effect on the liberal Catholic school of thought, and for that matter, on laissez-faire liberals generally, Catholic or otherwise, the pope established the ground rules upon which any future dialogue was to be held. With these groups in particular, there was now a basis for a new beginning. This was a necessary step before a theoretical framework could emerge to address the uniformly materialist complexities of the modern strife, in which the politics of the modern state had become reduced to a struggle among conflicting interest groups. *Dei Filius*, the dogmatic constitution approved by the Vatican I ecumenical council in 1870, embraced the harmony of faith and reason, just as a generation of neo-Thomists were advancing in theological influence during Pius IX's pontificate.[94] Even so, natural law reasoning, as the basis for an affirmative social teaching, was still absent from magisterial pronouncements. This is not to say that Pius IX did not occasionally refer to the law of nature or insights from historical experience, but systematic reference to Aquinas's natural law reasoning was not a part of the encyclical tradition, and it could not become a consistent feature of CST until the formal rehabilitation of Scholastic philosophy with the ascension of Leo XIII and the publication of his encyclical *Aeterni Patris* (1879).

93. Pius IX, Encyclical Letter *Quanta Cura* (December 8, 1864), 4.
94. Vatican Council I, Dogmatic Constitution *Dei Filius* (1870), chap. IV, "On Faith and Reason." See McCool, *Nineteenth-Century Scholasticism*, 216–22.

Leo XIII *from* Aeterni Patris *to* Rerum Novarum

The future Pope Leo XIII, Vincenzo Gioacchino Pecci, was a student at the Collegio Romano in 1828, where he was also a student assistant to Taparelli and undoubtedly a participant in Taparelli's clandestine study circle on the works of Aquinas. Perhaps pessimistic about the reigning philosophical confusion in the school, Pecci changed the focus of his studies from the philosophy of Aquinas to diplomacy and languages. He completed his degree in canon and civil law at the Università "La Sapienza" in 1835. Pecci then gained valuable practical experience in various administrative and diplomatic contexts, in Benevento (in the Papal States), Belgium, and for thirty years as archbishop of Perugia, including at the time it came under the sovereignty of the Italian national government.

Once pope, in 1878, after the capture of Rome by the unitary Italian state (1870) and the death of Pius IX, and after the rise of an anticlerical, largely antireligious Italian national government, the Holy See faced historic dangers. Intransigence and the *non expedit* banning Catholic political participation in the Italian government, first issued by Pius IX in 1861, remained papal policy. Liberal Catholics continued to hope for conciliation with the new state, and indeed some hoped for some sort of modernization of the Church itself. These hopes exposed the ongoing cleavages between liberal Catholics, moderate Catholic Liberals, and Catholic Conservatives, cleavages that made the emergence of any policy of conciliation difficult.[95] Fr. Curci, believing himself to be following Taparellian principles of adaptation to de facto concrete circumstances, moved to the conciliationist side, and increasingly to the liberal Catholic and then Socialist side, in the early 1880's.[96] Leo XIII, with greater political savvy, understood that until the electoral franchise in Italy was expanded to include a broader popular base, which would not happen until the end of WWI, Catholics were in no position to have a constructive impact on the national level.[97]

---

95. Giorgio Candeloro, *Il movimento cattolico in Italia* (Rome: Editori Riuniti, 1982), 160–64, 192–99, 201–14; De Rosa, *Storia del movimento cattolico in Italia*, 99–118.

96. Curci repented of certain of his accusations against the Vatican in 1884. He was readmitted to the Society of Jesus a few months before his death in 1891.

97. Universal male suffrage for persons over the age of thirty was introduced in 1912, for war veterans over the age of twenty-one in 1918, and for all adults, including women, only in 1945.

Over the course of his long pontificate, Leo demonstrated his diplomatic and real-world experience in his approach to the new realities of the modern state and international politics. He was able to reach a modus vivendi with both Bismarck's and the Kaiser's Germany, recalling the original Investiture controversy,[98] and in *Au milieu des sollicitudes* called for a *railliement* of French Catholics, majoritarian conservatives, and monarchists, to join with liberals against the anticlerical and authoritarian policies of the Third Republic.[99] After the suppression of the Paris Commune revolution (March 18 to May 28, 1871) a confluence of interests of monarchist, Bonapartist-Boulangist, fascist, progressive, and anti-Semitic factions arose in French politics that was probably not foreseeable. It became consolidated around the failed coup d'état of Boulanger in 1889 and the Dreyfus Affair from 1894 to 1906, all of which contributed to a radical Republican grip on the Third Republic and led to a series of secularizing laws in the 1870s and 1880s affecting religious education and religious freedom. These culminated in the anticlerical laws of 1905, which subordinated the clergy and the church generally to a state hegemony unmatched since the Revolution. The pontiff had understood during the course of the 1870s (he became pope in 1878) and 80s that the church could no longer stand on the sidelines, and it was clear that efforts had to be made to reconcile Catholic principles and sound reason with the new political realities. Leo's efforts in these and other political contexts revealed he was adopting a new way of thinking about the church's relations with the modern state, society, and culture, which was derived in no small part from Taparelli's appropriation and adaptation of his Scholastic sources.[100]

In *Quod Apostolici Muneris* (1878), Leo XIII's encyclical on socialism, Leo made clear that the faithful could not be politically indifferent with

---

98. With an extremely adept understanding of the German political situation, Leo and his secretary Cardinal Jacobini were able to muster the support of the Catholic Center Party for Bismarck's government in return for repeal of the Falk laws and favoring Bismarck's "peace laws" of 1887—but only after considerable horse trading and concessions to state authority. For general context, see Ernst Christian Helmreich, ed., *A Free Church in a Free State? The Catholic Church, Italy, Germany, France, 1864–1914* (Boston: Heath Publishers, 1964).

99. Leo XIII, Encyclical Letter *Au Milieu des Sollicitudes* (February 16, 1892).

100. Hittinger, "Introduction to Modern Catholicism" and "Pope Leo XIII (1810–1903)," in *The Teachings of Modern Roman Catholicism*.

respect to ideologies that were destructive of the common good; or more specifically, that embraced a conception of the common good that was contrary to the objective nature of society itself. This is an argument from Taparelli, who defended the personal rights of life, liberty, and the pursuit of happiness against potential collectivist claims on similar grounds: undermining those rights in one person undermines the reason for society in the first place. Leo's critique of socialism touches on the natural and divine constitution of society, which is based on the foundation of the family and private property. Christian principles of charity, true justice, and moral equality were, according to the encyclical, being perverted into claims for equality in material deserts. As Leo wrote:

> They leave nothing untouched or whole which by both human and divine laws has been wisely decreed for the health and beauty of life. They refuse obedience to the higher powers, to whom, according to the admonition of the Apostle, every soul ought to be subject, and who derive the right of governing from God; and they proclaim the absolute equality of all men in rights and duties. They debase the natural union of man and woman, which is held sacred even among barbarous peoples; and its bond, by which the family is chiefly held together, they weaken, or even deliver up to lust. Lured, in fine, by the greed of present goods, which is "the root of all evils, which some coveting have erred from the faith" (1 Tim. 6:10), they assail the right of property sanctioned by natural law; and by a scheme of horrible wickedness, while they seem desirous of caring for the needs and satisfying the desires of all men, they strive to seize and hold in common whatever has been acquired either by title of lawful inheritance, or by labor of brain and hands, or by thrift in one's mode of life. These are the startling theories they utter in their meetings, set forth in their pamphlets, and scatter abroad in a cloud of journals and tracts.[101]

In part a restatement and elaboration of Pius IX's condemnation of socialism and communism in *Nostis et nobiscum* (1849), Leo's criticisms in *Quod Apostolici Muneris* emphasize that the rejection of divine authority is the

---

101. Leo XIII, Encyclical Letter *Quod Apostolici Muneris* (December 28, 1878), 2.

starting point of intellectual and moral chaos. He also defends private property as "sanctioned by natural law" on the basis of inheritance and the fruits of labor. With this encyclical, Leo takes the first steps toward formulating a remedy for "the social question." The pope recognized the subsidiary structure of society, which was so fundamental for Taparelli's natural law social science.

> For, He who created and governs all things has, in His wise providence, appointed that the things which are lowest should attain their ends by those which are intermediate, and these again by the highest. Thus, as even in the kingdom of heaven He hath willed that the choirs of angels be distinct and some subject to others, and also in the Church has instituted various orders and a diversity of offices, so that all are not apostles or doctors or pastors, (1 Cor 12:28) so also has He appointed that there should be various orders in civil society, differing in dignity, rights, and power, whereby the State, like the Church, should be one body, consisting of many members, some nobler than others, but all necessary to each other and solicitous for the common good.[102]

Leo contends that the Church "sustained by the precepts of natural and divine law, provides with especial care for public and private tranquility in its doctrines and teachings regarding the duty of government and the distribution of the goods which are necessary for life and use."[103] Against false and destructive claims of entitlement to a community of goods, the Church teaches respect for the obligations of justice but also promotes provision for the needs of the poor through charitable associations, all in the context of reminding man of his eternal destiny. An approach combining natural and divine law is proposed as the "best way" to solve the social problems of the day. Leo was keenly sensitive to the inevitable totalitarian consequences of socialism.

> For, as the very evidence of facts and events shows, if this method is rejected or disregarded, one of two things must occur: either the

---

102. Leo XIII, *Quod Apostolici Muneris*, 6.
103. Leo XIII, *Quod Apostolici Muneris*, 9.

greater portion of the human race will fall back into the vile condition of slavery which so long prevailed among the pagan nations, or human society must continue to be disturbed by constant eruptions, to be disgraced by rapine and strife, as we have had sad witness even in recent times.[104]

It was a simple conclusion from abstract reason and confirmed in concrete experience that socialism inevitably led to strife and poverty, and that tyranny and slavery follow.

In his first two encyclicals, Leo XIII manifested his understanding of the case that Taparelli had been making since the 1820s generally, and specifically in the pages of the *Civiltà Cattolica* since the 1850s: that the great conflict of ideologies in industrial society was not between competing political forms with greater or lesser popular participation, nor in general about whether the state should take a lesser or greater role in the regulation of civil society. Political ideologies, political parties, and policy prescriptions were surface matters, consequences of and derivations from competing beliefs about the nature of man and society, of the common good, and of happiness. Therefore, the challenges of industrial society that the church was forced to confront at that time were not merely, or even primarily, economic, social, or political, but philosophical, cultural, and moral. In his next encyclical, *Aeterni Patris* (*On the Restoration of Christian Philosophy*), Leo adopted the line of reasoning that so motivated Taparelli's work of some forty years earlier—namely that confused metaphysical and anthropological beliefs were at the root of the modern crisis.

> Whoso turns his attention to the bitter strifes of these days and seeks a reason for the troubles that vex public and private life must come to the conclusion that a fruitful cause of the evils which now afflict, as well as those which threaten, us lies in this: that false conclusions concerning divine and human things, which originated in the schools of philosophy, have now crept into all the orders of the State, and have been accepted by the common consent of the masses. For, since it is in the very nature of man to follow the guide

104. Ibid.

of reason in his actions, if his intellect sins at all his will soon follows; and thus it happens that false opinions, whose seat is in the understanding, influence human actions and pervert them.[105]

In calling for a restoration of "Christian" philosophy in *Aeterni Patris*, Leo invokes the example of the early church fathers. Philosophy as the product of human reason, implanted in us by God, "if rightly made use of by the wise," has multiple purposes in the divine plan: as a *preparatio evangelicum* in complementing and deepening the understanding of faith, as a preparation for advanced theological thought, and for apologetics in defense of the faith against attacks from philosophical critics.[106] The medieval Scholastic philosophers are singled out for the coherence, clarity, and strength of their reasoning, and Aquinas is especially singled out as the most excellent among them in breadth and depth of thought.

> Philosophy has no part which he did not touch finely at once and thoroughly; on the laws of reasoning, on God and incorporeal substances, on man and other sensible things, on human actions and their principles, he reasoned in such a manner that in him there is wanting neither a full array of questions, nor an apt disposal of the various parts, nor the best method of proceeding, nor soundness of principles or strength of argument, nor clearness and elegance of style, nor a facility for explaining what is abstruse.[107]

Leo XIII had acquired a deep appreciation for Aquinas's comprehensive philosophical enterprise since his time at the Collegio Romano in the late 1820s, when Taparelli was first proposing a return to the Scholastics there. Liberatore was among the drafters of *Aeterni Patris*, and there is a strong reverberation of Taparelli's arguments from when he was the rector at the Collegio, fifty years earlier. The intellectual synthesis and work of that second generation of trained neo-Thomist philosophers and theologians had been accomplished.[108]

---

105. Leo XIII, Encyclical Letter *Aeterni Patris* (August 4, 1879), 2.
106. Leo XIII, *Aeterni Patris*, 4–7.
107. Leo XIII, *Aeterni Patris*, 17.
108. See generally for the influence of Taparelli's protégé, Liberatore, and an evaluation of the

Taparelli's unique contribution of a natural law social scientific theory and methodology to the launching of modern CST was, however, still ahead, now that the intellectual foundation had been laid. Taparelli died in 1862, before Pius IX's *Quanta Cura* (1864) and before *Dei Filius* (1870), let alone Leo XIII's *Aeterni Patris*. Meanwhile, the historical situation from the 1860s through the 1880s, in Europe and globally, presented "new things" that called for an elaboration of principles to guide Catholics of all political leanings and to reach beyond Catholics to the rest of an increasingly secular modern world. While the influence of Taparelli's realist social science is pervasive in *Rerum Novarum*, it is not controlling. In *Rerum Novarum*, the right of private property, which Leo had previously described in *Quod Apostolici Muneris* as "springing from" nature and "sanctioned" by natural law, is heralded as nearly "sacred" and explicitly "inviolable"; as formally a part of the natural law, not merely "springing from" it. This attitude marks the extent to which the neo-Thomists after Taparelli, of Liberatore's generation, believed it crucial to secure the advantages of capitalist development against a rising socialist tide while at the same time recognizing the need for some forms of state intervention, but without specifying principles of "due measure and degree" that might apply so that its reasonableness could be judged.[109]

If *Rerum Novarum* speaks with insufficient clarity on the foundation of individual or subjective rights "from nature," the fault has more to do with the genre of the encyclical as compared to a philosophical treatise, and with the historical context of its composition, and so it is little wonder that later Pope Pius XI so warmly advocated the study of Taparelli's work, ranked behind that of only the Angelic Doctor himself. Pius XI's adoption of Taparellian social and political principles in *Quadragesimo Anno* (1931), on the fortieth anniversary of *Rerum Novarum*, will be considered below. Modern CST, beginning with *Rerum Novarum*, was only made possible by restoring a framework of Thomist natural law, and in particular of the realist natural law reasoning about man and society "based on fact" that Taparelli pioneered from the 1840s.

---

content and impact of *Aeterni Patris*, see McCool, *Nineteenth-Century Scholasticism*, 145–66, 226–40.

109. Leo XIII, *Rerum Novarum*, 16.

CHAPTER III

SOCIAL JUSTICE AND SUBSIDIARITY

THE FOUNDERS OF MODERN social science claimed they were offering a value-free study of society, modeled on the natural sciences. Although such views on social science can still be found, by the twenty-first century, modernist, postmodernist, and critical theory agree that there is no escaping theory in scientific investigation, whether this "theory" is described as worldview, ideology, paradigm, or narrative framework. According to this view, normative or poetic prefiguration of paradigms is actually the condition for any theoretical inquiry and the progress of any science, whether natural or social. Theories of "the way things are" do not emerge as the product of scientific endeavor but rather are the necessary preconditions of such endeavor. One of the most frequently cited authors on the theory of science, Thomas Kuhn makes a compelling case that the organization of data in scientific thinking requires preexisting axiomatic models, or paradigms, that determine which facts and theories can be counted as facts and theories.[1]

Taparelli was thus ahead of his time in criticizing these claims as being abstract, reductionist, misleading in theory, and having devastating consequences in practice—in a word, ideological. It was obvious to Taparelli that every science is founded on ideas that lay outside its formally identified object of study; in fact, founded on a theory of existence itself. The perspectives offered by Classical thinkers in the realist tradition understood the necessity for axiomatic starting points for scientific inquiry; Taparelli understood, with Aristotle and Aquinas, for instance, that

---

1. Kuhn, *The Structure of Scientific Revolutions*. Kuhn arrived at his conclusion from an historical study of how science has actually been practiced, beginning with *The Copernican Revolution* (Cambridge, Mass.: Harvard University Press, 1957).

theoretical assumptions about the essential nature of the object under study are necessary guides to inquiries, explanations, and conclusions.

Taparelli would assert that the same axiomatic foundations—recognized by theorists as being essential to scientific inquiry specifically—are just as relevant to everyday cognition and human reasoning. In the case of the *social* sciences, it is almost self-evident that no data can be collected, nor analyzed, nor conclusions reached, without axiomatic assumptions regarding the operation of human nature and action. Whether tied to a materialist metaphysical belief, or merely to a somewhat effective heuristic, like choice theory, these assumptions in modern social science are often reduced to a single fundamental mechanism: arbitrarily defined materialistic self-interest. Reliance on belief in this one mechanism involves a methodological reductionism, which, while heuristically convenient, predetermines a materialistic result. Likewise, the further social scientific assumption of methodological individualism, with its premises and conclusions, reiterates a narrative framework concerning the relations between individuals and society that Taparelli found to be far from complete. In the absence of critical self-reflection, these metaphysically materialistic and anthropologically individualistic axioms are ideological in the negative sense: they belie considerable data human beings have gained from lived experience.[2]

Taparelli's realist natural law social science requires reasoning about human action from the point of view of a hylomorphic anthropology of composite human nature, which holds that man has a material, an efficient, a formal, and a final cause. Taparelli reasons from the starting

---

2. The term "ideology" is used here not as a term of Marxian economic determinism but rather as Yves Simon uses it—to describe the assumptions and aspirations of a given group of people at a given time who claim that they have universal application and explanatory value. This is not entirely dissimilar to Kuhn's "paradigms" in the context of professional science, including the social or human sciences, but Simon's term has an explicitly broader scope that applies to the cultural, cognitive-operative axioms of people at any time and place which are used in their reasoning generally about reality. Yves Simon, *The Tradition of Natural Law*, ed. Vukan Kuic (New York: Fordham University Press, 1992), 16–27. Indeed, and Taparelli would agree, these shared axioms, or "ideologies," as Simon calls them (which could also be referred to as "worldviews," "beliefs," or "values") are a formal precondition for any society of persons to distinguish themselves from a randomly chosen group of individuals who accidentally happen to be sharing time and geography. For evidence and cogent arguments opposing various materialistic paradigms (Marxian, Nietzschean, or Freudian), see C. S. Lewis, *The Abolition of Man* (Oxford: Oxford University Press, 1943).

point that human beings are material organisms, sociobiological animals, endowed with reason, and that human fulfillment ("perfection") consists in the flourishing of the multidimensional goods of health and prosperity, ordered liberty, and the advancement of knowledge and true happiness. Taparelli drew his thinking primarily from the Aristotle of the *Nicomachean Ethics* and from the Aquinas of the Treatise on Law[3] but also engaged the thinking of later Scholastics as well as a wide range of modern natural law and sociopolitical theorists.

Contemporary historical developments and Taparelli's professional and intellectual engagements, as we have seen, led him to attempt a reformation of natural law and social scientific thinking on a neoscholastic basis. The social and political crisis of modernity would never be solved, he believed, by employing the prevailing reductionist theorizing—the content of which was assumed by most of Taparelli's educated contemporaries to be the basis for future efforts in this regard. Taparelli's realist social theory—his abstract natural law reasoning applied to concrete historical contexts and his theories concerning correlative duties and rights manifested in conscience—takes the composite nature of human persons, with their material, social, and intellectual dimensions, as its foundation.

The Problem of Social Justice

The terms "social justice" and "subsidiarity" as coined in Taparelli's work have been the subject of much comment and misapprehension. Both terms were enunciated in Pius XI's social encyclical *Quadragesimo Anno*[4]

---

3. This "treatise" is found in *ST*, I-II, traditionally considered to encompass Questions 90–108, but identified by some scholars as relating only to Questions 90–97.

4. With respect to "social justice," see Pius XI, Encyclical Letter *Quadragesimo Anno* (May 15, 1931), 57–58, as follows:

> 57. But not every distribution among human beings of property and wealth is of a character to attain either completely or to a satisfactory degree of perfection the end which God intends. Therefore, the riches that economic-social developments constantly increase ought to be so distributed among individual persons and classes that the common advantage of all, which Leo XIII had praised, will be safeguarded; in other words, that the common good of all society will be kept inviolate. By this law of social justice, one class is forbidden to exclude the other from sharing in the benefits.
>
> 58. To each, therefore, must be given his own share of goods, and the distribution of created goods, which, as every discerning person knows, is laboring today under the gravest evils due to the huge disparity between the few exceedingly rich and the unnumbered propertyless,

in 1931, forty years after they were presented in their essential dimensions in *Rerum Novarum*. *Quadragesimo Anno* was primarily written by the German Jesuit Oswald von Nell-Breuning,[5] and it may well be that Nell-Breuning was not able to clarify the problem of what makes social justice (the term from Taparelli) different from simple distributive justice, or even what a social virtue is, and how it relates to individual moral conduct. Using the adjective "social" itself seems redundant in that justice always refers to individuals in some sort of relationship.[6] The reference in notes 57 and 58 of *Quadragesimo Anno* to the "distribution" and "share" of "riches" and "goods," equating the "norms of the common good" with "social justice," are altogether un-Taparellian formulations, as shall be seen. Michael Novak points out the problem with the concept of social

---

must be effectively called back to and brought into conformity with the norms of the common good, that is, social justice.

With respect to "subsidiarity," ibid., 79–80:

79. As history abundantly proves, it is true that on account of changed conditions many things which were done by small associations in former times cannot be done now save by large associations. Still, that most weighty principle, which cannot be set aside or changed, remains fixed and unshaken in social philosophy: Just as it is gravely wrong to take from individuals what they can accomplish by their own initiative and industry and give it to the community, so also it is an injustice and at the same time a grave evil and disturbance of right order to assign to a greater and higher association what lesser and subordinate organizations can do. For every social activity ought of its very nature to furnish help to the members of the body social, and never destroy and absorb them.

80. The supreme authority of the State ought, therefore, to let subordinate groups handle matters and concerns of lesser importance, which would otherwise dissipate its efforts greatly. Thereby the State will more freely, powerfully, and effectively do all those things that belong to it alone because it alone can do them: directing, watching, urging, restraining, as occasion requires and necessity demands. Therefore, those in power should be sure that the more perfectly a graduated order is kept among the various associations, in observance of the principle of 'subsidiary function,' the stronger social authority and effectiveness will be the happier and more prosperous the condition of the State.

5. See Novak, *Social Justice*, 107; Oswald von Nell-Breuning, *Reorganization of Social Economy*, trans. and ed. Bernard William Dempsey (New York: Bruce Publishing, 1936, expanded 1937, repr. 1939). Only in the 1937 and 1939 editions is the section titled "Subsidiarity," 205–6, followed by a lengthy footnote not in the original German text explaining subsidiarity in Taparellian terms, and identifying what the translator calls the "Principle of Autonomy," the "Principle of Intervention," and the "Principle of Hierarchy." The name "Taparelli" is placed in parentheses in the middle of this long note, following a quotation, with no other explanation. The quotation in this note, apparently penned by Dempsey, that references Taparelli is: "The activity of the supreme administrator will be the more effective and the more beneficial the more it affects the individual by means of subordinate authorities."

6. *ST*, II-II, q. 58, a. 2.

justice as it seems to be formulated in *Quadragesimo Anno*: Pius XI makes the argument that social justice is a normative social law, which seems inherently problematic without positing a collective mind, consciousness, and conscience. The regulative principles of social organization (such as laws) are themselves impersonal and not therefore subject to characterization as virtuous or vicious themselves. Rather, they are good or bad as they are conducive to virtue or vice and can also be implemented in virtuous or vicious ways.[7] Friedrich Hayek had already elaborated the point that, with respect to the common uses of the term "social justice," virtue and moral reasoning require the operation of a conscience.[8]

Aquinas adopts a definition of the virtue of justice that includes the will, calling it "a constant and perpetual will to render to each his right," adding:

> The definition of justice given above is suitable if it is rightly understood. For since every virtue is a habit which is the guiding principle of good acts, it is necessary that a virtue be defined in terms of the good acts specific to that virtue. Now justice is properly concerned with those things which have to do with our relations with others, as will be made clear below. [a. 2] Hence by the words 'to render to each his right' justice is defined in terms of both the act specific to it and its object. For, as Isidore says in the book Etymologies, 'someone is called just [iustus] because he upholds the right [ius]'.
>
> But if an act of any kind whatsoever is to be virtuous, it must be voluntary, and it must moreover be stable and unwavering. For the Philosopher says at Ethics II that if an act is to be virtuous it must be done, first, knowingly; second, voluntarily and for a proper end; and, third, resolutely. Now the first of these things is included in the second, since, as is said at Ethics III, what is done unknowingly is done involuntarily. Hence the definition of justice mentions first the 'will' [voluntas], in order to show that an act of justice must be voluntary; and the words 'constant' and 'perpetual' are then added, to indicate that the act must also be unwavering.

---

7. Michael Novak, *The Catholic Ethic and the Spirit of Capitalism* (New York: Free Press, 1993), 77.
8. Friedrich Hayek, *The Mirage of Social Justice* (Chicago: Regnery, 1976), 60–100.

The definition given above is, therefore, a complete definition of justice apart from the fact that the act of justice is mentioned instead of the habit which takes its species from acts of that kind: that is, the habit which is defined in terms of such acts. And if anyone should wish to reduce it to the proper form of a definition, he might say that 'justice is the habit according to which someone has a constant and perpetual will to render to each his right'. This is, in effect, the same definition as that proposed by the Philosopher at Ethics V, where he says that justice is 'a habit according to which someone is disposed to do what is just, and to be just in act and intention'.[9]

What does "social" add to "justice"? It is not to de-personalize the concept of justice: for Taparelli social justice is indeed a virtue of individual conscience, a constant and perpetual will to render to each his right. The principal point that makes it "social" is that it is such a will to render what is due to others in society *simply on account of their participation in that society*, a conception distinct from the traditional categories of justice. This point has been missed by commentators. Secondarily, social justice language is used by Taparelli, somewhat figuratively, to characterize governmental actions (institutions, policies, laws) that ought to protect and promote the fulfillment of duties and the exercise of the inalienable rights of persons in society, as these are the purposes for which society exists—but institutions, policies, and laws are in any case manifestations of the will of individuals, however authoritatively transmitted.[10]

As has been noted, Taparelli has come under criticism for introducing the concept of social justice and subjective rights talk into CST. A proper understanding of the meaning of the term "social justice" as intended by Taparelli in his elaboration of a normative science of economy, society, and

9. *ST*, II-II, q. 58, a. 1, in Dyson, *Aquinas*, 168–70.
10. As will be seen, Taparelli's conception of social justice is the virtue that corresponds to the ethical duty of solidarity, "social charity" or love of neighbor as oneself, and is anticipated in Aquinas: "Wherefore in matters pertaining to nature we should love our kindred most, in matters pertaining to the relations between citizens, we should prefer our fellow-citizens, and on the battlefield our fellow-soldiers. Hence the Philosopher says (Ethics ix, 2) that 'it is our duty to render to each class of people such respect as is natural and appropriate. This is in fact the principle upon which we seem to act.'" *ST*, II-II, q. 26.

politics, deriving its direction and moral foundation from nature, must begin with an understanding of what is socially "due." In other words, what is the nature of the rights, if any, of the members of a society deriving from the mere fact of their participation in society? What is objectively right in relating to other persons, and what are the subjective *rights* of persons as individuals—and, for Taparelli, also of the intermediary associations individual persons form in civil society that stand between themselves and the state—as they engage in the universal pursuit of happiness?

It is important to point out what social justice clearly is *not*, according to Taparelli and those following him: it is not social and/or economic egalitarianism guaranteed by a leviathan state. Nell-Breuning highlights this fundamental caveat intended by Pius XI, noting that the pope "puts his greatest and highest expectations on the state—not a state that intends to take care of everything, but a state strictly following the principle of subsidiarity."[11] The concept of subsidiarity must be introduced therefore in order to to gain a proper understanding of social duties and rights. For Taparelli, subsidiarity is the regulative principle of social justice.

In Michael Novak's last word on the subject of social justice, written with coauthor Paul Adams, he takes an historical approach to the evolution of the term "social justice" in political thought, and particularly in CST. He addresses, as had Hayek, the rhetorical imperialism the term has supported, noting how it has come to be used as a moral bludgeon and political conversation-stopper. Novak's own conclusion is that

> Rightly understood, social justice is a social virtue learned in painstaking practice by individuals—a social virtue both in its method and in its purposes. It is a noble habit truly worthy of the name "virtue." It is the living energy of the practice of democracy in America. It stands among the "habits of the heart" that Tocqueville so highly praised. It is, in fact, the habit that Tocqueville singles out as the "first law of democracy": the habit of forming associations to attend to the public needs of a democratic people.[12]

---

11. Nell-Breuning, *Reorganization of Social Economy*, 251 (discussed in Novak, *Catholic Ethic*, 76–77, 80).
12. Novak, *Social Justice*, 26–27.

This conclusion accords well enough with Taparelli's definition, as will be seen, but the differences over the form, means, and end of social justice as between Taparelli and Tocqueville have already been remarked. Working from Nell-Breuning's interpretation of social justice handicapped Novak in his effort to rescue a more definite sense of the term used so frequently in CST and in general political rhetoric.[13] Novak analyzes how Nell-Breuning treats social justice

> both as a virtue and as a principle, but ends by treating it almost solely as a principle. ...Social justice appears at best to be an institutional ideal—of indeterminate shape or location—against which concrete institutions are measured. Social justice seems to characterize no society that has yet been seen. Indeed, the use of the term is left slippery.[14]

Nell-Breuning's lack of clarity about the meaning of "social justice," and a similar lack of clarity among others working in social ethics and social economy in the late nineteenth century and into the twentieth (including Pesch, Antoine, and Messner) is understandable. While these thinkers were familiar with Taparelli's neoscholastic natural law social theories, they brought their own cultural-historical (ideological) thinking to their analyses of social problems and proposals for solutions—with views that might well strike one as idealistic, in both the pedestrian and the philosophical sense. German conservative thinkers on the social question, for instance, were more anti-capitalist than either Taparelli or Pius XI ever were. While they opposed state socialism, thinkers like Nell-Breuning favored a broad restructuring of the whole of society on corporative paradigms.[15] In any case, at the same time Nell-Breuning influenced Pius XI, the pope directly appreciated Taparelli's work.[16]

---

13. Nell-Breuning was chosen for analysis by Novak because he was the chief drafter of *Quadragesimo Anno*.
14. Ibid., 115.
15. Stefano Solari, "The Corporative Third Way in Social Catholicism (1830–1918)," *European Journal of the History of Economic Thought* 17, no. 1 (February 2010): 87–113.
16. On the influence of Taparelli's work on Pius XI, see Hittinger, "Introduction to Modern Catholicism," 11–16.

Taparelli's biographer Jacquin recalls the conversation he had with Pius XI in 1936 in which the Pope declared, "Taparelli is an author that we highly esteem, and will never be esteemed to the merit he is worth."[17] Earlier, in 1929, in the encyclical *Divini Illius Magistri* on Christian education, Pius XI referred students to the *Saggio*, which he described as "a work never sufficiently praised and recommended to university students,"[18] and referenced his comments from an address to Catholic educators and students in an allocution of December 18, 1927, in which he made the following observation.

> But beyond the works of [Aquinas], there are others that have no less excellence, and freshness of doctrine, that can be studied and consulted in every time. One of these works is certainly the *Saggio teoretico di dritto naturale* of Fr. Taparelli D'Azeglio, of the Company of Jesus. Unfortunately there are not many who know him, while not a few foreigners know him and declare him insuperable and unsurpassed.[19]

On the question of the relationship between social justice and the common good, often linked in secular uses of the term "social justice," Novak rightly raises the issue of who gets to identify the common good, with the dangers of tyranny and threats to personal freedom that this crucial question implies.[20] Here it is fundamental to note that in Taparelli's system it is clear that the common good of society does not consist of any particular arrangement or distribution of goods, but rather the term refers to the good—the end—that persons in society seek in common, the common purpose for which society is formed: that is, the protection,

---

17. "Taparelli è un autore che Noi stimiamo molto e che non si stimerà mai al merito del valore." Jacquin, *Taparelli*, 157.
18. Pius XI, Encyclical Letter *Divini Illius Magistri* (December 31, 1929), 33.
19. Ma oltre le opere dell'Aquinate, altre ve ne sono che hanno non meno eccelenza e freschezza di dottrina, che possono essere studiate e consultate in ogni tempo. Una di queste opere è certamente il *Saggio teoretico di dritto naturale* del P. Taparelli D'Azeglio, d.C.d.G. Purtroppo non sono molti quelli che lo conoscono, mentre non pochi stranieri le conoscono e lo dichiarono insuperabile e insuperato...
Jacquin, *Taparelli*, 342n7.
20. Novak, *Social Justice*, 31–33.

at the very least, of those natural rights of each person to pursue particular goods, with natural social happiness as the end toward which all temporal societies aim. The advancement of social happiness, identified as the common good, is promoted when in a free society the exercise of each person's inalienable human rights is protected. For the exercise of those abstract rights to be meaningful, it must be facilitated by the kinds of social help that overcome concrete historical impediments; persons enter into or remain in society to receive this help. Social help however must not intrude on personal dignity and liberty. For Taparelli, social justice requires that individuals protect and facilitate the fulfillment of duties and the exercise of rights to life, liberty, and the rational pursuit of happiness of concrete human persons. This is the definition of the personally held "habit according to which someone has a constant and perpetual will to render to each his right," as Aquinas stated above. Figuratively, to reiterate, Taparelli also refers to just socio-political arrangements.[21] Taparelli's use of the term "social justice" in this secondary sense, referring to "socially just" acts of government, in his description of the natural law of social existence, is not utopian, but practical, providing norms when applied prudentially to hypothetical concrete conditions.

How does social justice arise as a personal virtue? Taparelli takes as his ontological starting point the social nature of persons. Every person is born into a situation of total dependence on society, a condition that, in its first effects, is called physiological sociality. Physiological sociality is stamped on the human person (as a rule and measure). With the development of experience and reason, sociality develops into a more complex understanding of the reciprocity of social relations referring to ideas of simple justice, and then, with the advancement of abstract reasoning and conscience, sociality becomes a dictate of reason, a secondary precept of the prescription of natural law "to do the good" with regard to others.[22]

21. *Saggio*, §354, and see, e.g., §714, where just government follows the natural laws of subsidiarity.
22. Taparelli rejects the view of other theorists on sociality or sociability regarded as a primary principle of human action (he points to Puffendorff [sic]), or as one among other primary impulses or instincts. For Taparelli, as for Aquinas, the first principle of human action, the action of a reasoning human being, is to do the good—the fact of sociality establishes a universally evident good of social interdependence. *Saggio*, Note XXII. Knowledge of and habits directed toward essential goods and ends follow from an understanding of the first precept.

Physiological sociality in the reasoning person attains a psychological dimension in the developing awareness of his need for help from others in pursuit of even the barest of human goods—survival, not to mention flourishing. The morally reasoning person, having recognized that one's obligation to provide for oneself requires the help of others, and that others must do the same for themselves, to which is added an understanding of the abstract equality and identity of human persons, observes a duty of noninterference in the fulfillment of the duties of others for themselves. This moral obligation of noninterference is called by Taparelli a (subjectively held) right in that individuals can lay claim to it in the conscience of others.[23] Subsequently, the first precepts of right reason (that the good should be done and evil avoided; specifically, doing one's own good and avoiding one's own evil) become explicitly understood in the morally reasoning person in light of the recognition of our "replicated selves," as social duties: doing the good of others and avoiding doing them evil. Sociality then becomes transformed in conscience from a human need in the material and social order (physiological and psychological sociality) into a further principle of natural right (moral sociality) applied as among individuals simply by the fact of their being, necessarily, in society. From there, as a result of their power to bind others in conscience, Taparelli calls these social rights. Physiological sociality (as a de facto condition of human existence), develops into psychological sociality (as a means of pursuing one's own perceived good), and then leads to moral sociality (a sense of obligation to work for the good of others). From sociality as a human necessity comes sociality as a human virtue, involving respect for the necessities of others in society; and the freedoms exercised in fulfillment of duties claimed for oneself transform into "rights" held by oneself and others. This is how the fact of sociality leads to the obligations of social rights and the precepts of social justice.

23. Without trivializing this realization in the developing conscience, this amounts to recognizing that "we are all in this together." This point also is anticipated by Aquinas.
> Thirdly, there is in man an inclination to good, according to the nature of his reason, which nature is proper to him: thus man has a natural inclination to know the truth about God, and to live in society: and in this respect, whatever pertains to this inclination belongs to the natural law; for instance, to shun ignorance, to avoid offending those among whom one has to live, and other such things regarding the above inclination.

ST, I-II, q. 94, art. 2.

Regard for social justice, for the protection and promotion of our fulfillment of duties and exercise of rights, is closely connected in CST to the ethical principle of "solidarity." Solidarity, or social charity, goes beyond what the natural law demands of all forms of justice, based on what is due in the context of social order and simple justice. Solidarity as social charity introduces the idea of the sacrifice of one's own interests. The term "solidarity" comes to us through the work of those same German theorists who borrowed heavily from Taparelli's thinking, especially Heinrich Pesch.[24] "Solidarity" has gained importance in modern CST, from its first uses by Pius XI in *Quadragesimo Anno*, to the encyclicals of John-Paul II[25] and Benedict XVI,[26] as another way of thinking about questions of social morality. If it is understood as an elevated obligation of moral sociality, as in Taparelli's theory, arising from the recognition of abstract human identity and equality, moved by compassion, aided by piety and charity (love) and rising to the level of self-sacrifice for others, then a life of solidarity would characterize the supremely socially just person. Obviously, charitable associations are engaged in the work of social justice and solidarity. Political societies, with their particular ends and particular means, are also subject to the dictates of social justice, including the protection and promotion of solidarity—indeed it is their raison d'être. While Taparelli does not use the term "solidarity," he does discuss how the perfection of social duty culminates in the sacrificial love of neighbor.

---

24. Pesch introduces the term "solidarism" to describe another sort of corporative vision for society and opposes this theory to individualism and socialism—but his definition of "social justice" is fundamentally different from that of Taparelli. The concept of "solidarism" in Pesch is just as slippery as is his idea of social justice.
> It is precisely this *universality of energies, means, and motives* which is peculiar to solidarism, the breadth of vision with which it takes into account the wide variety and the shifting historical contexts in which economic phenomena operate, which is its best endorsement and which sets it apart from the essentially one-sided individualist and socialist systems. At the very heart of the [solidarist] system, however is *social justice*, justice toward the community, toward the whole, for all classes, all citizens, which is firmly rooted in the moral order of things.

Rupert J. Ederer, ed. and trans., *Heinrich Pesch on Solidarist Economics: Excerpts from the Lehrbuch der Nationalökonomie* (Lanham: University Press of America, 1998), 88. For Pesch's extended explanation of his choice of the term "solidarism," see ibid., 85.

25. Including twenty-two encyclicals from *Redemptor Hominis* (1979) to *Sollicitudo Rei Socialis* (1987) and *Centesimus Annus* (1991), among others.

26. *Caritas in Veritate* (2009), *Deus Caritas Est* (2005).

To determine my duties toward men I have only to act such as to will for them the various forms that I present to myself of the universal principle [do the good] considered relative to myself. By this material transformation I will obtain by analogy the following formulas, all substantially equal: *do the good of others, act that the other tend toward his end, that he retains order, that he lives honestly, fittingly, that he obtains his perfection, that he finds happiness, that he tends toward God, that he manifests divine perfection, that he gives glory to his God.* ...you will see the social principle reduce itself to the noted formula – *to love others as oneself.*[27]

Introduction to Subsidiarity

The complementary principle of natural law governing social organization is that of subsidiarity—which Taparelli calls "hypotactical right." Subsidiarity defines the contextual requirements and modes of social justice. Indeed, in terms of solidarity and social charity, the principles of subsidiarity clarify how best, prudently and effectively, to advance social justice, but also how to direct the sacrifice of material self-interest. To briefly introduce the concept, it must be pointed out that Taparelli was charting new, natural law territory from an Aristotelian and Thomistic philosophical starting point, and he was compelled to coin technical terms, including "hypotactical association," to describe the complex relations of intermediary associations, or societies, in the larger society.[28] He called an association of individuals or of groups generically a "consortium" (*consorzio*). Intermediary associations, describing all such consortia (*consorzii*) situated between the individual and the state, exist in determinate relations of interdependence or subordination; thus consortia that together comprise higher, more comprehensive, associations were "deutarchies"; while broader societies culminating in

---

27. *Saggio*, §314. Taparelli finds confirmation and evidentiary weight for his theories in the divine law but does not derive details from revelation other than from the acknowledgment of the creative power of the "Grand Artificer"—knowledge of which, following Aquinas and Aristotle, he was persuaded was accessible to natural reason.

28. "Non ci s'imputi a colpa la novità del vocabolo..." [Please don't blame us for the novelty of the term.], *Saggio*, §688, note 'a.'

political states, formed by a conglomeration of deutarchies, were called "protarchies." Deutarchies and protarchies may be of synthetic or analytic formation, which is to say they may be formed by individuals or by associations as higher orders of organization (composition), or by higher level associations as diverse lower levels of organization (division). The mode of formation of the association at any level carries with it principles of relative rights and legitimate authority. Any society of a certain size implies, Taparelli suggests, complex association, carrying within it both vertical and horizontal intermediary associations. In such an arrangement, the deutarchies are not subordinate to the protarchy insofar as their own ends are concerned: they each have their own rights as associations to pursue their proper ends, the "universal law, principle of all hypotactical right, born from the essence of these relations."[29] Thus the abstract natural law of complex social organization establishing the duties and rights of association is that "every consortium must conserve its proper unity in such a way as to not diminish the unity of the whole; and every higher society provides for the unity of the whole without destroying the unity of the consortia."[30]

Taparelli's theoretical social order would culminate, ideally, in a future international order of the "ethnarchy," or "society of peoples" emerging from the "polyarchy" of independent state protarchies—a brotherhood of nation-states characterized by their own rights to existence, and by their own orientation and authority in support of the common good (that is, protecting and facilitating the exercise of inalienable human rights) of the whole of humanity,[31] subject to the principles of subsidiarity.

Realist social and political theory starts with a conception of human nature in its composite material, social, and intellectual aspects, and it develops an approach to the question of the best-suited political arrangement in a given society based on a regime's utility or expedience towards achieving the satisfaction of human needs and goods conceived of as

---

29. *Saggio*, §§685–93, generally.
30. "Ogni consorzio dee conservare la propria unità in modo da non perdere la unità del tutto: ed ogni società maggiore provvedr all unità del tutto senza distruggere la unità dei consorzii." *Saggio*, §694.
31. *Saggio*, §§1363–68.

ends.[32] Comparing the utility of regimes towards the fulfillment of human nature understood as ends is radically different from Epicurean utilitarianism: the latter takes both the "autonomous individual" and material self-interest (measured in units of pleasure) as its starting points and sees social and political organization as necessary evils at best, because they are infringements on the unlimited gratification of material self-interest, which are seen by it as the proper end of individual action. In contrast, for realists, human social existence at its core is biological, based on human sexual and developmental requirements; social and political arrangements are natural extensions of the limited power of individual human beings to satisfy their personal composite needs; in this sense, politics is a positive good for the facilitation of the greater fulfillment of, for the perfection of, not merely material, but also social and intellectual goods, all tending toward a conception of happiness—the perfection of body, will, and intellect—that serves as a guide for a person's reasoning and actions. Nature establishes in humans a range of needs with reference to the goods that satisfy them but unfortunately limits their capacity for satisfying them in myriad ways; therefore, humans are naturally dependent, in this natural order not of their own making, on forming associations for support. According to Taparelli, the needs of physiological sociality are met by "social support" (*sussidio sociale*) by associating with others to fulfill first and foremost the duty to oneself of self-preservation, the sine qua non of animal survival and basic condition of any other human flourishing.[33]

Taparelli's natural law thought justifies the conceptual move from natural right (*dritto naturale*) to subjectively possessed natural rights, by means of the movement in a well-formed conscience from the abstract

32. "If you tell me: act in such a way because it is useful—I will ask you right away: useful for what?" *Saggio*, Note VII, Taparelli suggests that moral philosophies can be classified as they reason from pleasure or to happiness: they say "such an act gives pleasure, *therefore* it is appropriate (honest, good), others say such an act is appropriate (honest, good) *therefore* it will make you happy." See also Note IX where every "utility" must be defined by the ends of human action identified in what Taparelli calls the universal division of philosophy into the *sensist* (*materialist*), *spiritualist* (*idealist*), or *mixed* (*realist*) systems. Taparelli's elaboration of traditional indifference in Catholic political philosophy with regard to regime forms (seeing government as merely useful to the pursuit of the common good, as the good of fully human persons) should not be confused with Epicurean utilitarianism (a philosophy Taparelli regularly criticizes by name).

33. *Saggio*, §691.

apprehension of "right" in the contemplation of being and of the order of the natural world to the subjective apprehension of corresponding and reciprocal duties for the common good of social order.[34] The intellectual apprehension of common human experience, including the experience of effort and suffering, and their opposites, cooperation and pleasure, lead to the identification of the goodness of sociality as an object of the will. It is when the human person recognizes in other persons in society the same duties to preserve life, to associate with others, and to pursue happiness in this world that the person sees in themselves, that the dictate of noninterference in those pursuits becomes a right that one extends to others in conscience. For Taparelli, subjective rights, not rational calculations of self-interest (however they might be defined) are the natural product of moral reasoning. To reiterate, according to the natural law of sociality, the duty to seek and the right to receive social help is expressed in the human right of freedom of association. The duty and right of association does not require agreement on the ultimate good to be pursued but merely on an appropriate good that is not contrary to ultimate Good. In other words, freedom of association is a necessary but not sufficient condition for persons to fulfill their true good, which is perfect happiness in the divine beatitude—but consensus on the exact content of that conclusion or belief can in fact be bracketed, so long as the useful good pursued in any society is not contrary to it.[35]

And so it is that from the pursuit of happiness that each person recognizes his intellectual, social, and material needs, as well as the goodness of the social order that makes the pursuit of those other goods for oneself and for other selves possible, and which reveals the natural law of sociality as a necessary (but not sufficient) condition for the ultimate good of free intellectual persons. Based on his metaphysical and anthropological understandings, and finding confirmation in Socrates, Plato, Aristotle, Cicero, and Saint Augustine, Taparelli identifies the highest end of human activity, the highest human happiness, as the intellectual

---

34. *Saggio*, §349.
35. *Saggio*, §28; see also ibid., Note XX.

contemplation of the truth.[36] Considering that no person wants to believe a falsehood, the pursuit of happiness, human flourishing, and self-actualization do not imply open-ended possibilities. No person has a right to define the universe and the meaning of life as he wishes: there is a finite range of rational possibilities, from the strictly materialist to the strictly spiritualist, and one can dare to say that the effects of any given set of metaphysical/anthropological/ethical beliefs are subject to pragmatic empirical evaluation. Taparelli contended that the flaws of the modern political theorists were their mistaken theories on morality and ethics, the product of their elevation of one or another limited end of human activity—focusing on material needs primarily, and physical pleasure—as the ultimate good, and that they imagine that ideology is able to perfect society.[37] In contrast, in Taparelli's system of social science, every particular society, no matter its particular scope or end, is never more than a means to the true end and ultimate happiness of mankind and is subject to evaluation on that basis.[38]

Taparelli's determination to reconcile the notions of natural right and subjective rights was driven by the need he felt to counter the social contract theories of rights, which were based on false axioms of moral autonomy and sovereign will. He saw these metaphysical and anthropological beliefs as being at the root of nearly the whole of the modern crisis, affecting every dimension of life—spiritual, intellectual, moral, economic, social, and political. He saw the ideals of the modern theorists, especially Hobbes, Rousseau, and Kant, as vain attempts for plural attempts to establish society on the clean slate of a rationally constructed system. Taparelli, like other Catholic Conservatives of the Restoration period, saw this spirit of independent reason as the root of the Reign of Terror and a signpost pointing to future moral chaos and totalitarian avatars. Instead, as has been seen, Taparelli's natural law human rights are derived from an understanding of composite, material, social, and intellectual human nature—and from there to the recognition of our replicated selves in others, bound together in sociality.

36. *Saggio*, Note X. Taparelli also finds confirmation for this point from the Hindu doctrines of *maia* and *nirvana*.
37. *Saggio*, Notes VIII–IX.
38. *Saggio*, Note XXXVIII.

Duty to oneself, and the recognition of this duty equally and reciprocally as respects others, leads in conscience to extending subjective rights to the humanity in those others, originally identified in the abstract as other selves. In this way, subjective rights are established in the abstract. Natural right or natural law is a product of right reason, while subjective rights are the intersubjective products of moral judgment, exercising their force in the arena of conscience and will, based on the appreciation of abstract human identity. The fundamental needs of human nature—material, social, and intellectual (or spiritual)—correspond to what Taparelli referred to later in his social economic writings as the "three motors" of human action, or the three distinct ends/goods that inform human action; namely, physical perfection (life and health), social perfection (order and justice), and intellectual perfection (truth, piety, and love). Understanding this composite motivation of human action is the basis for Taparelli's realist, normative-ethical social science in which the advancement of social justice according to the principles of subsidiarity, along with the expansion in general of the material circumstances of life, are the measures of authentic civilizational progress and of human felicity.

Genealogy of the Idea of Subsidiarity

The origins of the term "subsidiarity" and the formal expression of the concept in Catholic thought is generally traced back to Pius XI's statements in *Quadragesimo Anno* from 1931. Its more precise genealogy is obscure in the literature, some tracing it to discussions in German jurisprudence between the World Wars, some to the writings of Bishop Wilhelm Emmanuel von Ketteler in the mid-nineteenth century. Others find seminal formulations of it in Aquinas and Aristotle; Finnis identified the principle in *Summa Contra Gentiles*.[39]

> In every government the best thing is that provision be made for the things governed according to their mode, for in this consists the justice of the regime. Consequently, even as it would be contrary to the nature of human rule, if the governor of a state were to forbid men

---

39. John Finnis, *Aquinas: Moral, Political, and Legal Theory* (Oxford: Oxford University Press, 1998), 121.

to act according to their various duties,—except perhaps for a time, because of some particular urgency—so it would be contrary to the notion of God's government, if he did not allow creatures to act in accordance with the mode of their respective natures.[40]

And Finnis finds an important anticipation of the principle of subsidiarity as well in the *Summa Theologiae*: "Neither in one's whole being nor in all one's belongings is one subordinate to the political community."[41] These statements from the two *Summae* taken together identify aspects of subsidiarity as an exercise in political prudence aimed at the common good of human life as a whole.[42] Nevertheless, identifying scholastic antecedents to subsidiarity does not establish how the concept came to be used in the 19th and 20th centuries. On classical roots of the principle of subsidiarity, Finnis points out that Aristotle probably rejected Plato's apparent argument in the *Republic* respecting state centralization and control that more is better.[43] Aristotle appreciated the complex makeup of the polis and of households and villages in the *Politics*,[44] but there and in the *Nicomachean Ethics*[45] he took as fundamental the natural priority of the city-state (the "whole precedes the parts") and the superiority of the common good of the polis (its flourishing) over that of the individuals comprising it. The exact balance in Aristotle of uniformity and control versus the freedom of individuals and their joint enterprises remains a contested point beyond the scope of this study. The natural law and principles of justice that should apply in complex societies were essentially open questions that Taparelli addressed with his natural law theory of social duties and rights. Although Taparelli did not use the term "subsidiarity," preferring the Greek term of his own coinage "hypotactical right," Taparelli had a conception of subsidiarity that arose from his view of the social nature of man and establishes

---

40. SCG, III, 71, para. 4.
41. ST, I-II, q. 21, a. 4, ad. 3.
42. Finnis, *Aquinas*, 121, 237.
43. John Finnis, "Subsidiarity's Roots and History: Some Observations," *The American Journal of Jurisprudence* 61, no. 1 (2016): 136.
44. Aristotle, *Politics*, I, 1–2.
45. NE, I, 2.

principles of association that must be respected as rights in the political order; it entered into CST in this form and became an operative principle of social justice.[46]

The language of *Quadragesimo Anno* reflects the direct, at times verbatim, influence of Taparelli on the concept of subsidiarity. Such an influence was obscured by Nell-Breuning, identified as the chief drafter of the encyclical, who explained the concept of subsidiarity in his subsequent book on the encyclical in clearly Taparellian terms without referring to Taparelli at all.[47] Apparently such was still the reluctance to refer in any larger public context to Taparelli as an authority for such matters, perhaps especially among the Jesuits (other than contributors to *Civiltà Cattolica*). Moreover, in a later writing, Nell-Breuning additionally obscured Taparelli's influence by tracing the concept more vaguely back to a time "well before Pius XI" formulated it in Catholic teaching, even locating its roots in the political thought of Abraham Lincoln. Nell-Breuning quotes Lincoln as stating that "the legitimate object of government is to do for a community of people whatever they need to have done but cannot do at all, or cannot so well do for themselves in their separate and individual capacities. In all that people can individually do as well for themselves, governments ought not to interfere."[48] Nell-Breuning strains to posit a connection between the idea of limited government as a general political principle and subsidiarity as a fully developed sociopolitical theory of the rights and duties of intermediary associations in complex societies.[49]

---

46. Subsidiarity has been described as "neither a theological nor even really a philosophical principle, but a piece of congealed historical wisdom." John Coleman, SJ, ed., *The Development of Church Social Teaching* (New York: Paulist Press, 1986), 183, cited in Thomas Kohler, "Quadragesimo Anno," in *A Century of Catholic Social Thought*, ed. George Weigel and Robert Royal (Washington, D. C.: Ethics and Public Policy Center, 1991), 31. For the historical sources of the concept, see Ilenia Massa Pinto, "La Concezione Antica."

47. Nell-Bruening, *Reorganization of Social Economy*, 206. This citation is to the 1937 expanded edition. See note 5 above.

48. Nell-Breuning, "Social Movements: Christian Social Doctrine," in *Sacramentum Mundi: An Encyclopedia of Theology*, vol. 6, ed. Karl Rahner (New York: Herder & Herder, 1968–70), 114–16, cited in Novak, *Catholic Ethic*, 76n36.

49. It would have been better had Nell-Breuning focused on relating subsidiarity to the principle of federalism if he wanted to draw upon the American experience. See, for example, David Golemboski, "Federalism and the Catholic Priniciple of Subsidiarity," *Publius: The Journal of*

Pius XI was obliged to address these very issues by the rise of the statist systems of the Fascists and Communists, including their absorption or elimination of private associational freedoms and initiatives, particularly those of organizations connected to the Catholic Church. The twentieth century was giving birth to regimes that Taparelli had in the 1840s accurately predicted—more presciently even than had Tocqueville—as the inevitable result of the secularization of culture, rationalization of government, and atomization of the economy and society. Pius XI spelled out the relevant principles of subsidiarity in *Quadragesimo Anno*, noting that the mere technological ability of modern states to assume many tasks formerly performed by lesser associations, enterprises, and individuals does not make it good or even efficient for them to do so, keeping in mind that

> just as it is gravely wrong to take from individuals what they can accomplish by their own initiative and industry and give it to the community, so also it is an injustice and at the same time a grave evil and disturbance of right order to assign to a greater and higher association what lesser and subordinate organizations can do. For every social activity ought of its very nature to furnish *help* to the members of the body social, and never destroy and absorb them.[50] (italics added)

Thus, an attack on the independent existence of these lower associations is an attack against the social body itself; that is, against the foundation of its authority. These formulations follow Taparelli on subsidiarity very closely. What is unformulated is how the destruction and absorption of these subordinate associations is a violation of social justice—described by Taparelli as following from a violation of the necessary respect owed by the state for the duties and rights of intermediary associations and individual persons.

Pius XI endorsed Taparelli's reasoning also on the utility and efficiency to be gained from respecting this natural mode of social organization. But

---

Federalism 45, no. 4 (October 1, 2015): 526–51.
50. Pius XI, *Quadragesimo Anno*, 79.

it must be noted that the focus on the word "help" (*subsidium*) encourages a potential misunderstanding of subsidiarity. Taparelli's concept of subsidiarity comes from a realist utilitarian conception of the state as the necessary means for the pursuit of the common good, as we have seen, and so the idea of "helping," even from the top down, so to speak, is not without some sense. But the proper "help" that Taparelli argues the larger society can offer to individuals and lower associations is in protecting the exercise of their rights and facilitating their own agency in the fulfillment of their duties.

"Help" is actually the secondary meaning of the term *subsidium*; it comes from the figurative use of one of its primary meanings, which is an "auxiliary troop," derived from the prefix *sub*, meaning below, and *sedeo*, meaning "sit." These were reserve forces, such as the *triarii*, in Roman legionary battle formations and tactics. Thus, the term specifically comes from a tactical arrangement of forces, connected and interrelated to support the common purpose of the cohort, century, and legion. The support is from the bottom up, "helping" the larger grouping in its pursuit of a common good. That is the primary meaning and provides a very useful context for describing the principles of the arrangement of lower-level forces toward a common purpose, taking into account their proper makeup, purpose, and authority. Indeed, the success of the whole depends on respecting the relative autonomy of the lower units. Although Taparelli uses a reference to the centuries of soldiers constituting the Roman legion as an example of "hypotactical association," he chose not to adapt the Roman military terminology, but rather to employ a Greek term for setting forth the natural law principles of complex society—"hypotactical right," which primarily relates to Greek grammar. "Subsidiarity" was not his expression at all but instead was the renaming of Taparelli's term by perhaps Nell-Breuning and/or others—possibly to avoid an obvious reference to Taparelli, which "hypotactical right" surely would have been. It is not clear whether Nell-Breuning introduced this linguistic transition when he advanced Taparelli's natural law social theory in the course of drafting *Quadragesimo Anno*; any number of German, French, or Italian Jesuits may have made the crucial suggestion.

The adjective *"ipotattico"* (hypotactical) chosen by Taparelli was undoubtedly inspired by the Greek term "ὑπόταξις" (hupotaxis), which had both military and grammatical senses. In its variable forms and uses, the adjectival hypotactical, "ὑποτακτικός" (hupotaktikós), relates in grammar to what is "necessarily placed after" (behind, under) "something with which it is combined."[51] It comes from the Greek *"hupo-,"* ("hypo-") meaning under or behind, and *"taktikos"* meaning (obviously) "tactics," strategic coordination, or arrangement. Hypotaxis and hypotactical as grammatical terms have been in common use since antiquity. The term refers to "postpositions" (the opposite of prepositions), which are adjectival or adverbial terms that give meaning to their complement from behind it in the order of the sentence. It refers also to the position of vowels that must come second in a diphthong; that is, the necessary coordination of vowels to provide for a word's proper sound, and it also relates to verbs requiring the subjunctive mood generally. Taparelli would also have appreciated the other substantive meanings of hypotaxis relating to military organization, as with the Roman legion, and the more lightly armed Greek military troops that supported, or followed, the phalanx. While inspired by these terms, both for their grammatical meanings and military organizational imagery, Taparelli uses only the adjectival form *"ipotattico"* from ὑποτακτικός, (hypotactical). The neologism that Taparelli uses—*"società ipotattica"* ("hypotactical society") and *"dritto ipotattico"* ("hypotactical right")—conveys the idea of the cooperative ordering of parts in society, and the duties and rights pertaining to the interdependent, necessarily coordinated integrity of social relations. The coordination is essential: the whole cannot, even conceptually, take priority over the parts. The parts and the whole are mutually bound together by the natural law of social relations, like the parts of speech and clauses in a sentence, without which the sentence as a whole is without meaning or confused. Similarly, the larger society, let alone the state that exercises political authority, has no meaning or purpose independent of the individuals and associations within it, the purposes of their associating in

---

51. Henry George Liddell and Robert Scott, *A Greek-English Lexicon*, 9th ed., revised supplement by Henry Stuart Jones (First edition, 1843; Oxford: Oxford University Press, 1996), 1897.

the first place.[52] Thus, while the Greek etymologies generally imply a sort of submission or subordination in the arrangement of parts of a whole, Taparelli writes that the problem is precisely to determine the natural laws, the duties and rights, of the complex of what has been confusedly called a "*subordinate* society."[53]

"Subsidiarity," as the principle came to be known, is etymologically a fair latinization, on the one hand, from the Greek *hupotaxis*. But, on the other hand, as has been seen, the translation *sub-* ("below") plus *sedeo* ("sit") involves a shift; whether this was understood or not at the time of the shift is probably not knowable at this point. The shift comes with advantages and disadvantages. On the one hand it seems to accord with other language used by Taparelli concerning how associations of individuals and associations of associations exist for the purposes of social subsidy (*sussidio sociale*)—that is, they facilitate the fuller exercise of the rights and fulfillment of the duties of individuals and their subsequent associations. But the new wording also invites a top-down interpretation, as if the intermediary associations and even persons exist to support the greater society. Or, if the term "social subsidy" is not understood at all properly in the Taparellian sense, one could imagine subsidiarity meaning that the larger society sends "*sussidio sociale*" as it "subsidizes" individuals, an interpretation that reinforces rhetorical uses of the term social justice as another name for distributive, or redistributive, justice. This understanding of the term runs directly contrary to Taparelli's theory of hypotactical association and to Pope Pius XI's articulation of the teaching in *Quadragesimo Anno*, where the pope explicitly defends the independent rights and authority of intermediary associations in matters where the state has no right to meddle, calling it "a grave evil and disturbance of right." One must imagine the force of this remark being proclaimed in the capital of Mussolini's Italy.

---

52. That is, the purposes of individuals in forming the deutarchies, and of deutarchies in forming the protarchy. Protarchies cannot ever be formed by individuals—there's always at least the association of families at the base of any and all higher levels of social and socio-political organization.

53. *Saggio*, §685. Concerning those "società *subordinate*" that make up another larger society in pursuit of a common good, "le leggi della lor *subordinazione* non sono state mai contemplate" [the laws of their *subordination* have never been contemplated]

Certainly the Latinization of the term into "subsidiarity" was a mellifluous choice over "hypotactical right." Another risk of not changing the term, moreover, would have been a mistranslation or conflation with the word "hypostatic"—a confusion to be avoided at all costs. A "hypostatic" notion of the absorption of the individual into the machinery of the state, or of individual wills into a Rousseauian General Will, would be the very opposite of Taparelli's meaning. A conception of the state as representing a higher level of being, with persons defined fundamentally by their relationship to it, would be diametrically opposed to Taparelli's idea of the dignity of the human person endowed by nature, and nature's creator, with certain inalienable rights. It would be the difference between an organic and an *organicist* conception of social nature,[54] which is to say the difference between a state conceived as an extension of the natural order of family, clan, and tribe, for instance, and that of the state imagined as the pinnacle of human achievement, giving meaning and direction to all its parts.[55] Another fundamental difference between "hypotactical" and "hypostatic" is of course that *Quadragesimo Anno* drew a clear distinction between the necessarily voluntary character of professional associations[56] at a time when the *regime corporativista* (corporatist regime) of the

---

54. Cf. Rommen, *The State in Catholic Thought: A Treatise in Political Philosophy* (St. Louis: B. Herder, 1945), 36–38. For the contrast with a traditional Catholic view of the state as a moral organism, see ibid., 299–305.

55. Consider Pius XI's further distinction made in *Quadragesimo Anno*, 95:
We are compelled to say that to Our certain knowledge there are not wanting some who fear that the State, instead of confining itself as it ought to the furnishing of necessary and adequate assistance, is substituting itself for free activity; that the new syndical and corporative order savors too much of an involved and political system of administration; and that (in spite of those more general advantages mentioned above, which are of course fully admitted) it rather serves particular political ends than leads to the reconstruction and promotion of a better social order.

56. Moreover, just as inhabitants of a town are wont to found associations with the widest diversity of purposes, which each is quite free to join or not, so those engaged in the same industry or profession will combine with one another into associations equally free for purposes connected in some manner with the pursuit of the calling itself. Since these free associations are clearly and lucidly explained by Our Predecessor of illustrious memory, We consider it enough to emphasize this one point: People are quite free not only to found such associations, which are a matter of private order and private right, but also in respect to them 'freely to adopt the organization and the rules which they judge most appropriate to achieve their purpose.' *Quadragesimo Anno*, 87.

Fascists was mandating social reorganization according to state policy.[57]

The principle of subsidiarity in modern CST had been first expressed, although not formally identified by name, by Leo XIII in *Rerum Novarum*. Concerned to support religious and worker's associations, he made the following claim based on natural law.

> These lesser societies and the larger society differ in many respects, because their immediate purpose and aim are different. Civil society exists for the common good, and hence is concerned with the interests of all in general, albeit with individual interests also in their due place and degree. It is therefore called a public society, because by its agency, as St. Thomas of Aquinas says, "Men establish relations in common with one another in the setting up of a commonwealth." But societies which are formed in the bosom of the commonwealth are styled *private*, and rightly so, since their immediate purpose is the private advantage of the associates. "Now, a private society," says St. Thomas again, "is one which is formed for the purpose of carrying out private objects; as when two or three enter into partnership with the view of trading in common." Private societies, then, although they exist within the body politic, and are severally part of the commonwealth, cannot nevertheless be absolutely, and as such, prohibited by public authority. For, to enter into a "society" of this kind is the natural right of man; and the State has for its office to protect natural rights, not to destroy them; and, if it forbid its citizens to form associations, it contradicts the very principle of its own existence, for both they and it exist in virtue of the like principle, namely, the natural tendency of man to dwell in society.[58]

---

57. Cf. Novak, *Catholic Ethic*, 63n3; and *Social Justice*, 112–13. Note the fascist/socialist statist and collectivist orientation of Mussolini's declaration, "Tutto nello Stato, niente al di fuori dello Stato, nulla contro lo Stato" [Everything in the state, nothing outside the state, nothing against the state], Speech before the Chamber of Deputies, May 26, 1927, in Benito Mussolini, *Discorsi del 1927* (Milan: Alpes, 1928), 157.

58. Leo XIII, *Rerum Novarum*, 51.

Though Leo XIII does not use the Taparellian terms, he clearly describes the principles of sociality and hypotactical right in explicitly Taparellian formulations. The conditions under which *Rerum Novarum* was written were very complex. There is no doubt that the "Magna Carta" of modern CST was greatly influenced by historical circumstances, having evolved in the context of worsening social conditions, political upheavals, anti-clerical liberal regimes, and the rise of hostile atheistic communism. The tensions and conflicting ideas present in these circumstances make the accomplishments of the encyclical all the more remarkable, notwithstanding certain uneven and frankly partisan sections.[59] It is no wonder that many concepts could not be explicitly formulated from the first principles, since there was in fact wide disagreement over those principles, not to mention over specific remedies to be proposed.

Jacquin in his article on the significance of the principle of "droit hypotactique" that appeared in a volume of studies commemorating the hundredth anniversary of Taparelli's death, points to the presence of Taparelli's social theories in the encyclical tradition beginning with *Rerum Novarum*. It is interesting to note that in the French translation of *Rerum Novarum*, the Taparellian term "sociability" is used. As Jacquin comments on the text, "Leo XIII, in his encyclical *Rerum Novarum*, wrote these lines confirming the position of Taparelli on

---

59. Antonazzi authoritatively depicts the situation thus, "Tutti naturalmente condannavano le teorie socialiste e, sia pure più blandamente, disapprovavono la politica liberale. Ma sul piano costruttivo ci si esauriva spesso in dibattiti infecondi, creando nelle coscienze un diffuso senso di disagio. Non era davvero agevole porsi al disopra delle parti, indicare un orientamento, impartire direttive chiare, precise e vincolanti per tutti." [Everyone naturally condemned the socialist theories and, perhaps more blandly, disapproved of liberal politics. But on the constructive level one often exhausted oneself in infertile debates, creating in consciences a diffuse sense of unease. There was really no easy placing oneself above the parties, to indicate an orientation, to impart clear directives, precise and binding for all.] And continuing: "Il significato della *Rerum novarum* e il suo merito precipuo sta, a mio parere, nell'aver individuato, attraverso il dinamismo di una dialecttica non sempre equanime e spassionata, quell'orientamento, di averlo additato con la tradizionale prudenza ma anche con profetica lungimiranza e di averlo avallato col sigillo del supremo magistero della Chiesa." [The significance of *Rerum Novarum* and its main merit stands, in my opinion, in having located, through the dynamism of a not always level-headed and dispassionate dialectic, that orientation, to have pointed it out with the traditional prudence but also prophetic farsightedness and to have guaranteed it by the supreme magisterium of the Church.] Giovanni Antonazzi, "Il laboratorio della *Rerum novarum*," in De Rosa, *I tempi della Rerum Novarum* (Roma: Rubbettino Ed., 2002), 294.

the *deutarchies* at the bosom of the protarchy: "The right to existence was authorized to them by nature itself, and the public society which would prohibit private societies would be attacking itself, since societies, public and private, draw their origin from a same principle, the natural sociability of man."[60]

Subsidiarity as a formal principle of CST was subsequently reiterated many times, beginning in 1931 when it first appeared in *Quadragesimo Anno* (as "the principle of 'subsidiary function'"), but especially after Vatican II and John XXIII.[61] Taparelli's biographer, Jacquin, does not connect Taparelli's *dritto hypotattico* with the principle of subsidiarity; in fact, he

---

60. Robert Jacquin, "L'actualité du 'Droit Hypotactique,'" in *Miscellanea Taparelli*, ed. P. Ciprotti and J. D. Algeria (Roma: Libreria Editrice Dell'Università Gregoriana, 1964), 191–205, especially 205, quoting from *RN* 51. In the official French edition of *Rerum Novarum*, versus the official English translation quoted above, the phrase from *RN* 51, "homines sunt natura congregabiles" is translated at footnote 59 as "la naturelle sociabilité de l'homme."

61. After Pius XI, the doctrine was confirmed and further elaborated by magisterial statements. John XXIII quoted Pius XI's formulation from *Quadragesimo Anno* in his encyclical *Mater et Magister* (May 15, 1961), 53. Paul VI elaborated the concept as necessarily relating to the free formation and expression of cultural and religious ideals:

> Political activity ... should be the projection of a plan of society ... which springs from a complete conception of man's vocation and of its differing social expressions.... It is for cultural and religious groupings, in the freedom of acceptance which they presume, to develop in the social body, disinterestedly and in their own ways, those ultimate convictions on the nature, origin and end of man and society.

Encyclical Letter *Octogesima Adveniens* (May 14, 1971), 25. Paul VI also cites Taparelli in his General Audience address of October 9, 1968, in reference to the natural law on human equality and the inviolability of the human person; and again in a General Audience address of August 9, 1972 on awakening consciences in light of the "disastrous myth" of "revolution" as compared to a right understanding of liberty and progress that respects objective duties and the common good, and in which he cites Aquinas, *ST* II-II, q. 42, along with the *Saggio*, §980. John Paul II in his consideration of CST after Leo XIII in *Centesimus Annus*, directly invoked "the principle of subsidiarity" in the context of a discussion of making the welfare state more efficient and more human, defining it thus: "A community of a higher order should not interfere in the internal life of a community of a lower order, depriving the latter of its functions, but rather should support it in case of need and help to coordinate its activity with the activities of the rest of society, always with a view to the common good." Encyclical Letter *Centesimus Annus* (May 1, 1991), 48. Of course this depends on Pius XI's formulation of the concept, which constituted a faithful application of Taparelli's principles. A comparison of Taparelli's reasoning on the natural law principles of subsidiarity, social justice, and solidarity, and their implications, to recent compendia of CST, either in the *Catechism of the Catholic Church* (Vatican City: Libreria Editrice Vaticana, 1993), §§1877–1948 or in the *Compendium of the Social Doctrine of the Church* (Vatican City: Libreria Editrice Vaticana, 2005), is beyond the scope of this study.

merely summarizes Taparelli's explication of hypotactical association in about one page of the biography.[62]

Jacquin's view in the 1940s was that the writings of Taparelli that held the greatest interest were in the area of political economy, and particularly his critique of laissez-faire capitalist principles divorced from ethical considerations. While Jacquin touched on the rights of families and schools, and on the limits of administrative regulations impacting the right to strike, in his 1964 contribution on *"droit hypotactique,"*[63] Jacquin's main interest seems to have been the theoretical foundation of and prospects for international integration that Taparelli had indicated should be based on the principles of subsidiarity: "The perfection of extensions in social communications introduce little by little a wise cosmopolitanism aimed at considering all the nations as families of universal society, without the loss, however, of the special love of their own."[64] The concept of subsidiarity has had implications far beyond CST, in many different areas of social reality: especially in economics, corporate organization, welfare, healthcare, education, and environmental policy; but also in urban development, criminal justice, governmental devolution generally, business operations, labor relations, ecclesial governance, and, not least, foreign aid and international organization.[65] For instance, as has been

---

62. Jacquin, *Taparelli*, 215. It can be recalled that Nell-Breuning made no reference to Taparelli in his commentary on *Quadragesimo Anno*, and certainly there was no footnote about Taparelli's contribution in the encyclical, but its language, as has been seen, was taken virtually verbatim from Taparelli, so this short shrift given by Jacquin in 1943 is difficult to comprehend.

63. See note 57 above.

64. *Saggio*, §937.

65. See Michelle Evans and Augusto Zimmerman, eds., *Global Perspectives on Subsidiarity* (Dordrecht: Springer, 2014), and see Domènec Melé, "Exploring the Principle of Subsidiarity in Organizational Forms," *Journal of Business Ethics* 60, no. 3 (2005): 293–305, for an overview of the applications of the principle. A simple internet search on any of the above topics, for example "subsidiarity and environmental policy" or "subsidiarity and foreign aid," turns up many titles. On the use of the term in CST, see, Russell Hittinger, "The Coherence of the Four Basic Principles of Catholic Social Doctrine: An Interpretation," in *Pursuing the Common Good: How Solidarity and Subsidiarity Can Work Together*, ed. Margaret S. Archer and Pierpaolo Donati, (Vatican City: Pontifical Academy of Social Science, 2008), 75–123; Roger Greenacre, "Subsidiarity in State and Church," *Contemporary Review* 260, no. 1517 (June 1, 1992): 287–91; Thomas Kohler, "Quadragesimo Anno," 29–43; Richard E. Mulcahy, "Subsidiarity," in *New Catholic Encyclopedia*, vol. 13, ed. William J. McDonald (New York: McGraw-Hill, 1967), 762; Jean-Yves Calvez and Jacques Perrin, *The Church and Social Justice: The Social Teaching of the Popes from Leo XIII to Pius XII (1878–1958)* (Chicago: Regnery, 1961), 122, 332–33; See also Pinto, *Il Principio di Sussidiarietà*, for the broad historical and constitutional background.

noted, Article V of the European Union Maastricht treaty establishes subsidiarity as a protocol for the protection of member state interests.[66]

Subsidiarity is the regulative principle of individual and associational protection and promotion of the fulfillment of duties and exercise of rights in the social order. Taparelli addressed such questions with theoretical precision in the *Saggio* and then in various applied contexts in his articles in *Civiltà Cattolica* in terms of abstract principles of right but also as matters of practical and prudential policy concerning how the exercise of rights might best be advanced. The most pertinent points from the CC articles as he applied them to his moderate liberal and personalist economics, which he called social economics, will be considered below.

The terms deutarchy, protarchy, and ethnarchy are necessary technical designations of specific levels of association, each having its proper functions and respective duties and rights, but it is probably understandable why these terms did not catch on in the encyclical tradition any more than "rights of hypotactical association." The prefix "deu-" (or "dys-") refers to the lower societies' imperfect ability to themselves fully satisfy human needs, that is, their lack of self-sufficiency. The prefix "pro-" refers to the higher societies' positioning "in front of" (or, "having precedence over") the lower societies, and "ethn-" refers to governance of all the peoples. The alternative to these terms is of course "lesser society," "greater society" and perhaps "global" or "international society," but there is a loss of specificity; and it is possible that "smaller"/"larger" and "inferior"/"superior" may have introduced confusion or even ideas contrary to the perfective relationships Taparelli had in mind. In fact "superior" is the technical term that Taparelli uses to designate the person (or persons) who exercise authority (the formal cause) of any society; the "superior" of an independent protarchy would be the sovereign, the person or body of persons who exercise authority. In other words, this is the case where the superior answers to no other authority on earth: "It acquires the name of Sovereignty or Majesty; and the society that it governs, especially if

---

66. See, Schütze, "EU Competences," for the legal and constitutional functioning of the principle of subsidiarity in European Union legislation and jurisprudence.

it is in a stable territory, becomes a State."⁶⁷ There is no fundamental distinction between civil society and political society for Taparelli—the state, charged with the exercise of political authority, is merely a national protarchy whose superior has independent, sovereign authority. Its formation is subject to the same conditions with respect to duties and rights that are applicable to other associations.

Hypotactical right (subsidiarity) represents Taparelli's conception of the proper balance between order and liberty in society. The principle prioritizes the dignity of individuals, and of the associations that individuals freely form, in order to protect both vis-à-vis the potentially unjust claims of higher levels of civil or political association. In the *Epilogo Ragionato* the principles are stated thus:

> 71. Prop. XIX. A society may be comprised of many smaller societies
>
> N. B. I will call these *deutarchies* or *consortiums*, the greater one *protarchy*.
>
> Proof: Every *deutarchy* is an intelligent being; the union of intelligent beings for tending toward an end is society; now many deutarchies can unite themselves to obtain an end of common good...
>
> 72. Coroll. 1°. The *deutarchies* in associating themselves do not lose being, if they do not abandon the anterior end that they had before associating themselves; and if, [as required for the deutarchy's independent ongoing existence], the deutarchy's superior [also] remains.
>
> Coroll. 2°. The end of the *protarchy* is different from that of the *deutarchies*.
>
> Coroll. 3°. In every large society a system of *deutarchies* must be found, it being necessary that there be diverse *ends* subordinate to the end of the *protarchy*: and diverse *superiors* that guide to *deutarchic* ends. We have called *hypotactical right* the complex of the laws resulting from such relations.
>
> Coroll. 4°. A Protarchy may compose itself either from preexisting deutarchies, and having their *own* authority; or of deutarchies

---

67. *Saggio*, §591.

created by the protarch authority, and therefore having from it all their authority.

N.B. The *complete* protarchy is usually called *public* society, and if it is *independent* it is usually called *state* (especially when in possession of a stable territory); the independent Protarch [is usually called] *sovereign*, [and] his authority *sovereignty*. The *complete* elemental society is usually called *family* or *domestic* society: and is [a] *deutarchy* relatively to public society.[68]

Thus, Taparelli has set himself the task of considering the laws governing the interdependence of societies that had not been undertaken before, and he created the term *"associazione ipotattica"* ("hypotactical association") in order to distinguish this interdependence from that of an individual's dependence on society (implied in the expression "social subordination"); confusion on this point might lead to an erroneous understanding of social cooperation and the needed balance between dependence and autonomy among these societies.[69] It is the multiplicity of the needs of human beings and their limited capacities as individuals (creating sociality) that cause them to look for help (*sussidio sociale*, "social help") in the formation of associations, in which the "cooperation of the associates" is

---

68. 71. Prop. XIX. Una società può comporsi di molte società minori
    N.B. Dirò queste *deutarchie* o *consorzi*, la maggiore *protarchia*.
    Prova: Ogni *deutarchia* è un essere intelligente; l'unione di esseri intelligenti per tendere ad un fine è società; or molte deutarchie possono unirsi per ottenere un fine di ben commune: dunque ecc.
    72. Coroll.1°. Le *deutarchie* nel consociarsi non perdono l'essere, se non abbandonano il fine anteriore che aveano prima di associarsi; e se per consequenza non vien meno il superiore deutarchico.
    Coroll.2°. Il fine della *protarchia* è diverso da quello delle *deutarchie*.
    Coroll.3°. In ogni gran società dee trovarsi un sistema di *deutarchie*, essendo necessario che vi sieno diversi *fini* subordinati al fine della *protarchia*: e diversi *superiori* che guidano ai fini *deutarchici*. Abbiam chiamato *dritto ipotattico* il complesso delle leggi risultanti da tali relazioni.
    Coroll.4°. Una Protarchia può comporsi o di deutarchie preesistenti, ed aventi un autorità loro *propria*; o di deutarchie create dall'autorità protarchica, e però aventi da lei ogni loro autorità.
    N.B. La protarchia *completa* suol dirsi società *pubblica*, e se sia *indipendente* suol dirsi *stato* (specialmente quando possiede stabile territorio); il Protarca indipendente *sovrano*, la sua autorità *sovranità*. La società *completa* elementare suol dirsi *famiglia* o società *domestica*: ed è *deutarchia* relativamente alla società pubblica.
    Taparelli, *Epilogo Ragionato*, §§71–72.
69. *Saggio*, §§685, 688, note 'a.'

directed by some "authority."[70] Associations are "intelligent beings" in that there is authority which coordinates, one way or another, the intelligences of associated persons, uniting and directing every association of intelligent persons, down to the lowest level of association—imparting duties and rights upon authorities.

In other words, the social "subsidy" that men seek in associating themselves with others in particular societies in forming *consortia*, or that smaller societies seek in associating themselves with higher societies (joining other consortia as *deutarchies*, up to, eventually, a protarchy), or that higher societies (protarchies or deutarchies) might provide when they subdivide into smaller administrative units, can only be given and received when guided by specific authorities oriented to and knowledgeable about the receiving association's particular ends. Associations are framed for the pursuit of the associating members' limited, common good, and the rights of these members are at least partly grounded in the principles determined by the facts giving rise to the association itself. All particular societies, including an international ethnarchy, are formed for the attainment of limited good, the natural happiness attainable in the natural world; namely, peace and orderly life together so that the individual associates can freely exercise their universal and inalienable human rights to life, liberty, and the pursuit of the ultimate good, that is, true happiness or the perfection of body, will, and intellect.[71]

The centrality, then, of the principle of subsidiarity in Taparelli's work can hardly be overstated. It is nothing less than the set of principles in realist social theory that gives practical content to the widely misunderstood virtue of social justice, as it gives practical content also to the moral obligation of solidarity.

Natural, Voluntary, and Dutiful Societies

For Taparelli, to understand subsidiarity and hence social justice, it is important to examine the nature of the different kinds of associations

---

70. "Questo sussidio sociale deve essere ottenuto mediante il concorso dei socii diretti dall'autorità." *Saggio*, §691.
71. *Saggio*, Note XXXVIII.

in order to ascertain their particular laws of operation. The three types of social formations he identifies are "natural," "voluntary," and "dutiful" societies. The duties and rights of the individual members of associations vary according to the type of association (society).[72]

Natural societies initially arise independently of the will of the associates. Natural societies include the family, into which newborns arrive without being consulted. Natural societies can form accidentally when other societies and authorities have somehow disappeared and circumstances throw a group of individuals upon their own resources, such as in a shipwreck or other catastrophe, but these are obviously unusual. In natural societies, the facts giving rise to the society determine the concrete effectuation of social dependence (sociality) and of social justice, including the obligations of solidarity. The particular facts of social dependence, and the possibilities of fulfilling duties and exercising rights and of expressing solidarity impose moral requirements on the collaboration among the de facto associates in the furtherance of their common pursuit of happiness.[73] Duties to help others and rights to be helped by others created by the natural law of social justice operate "in proportion to the true necessity";[74] the right to be helped carries with it the duty to help in return, to the full extent of one's ability. The law of necessity encourages the exercise of patience and the acceptance by the members that they will fulfill the required duties. Natural societies generally become *voluntary* societies over time (discussed in more detail below) because a particular associate or associates can decide to leave a voluntary society—but it is also possible that a natural society in which a prior right of command is present can become a *dutiful* society (also discussed in more detail below). Authority is required in order to constitute and direct the unity of every association and of any society, and in the case of natural associations, the right to authority will tend to attach where there is a propensity to exercise authority and effectiveness of authority, including the possession of "might,"[75] although in the case of accidentally formed societies, authority

---

72. See *Saggio*, §§ 701–20 (in Appendix herein) for how duties and rights are determined by the formational facts of any society.
73. *Saggio*, §609.
74. Ibid.
75. *Saggio*, §614. On the general theory of authority in the concrete, see §§466–86. In this

may vest in a particular person or regime in concrete circumstances also by prior possession—such as the captain of a ship.

A necessary corollary, so obvious to Taparelli that he does not mention it, is that newborn persons begin life in the natural society of the family with the abstract duties and rights of humanity, as well as the natural duties and rights of solidarity, regardless of the newborn's immediate lack of "social utility." The concrete duties of the newborn are at first obviously insubstantial, but they accrue over time and with the development of his capacity; his rights, however, are fully present even if the newborn cannot claim them for himself, as in the conscience of others it is enough to recognize their replicated selves in order that those rights be understood. There is a crucial difference for infants and the family between this conception of association and authority based on human needs, duties, and rights arising from nature, manifested in always-relevant concrete facts, versus the theories of authority, rights, and duties based on "social contract."[76]

---

way, in conferring authority on Pepin the Short and his heirs rather than on the decadent Merovingian dynasty, Pope Zachary reasoned in 751 that Pepin had the de facto support of the Franks, and it is better to confer right on might, where there is propensity and effectiveness, than to try to produce might from right.

76. This difference is fundamental to Taparelli's entire system. *Saggio*, Notes LXVIII-LXXI, §§483, 622. Consider the alternative idea of the rights and duties of citizens under Rousseau's social contract as it applies to newborns, children, and families:

> From the first moment of life, men ought to begin learning to deserve to live; and, as at the instant of birth we partake of the rights of citizenship, that instant ought to be the beginning of the exercise of our duty. If there are laws for the age of maturity, there ought to be laws for infancy, teaching obedience to others: and as the reason of each man is not left to be the sole arbiter of his duties, government ought the less indiscriminately to abandon to the intelligence and prejudices of fathers the education of their children, as that education is of still greater importance to the State than to the fathers: for, according to the course of nature, the death of the father often deprives him of the final fruits of education; but his country sooner or later perceives its effects. Families dissolve, but the State remains.
>
> Should the public authority, by taking the place of the father, and charging itself with that important function, acquire his rights by discharging his duties, he would have the less cause to complain, as he would only be changing his title, and would have in common, under the name of *citizen*, the same authority over his children, as he was exercising separately under the name of *father*, and would not be less obeyed when speaking in the name of the law, than when he spoke in that of nature. Public education, therefore, under regulations prescribed by the government, and under magistrates established by the Sovereign, is one of the fundamental rules of popular or legitimate government. If children are brought up in common in the bosom of equality; if they are imbued with the laws of the State and the precepts of the general will; if they are taught to respect these above all things; if they are surrounded

Natural societies are governed by the abstract duties and rights of the natural law, which are then articulated subject to the factual, concrete circumstances obtaining at the time of their formation—thesis and hypothesis connect the abstract right and the concrete right. *Voluntary* societies are formed as persons "move" from abstract conditions of sociality into determinate relationships with others for the common pursuit of some limited good. The factors conditioning voluntary social formation, which also describe the stages of the influence of sociality on conscience, fall under three interconnected categories

1. *Physiological*, or the genetic, immediate, inevitable nature of material social need.
2. *Psychological*, or specifically a person's reflection on the weight of material factors and the hardships that certain choices would entail, including on social relationships, which can often be supremely compelling.
3. *Moral*, or the operation of ideas of justice as they apply to rational and voluntary action.

The physiological category relates first and foremost to the material dimension of sociality; that is, that human individuals are born into a total concrete dependence on others, even though they have abstract rights of independence. That divergence between abstract independence and concrete dependence is at the base of the whole of Taparelli's reasoning about social formation, subsidiarity, subjective duties and rights, and social justice, yielding notions that inform moral reasoning in politics and economy. What must be considered when talking particularly about voluntary associations is the interaction of the psychological factors—what

---

by examples and objects which constantly remind them of the tender mother who nourishes them, of the love she bears them, of the inestimable benefits they receive from her, and of the return they owe her, we cannot doubt that they will learn to cherish one another mutually as brothers, to will nothing contrary to the will of society, to substitute the actions of men and citizens for the futile and vain babbling of sophists, and to become in time defenders and fathers of the country of which they will have been so long the children.

Jean-Jacques Rousseau, "A Discourse on Political Economy," in *The Social Contract and Discourses by Jean-Jacques Rousseau*, trans. G.D.H. Cole (London and Toronto: J.M. Dent and Sons, 1920), 268–69.

can fairly be called calculations of material and social self-interest—with the dictates of reason and the strength of moral judgment as these affect the will. These considerations allow a proper understanding of what "voluntary," understood as a freely made choice, means in concrete reality.[77] For Taparelli, order is an intrinsic quality of all being and is the precondition for all moral reasoning in the movement from the abstract good to the concrete good.

> In fact let us give the following truths as demonstrated, that is that the good is being; that being is furnished with an intrinsic order; that the mind recognizes the good in this its essential order; that by that the good is that which is appropriate to each nature: can we therefore conclude that when the will approves and wills this [order], [that] man becomes *morally* good? ... Now this is evidently false in the judgment of common sense and speaking. Therefore beyond the essential order of things, that binds the mind to assent, another element is needed that binds the will for the *moral* act; and this element cannot be other than *a good*, and good capable of bending *in some way* the will without violating its liberty. Now such is the *Good* in general, which the will cannot not will, but the will certainly can, with regard to the *concrete* object, freely decide.[78]

There is also an intrinsic order of all human associations, and the good of social order is the source of all social duties. Persons connaturally know and recognize the truth and goodness of being and of order. Our experience of sociality and social existence immediately recognizes social order as good—this is what Jacques Maritain refers to as

---

77. *Saggio*, §615.

78. Infatti diamo pure per dimostrate le sequenti verità, cioé che il bene è l'essere; che l'essere è fornito d'un ordine intrinseco; che la mente ravvisa il bene in questo suo ordine essenziale; che perciò il bene è ciò che conviene ciascuna natura: potremmo noi conchiuderene che quando la volontà approva e vuole questo bene, l'uomo diventa *moralmente* buono? ... Or questo è evidentamente falso per giudizio del sentire e del parlare commune. Dunque oltre l'ordine essenziale delle cose, che lega la mene ad assentire, ci vuole per l'atto *morale* anche un altro elementa che leghi la volontà; e questo elemento non può essere altro che *un bene*, e bene capace di piegare *in qualche modo* la volontà senza violarne la libertà. Or tal è il *Bene* in generale, cui la volontà non può non volere, ma ben può, quanto all'oggetto *concreto*, liberamente determinare. *Saggio*, §98.

connatural knowledge. Though Taparelli does not describe this apprehension of the intrinsic order of being with such a term, it is fitting to describe this knowledge of the truth and goodness of order as Maritain might: connatural knowledge is the prediscursive experimental knowledge—whether speculative or practical—of nature, is acquired by shared natural inclination or connaturality (not through explicit reasoning), and is the foundation for moral reasoning and prudence.[79] Order is understood subsequently by speculative reason as true (constitutive of society), and in practical reason as good (perfective of society), and the good in the abstract comes to be articulated in concrete conditions and choices.

This is true even in the case of dutiful (nonvoluntary) societies, which oblige one's association due to some prevailing right of another.[80] Duties are associated with every form of association—natural, voluntary, or dutiful—arising from the nature of the constraints of abstract sociality/solidarity and its articulation in concrete circumstances. The abstract rights of sociality/solidarity are always instantiated within those concrete circumstances. Dutiful societies, in which cases involving force are the most interesting,[81] include a people conquered in a just war, justly convicted criminals in prison, and, we may add, mandated education for minors—and in these cases, duties normally predominate over rights. But even in such involuntary cases (1) the prevailing right of the authority must be certain, (2) the authority must not use excessive force or claim more than is due, and (3) the proper end of the association must not detract from the universal end of human society, which would involve not a "concrete *application*, but a destruction of the

---

79. See, Jacques Maritain, *Man and the State* (Chicago: University of Chicago Press, 1951), 89–91, and Jacques Maritain, *The Range of Reason* (New York: Charles Scribner's Sons, 1952), 22–29. Taparelli considers this apprehension of being in general and of order as good and immediate, while concerning the application of this knowledge in conscience he accepts the term "synderesis," from Aquinas, *ST*, I, q. 79, a. 11–13, which applies to ulterior moral reasoning, the process of reasoning from an abstract duty derived from the nature of a thing to a concrete dutiful act. *Saggio*, §119.

80. *Saggio*, §§638–40. Note that there can also be the scenario where the de facto authority (the government) fails to provide properly for the common good; that is, it disregards those inalienable rights that society exists to foster and governments exist to protect, and therefore will only be maintained by means of brute force.

81. *Saggio*, §§641–58.

law of sociality."[82] Moreover, even involuntary or dutiful societies may become essentially voluntary because thinking persons with awareness of the physiological, psychological, and moral situation "decide" to accept participation in them. The three most important laws governing voluntary association (reflecting the natural law right of sociality, freedom of association) are 1) liberty of entrance, 2) liberty of setting one's terms of participation (the manner of decision-making, for instance), and 3) the conditionality of the agreement to obey; namely, the association is subject to dissolution should there be grave infractions of its proper purpose.[83] These laws are stated in the abstract of course, but in practice each associate weighs the physiological, psychological, and moral considerations of voluntarily remaining. The effective cause of voluntary association is the finite good that each of the associates hopes and asks for.[84] Each associate has made a calculation of interest (rightly understood) to sacrifice some minor good, some part of their abstract liberty for instance, in exchange for a greater good available by cooperating with others under the direction of authority (without which no association of independent persons is possible).

Taparelli seeks to clear up confusion around the abstract conception and concrete reality of liberty (or freedom) as an aspect of voluntary action.[85] His point that concerns us here is that every voluntary association is born of consent, based on a sort of pact. But, it must be reiterated, this pact is very different in origin, nature, and consequences from those of "the claimed *social contract* of Rousseau, Hobbes and their followers,"

> since [this social contract] ... simply determin[es] the individuals with whom we will live; and toward whom we will practice the social duties prescribed to us by human nature.... Reflect carefully please, O reader, on these two most diverse principles of association, which will give the key to dissolve the deplorable sophism that forms still today the deception of many politicians who having given to the

---

82. *Saggio*, §638.
83. *Saggio*, §624.
84. *Saggio*, §625.
85. *Saggio*, §§617, 619, 621.

> people the right to elect the governors, hail [the people] as sovereign and believe to have constituted it, as a jurist would say, *sui iuris*. . . . The election, the consensus, the foundation, etc., are causes of the material conjunction under this or that reigning individual [i.e. superior]: but the right to govern and the duty to obey are founded in social nature.[86]

Examining the physiological, psychological, and moral forces affecting freedom of human action yields a very different theory of social obligation in political society (a national protarchy) from that of the social contract theorists. In Taparelli's view, political legitimacy and obligation are determined as an extension of natural sociality, natural association, and the translation of natural duties and rights into the context of concrete historical reality. All political regimes, no matter the conditions of their formation, present to all those subject to them who were not consulted for their approval—those who were not present at the regime's formation, or, in other words, all those born subject to the regime after its formation—the aspect of a de facto, natural society, as unwilled as being born into a particular family.

So any given political society presents itself, in a sense, to newcomers under the aspect of a natural society. Sociality compels cooperation in an existing regime. However, as Taparelli describes, a natural society is essentially transitory by definition. It cannot last unless it becomes a voluntary society—or, rather exceptionally, a dutiful one, for instance by force. Once an unwilling newcomer (children, obviously, are born into and do not choose the natural society of the family or a political society) is able to exercise the use of reason, the question of voluntarily associating oneself with an unchosen regime arises (perhaps repeatedly over the course of one's lifetime). In deciding to associate voluntarily with others, human persons make a calculation of the good(s) that can be achieved thereby versus their loss in abstract independence. Abstract duties and rights, especially those that are inviolable, remain intact when persons associate voluntarily and submit conditionally to civil authority and to political authority as it may concretely exist in the sovereign. The

---

86. *Saggio*, §622.

persistence of these abstract rights alongside the concrete circumstances of historical existence is the grounds for the right of those participating in voluntary associations to alter the conditions of the association; that is, its laws and rules must be able to be amended within the bounds of justice and equity.[87] These are the conditions of the legitimate exercise of political authority.

Taparelli's theory on the conditions for "dissolving" a voluntary society conforms with Aquinas on the lawfulness of seeking to restore the order of a society to the common good when tyrannical rule reaches the level of sedition itself, and the prospects of restoring order outweigh the harm of disturbing the existing authority.[88]

Nature compels association and establishes the laws of association; connatural knowledge recognizes the goodness of order in association; and reflective reason weighs the alternatives and determines the reasonableness of voluntarily submitting to this or that unchosen regime. Whether to accept the concrete legal obligations attendant to remaining under the authority of a regime is fundamentally a voluntary act and remains voluntary so long as the regime respects the inviolable rights of its associates—the right to life, to freedom of association (implying the right to leave, even if leaving would entail greater or lesser hardships), and to the pursuit of happiness (a limited good not destructive of the pursuit of true and ultimate good).

Dutiful societies, those established by a prevailing right of others, are based, as has been pointed out, on a disproportionate balance of

---

87. *Saggio*, §§624–28.

88. *ST*, II-II, q. 42, esp., a. 2, ad. 3. Taparelli, not surprisingly in the "age of revolutions," provides a lengthy treatment of the problem of tyrannical rule in the abstract, whether it take the form of a monarchy or a "polyarchy," the latter referring to representative governments (Taparelli does not regard democratic government as possible for any large society in theory or practice and therefore considers it worth mentioning only the range of forms of rule from one person to several persons, however those several are chosen), *Saggio*, §§1000–11; how the conflict of rights principles that govern social justice, §742, apply in the abstract, §§1012–20; concerning the practical question of when a sovereign loses authority and what can be done in this situation based on the conditions of the formation of that authority (it is best to appeal to a higher authority), §§1021–38; and remedies that must be sought through legitimate authorities (for example, subordinate constitutional authorities of civil society), §§1039–43, "but with such equity that they do not trample private rights other than to the extent that they are suspended in the collision with public rights." §1043.

duties over rights. The restriction of rights and the imposition of duties in these kinds of associations depend upon the clear establishment of the right which compels the association, which may follow from a duty toward another more fundamental natural or voluntary association to which one belongs—for example, the family that sends a child to a boarding school or the religious superior that sends a religious to a particular convent or parish (with the boarding school and the convent being dutiful societies). But in any case, the authority that manages the dutiful association must still operate it in a way that does not assert more than the duty to which the individual has originally submitted.[89] An example of abuse might be compulsory military service or school attendance were officials to add restrictions unrelated to the organization's particular intent, for instance a prohibition on religious observances. In other words, the particular intent of any association with a potential claim to duty, even those founded on force, must never run contrary to the "universal end of human society"; that is, the fulfillment of duties to oneself and to God, including the pursuit of happiness in the perfection of body, will, and intellect.[90]

Authority and the Common Good

For Taparelli, human associations are composed of intelligent persons as the material cause, sociality as the efficient cause, authority as the formal cause, and a common good as the final cause—and the identification of the person or persons, or this or that regime structure, that will exercise authority in a given association, or who will be the sovereign authority in a state, remains subject to concrete historical circumstances and prudential determinations.[91] Taparelli's passionate opposition to relativism and to distorted conceptions of autonomy, which he saw, as had so many Restoration Conservatives, as the plague of modernity, informed all of his work and career. Sensitivity to the intellectual and moral confusion he saw develop after the declaration of independence of reason, and the

---

89. *Saggio*, §639.
90. *Saggio*, §641–58.
91. *Saggio*, §591.

consequences of this declaration he witnessed in that revolutionary age, explains the fervor with which he systematically opposed the then-ubiquitous acceptance of popular sovereignty as an axiom of political morality. While the nature of authority is key to Taparelli's sociopolitical theory, it was his series of articles in the *Civiltà Cattolica* on the theoretical principles and practical applications of popular sovereignty (published as a separate two-volume edition in 1854, *Esame critico degli ordini rappresentativi nella società moderna*) that doomed his reputation among Catholic Liberals and especially among liberal Catholics.[92]

Among the social contract theorists, there is of course a difference between Locke's limited and conditional relinquishment of presumed natural autonomy to achieve the end of the peaceful enjoyment of private property, and Rousseau's total and unconditional sublimation of individual wills in the General Will. Taparelli was determined to demonstrate both the theoretical error and the evil consequences of Rousseau's claim that the General Will formed through the transference of the sovereignty of individuals to the collective is the only legitimate basis for the exercise of sovereign authority, which was Rousseau's solution to the riddle that he set for himself at the beginning of the *Social Contract*.

Questions related to authority permeate every corner of the *Saggio*, and Taparelli takes every opportunity to refute, theoretically and practically, what he saw as the pernicious influence of the social contract theorists. He also takes care to demonstrate that his social theory is in accord with, or at least not in contradiction to, the Scholastic philosophers of natural law, on this and other questions. On the source of authority, Taparelli carefully looks at Aquinas's arguments in *ST*, I-II, Question 90, Article 3, that the making of law belongs to the whole people or to some public personage who has care for the whole people, in order to correct what he sees as a mistaken reading of that text supporting the thesis of popular sovereignty. He underscores that Aquinas must be referring to cases in which the people happen to be "free"; then the government is in effect their "vice-regent." Taparelli continues his analysis with *ST*, I-II, Question 97, Article 3 on whether custom can obtain the force of law, focusing on Aquinas's

---

92. Pius IX's *Quanta Cura* (1864) and its Syllabus of Errors, which reiterates many Taparellian propositions, had much the same effect on liberals' judgment of Pius IX.

phrasing in "Reply to Objection 3," to argue that for Aquinas sovereignty itself does not reside in the people in all cases, but is rather an historical contingency, and therefore, not an inviolable right.[93]

Article 1 of Question 97 relates to the idea of the historical potential of practical reason to govern the development and possible improvement of political institutions, so that they might be "less frequently deficient in respect of the common weal"; but Aquinas also includes this observation from St. Augustine on the contingent nature of popular self-government:

> If the people have a sense of moderation and responsibility, and are most careful guardians of the common weal, it is right to enact a law allowing such a people to choose their own magistrates for the government of the commonwealth. But if, as time goes on, the same people become so corrupt as to sell their votes, and entrust the government to scoundrels and criminals; then the right of appointing their public officials is rightly forfeit to such a people, and the choice devolves to a few good men.[94]

Certainly this argument would seem to support Taparelli's conviction that the exercise of sovereignty by a person or persons, in this or that regime form, should vary with the context. But Taparelli does not explore Aquinas's direct answer to the question of authority, which specifically supports the idea of historical contingency and prudence, and he misses the opportunity to highlight this point by St. Augustine; perhaps he skips over these things because the "I answer that" seems to endorse the idea that a progressive "improvement" of institutions was possible and desirable. In any case, it is also particularly telling in this regard that Taparelli

---

93. The people among whom a custom is introduced may be of two conditions. For if they are free, and able to make their own laws, the consent of the whole people expressed by a custom counts far more in favor of a particular observance, than does the authority of the sovereign, who has not the power to frame laws, except as representing the people. Wherefore although each individual cannot make laws, yet the whole people can. *If however the people have not the free power to make their own laws, or to abolish a law made by a higher authority*; nevertheless with such a people a prevailing custom obtains force of law, in so far as it is tolerated *by those to whom it belongs to make laws for that people*: because by the very fact that they tolerate it they seem to approve of that which is introduced by custom. (italics added) ST, I-II, q. 97, a. 3, ad. 3.

94. From Augustine, *De Libero Arbitrio*, i, 6; cited in ST, I-II, q. 97, a. 1.

does not refer to that section of the *Summa* where Aquinas suggests as a matter of political prudence, if not also of divine design, that

> accordingly, the best form of government is in a state or kingdom, where one is given the power to preside over all; while under him are others having governing powers: and yet a government of this kind is shared by all, both because all are eligible to govern, and because the rules are chosen by all. For this is the best form of polity, being partly kingdom, since there is one at the head of all; partly aristocracy, in so far as a number of persons are set in authority; partly democracy, i. e. government by the people, in so far as the rulers can be chosen from the people, and the people have the right to choose their rulers.[95]

Because of the lessons he had learned from his era, Taparelli was not convinced that the mixed government described by Aquinas was "best"—he felt that it was certainly not the "best" in the abstract, but also, often, not in practice. Taparelli would have had very much in mind the concerns of St. Augustine from *De Libero Arbitrio* quoted above concerning the moral capacity of the "people" in question—and like Augustine and Aquinas would have understood from the course of history and from the classical theorists of political cycles that the moral character of a people is far from constant. Taparelli had no theoretical opposition to mixed government as a hypothetical regime arrangement where the contexts of concrete social formation legitimized it, so long as in a particular case the arrangement meets the critical standard of serving the common good and the ultimate ends of universal human society. Taparelli was perhaps reluctant to take on *ST*, I-II, q. 90, a. 3, q. 97, a. 1, and q. 105, a. 1, since these passages leave room for being taken out of context and manipulated in favor of claims for popular sovereignty. The arguments in q. 105 are general and eminently prudential considerations, not relating to right; that the language is of "good ordering" (*bonum ordinationem*) and not "right ordering" can be clearly seen when Aquinas gives prudential reasons why "all should take some share in government: for this form of

---

95. *ST*, I-II, q. 105.

constitution ensures peace among the people, commends itself to all, and is most enduring, as stated in Polit. ii, 6."[96]

Taparelli is more willing to take on what he calls the "confused" arguments of Suarez on the subject of political authority, which many commentators were seeing as supportive of the doctrine of popular sovereignty. He does so in the section of the *Saggio* titled, "Other Scholastic doctrines in such matter."

> 1. These reasons [by which Taparelli had made the case from *ST*, I-II, Question 97, Article 3 that Aquinas may seem to but does not actually support the abstract right of popular sovereignty], that more than once have been raised as objections to me by those who sincerely wish to know the truth, were together supported by the authority of one of the greatest philosophers who flourished in the late Scholastic era, the distinguished Suarez, from whom they are taken nearly word for word. He asserts expressly:[97]
>   1st That *the power of political principality is from God*
>   2nd That *it is shown as a dictate of natural reason in the human community, as a property following creation*
>   3rd That [there is] *no reason why it should be limited to one person*
>   4th That consequently *it is given to the community for as long as [the community] does not otherwise decree, or so long as no change be made by another having the power*
>   5th That as ultimate consequence *democracy is quasi natural* but *a community with such power may be deprived [of it] by one having just title*
> 2. And these last two propositions show us that in substance he held, even if confusedly and without comprehending full reason of it, the doctrine sustained by us, and distinguishes an *abstract being of equal society,* from a *concrete* society where inequality could be introduced *by another having the power.* Otherwise who

---

96. *ST*, I-II, q. 105.
97. Here, Taparelli cites from an uncertain edition of Francisco Suarez, *Defensio fidei catholicae et apostolicae adversus anglicanae sectae errores* (orig. 1613), [Defense of the Catholic and apostolic faith against the errors of Anglicanism], specifically, Book III.

could have ever been able to take away from society something that belongs to it by nature? Equally [later], where he shows how [society] can be formed, indeed how perhaps it actually was formed in many kingdoms (*perhaps many kingdoms began this way*), he establishes that society could find itself from the beginning under a monarchical Government: *a monarchical power and a perfect community can begin at the same time.* And he offers in proof, as precisely we have done also, the natural propagation of the family, *as, for example, in the family of Adam or Abraham in the beginning they were obeyed as fathers of the family; later with an increase of population that subjection could be continued and consensus extended to obeying them as a king.*

3. Neither should it give surprise if in those centuries, even extraordinary minds were able to express themselves in this with lesser exactness; while yet they had not received in such matter, from experience, those terrible lessons, that [experience] gave so clearly to our era with a voice of thunder and light of lightning. The amazing thing is that so many, after such a lesson, can still be deaf to such a voice or blind to such a flash, and continue to vaunt the sovereignty of the people and the inalienable rights of man to govern himself by himself.[98]

---

98. 1. Queste ragioni, che più d'una volta mi sono state obiettate da chi volea sinceramenta consosciere il vero, venivano insieme appoggiate dall'autorità di uno dei più grandi filosofi che fiorissero nella ultima età scolastica, l'esimio Suarez, da cui sono tratte quasi a verbo a verbo. Egli asserisce espressamente (footnote to *Defens. contra Reg. Angl,* lib. III)

1° Che *potestas politici principis est a Deo* (c. 1, §6).

2° Che *agnoscitur dictamine naturalis rationis in humana communitate, ut proprietas consequenscreationem* (c. 2, §5).

3° Che *nulla ratio cur determinetur ad unam personam* (ib. §7).

4° Che per conseguenza *datur comunitati quamdiu... aliud non decreverit, vel ab aliquo potestatem haente mutatio facta non fuerit* (ib. §9).

5° Che per ultima conseguenza *democratia est quasi naturalist* (ib. §8), ma *potest communitas tali potestate privari ab habente titulum iustum* (ib. §9).

2. E queste ultima due proposizioni ci mostramo che in sostanza egli tenea, sebbene confusamente e senza rendersene piena ragione, le dottrine da noi sostenute, e distingua un *esssere astratto* (footnote *Vi solius rationis*) *di società uguale*, dalla società *concreta* ove potea *ab aliquo potestatem habente* introdursi la disugualianza. Altrimenti chi mai avrebbe potuto rapire all società ciò che le compete per natura? Parimente al §19, ove mostra come può formarsi, anzi come forse realmente si formò in molit regni (footnote *Fortasse multa regna ita incoeperunt*), stabilisce che la società potè trovarsi fin dal suo nascere sotto Governo monarchico: *regia potestas et communitas*

It is not surprising that Taparelli's opposition to the claim that the transfer of the sovereign autonomy of individuals to the sovereign is the moral basis for all legitimate authority made him as much anathema among secular-minded and liberal Catholic thinkers as the Syllabus of Errors had made Pius IX. Taparelli believed that this claim concerning the nature of political power, right, and authority ignored the facts of human nature, human society, and human history. He saw this intellectual error as the seed of many excessive claims asserted by theorists and demagogues, and of heinous crimes committed on behalf of "the people." As has been seen, Taparelli's social theory starts from a realist understanding of composite human nature; in light of that nature, society itself is inseparable from its own composite nature—that is, society has its own material, social, and intellectual or spiritual ends. Society is essentially a union of rational human beings established to further common ends; without a directing authority, however that authority may be established and under whatever form of regime it may operate, society cannot subsist. There is no question that some kind of authority must be present, both within individual human beings as persons (the authority of reason or some alternative) and within a given society. For Taparelli, authority is intrinsic to the composite nature of man and of society, and it is a reflection of the creator's purpose. The ultimately voluntary character of all earthly societies (except abstract, universal humanity), versus that of heavenly society, even of the protarchy of sovereign states or of the pluralistic ethnarchy, is a consequence of their limited ends. Authority may well be found to be vested *in* the people, or exercised *by* the people, in determinate factual situations, but it is not naturally in any particular person or group of persons; it is not created by the people, nor is it transferable by them in an exercise of will.[99]

---

perfecta simul incipere possunt. E ne reca in pruova, come appunto abbiam fatto ancor noi [509 segg.], il naturale propagamento della famiglia, *ut v.g. in familia Adae vel Abrahae principio obediebatur tamquam patrifamilias; postea crescente populo potuit subjection illa continuari et consensus extendi ad obediendum illi tamquam regi.*

3. Nè dee recar meraviglia se in quei secoli, ingegni anche straordinarii abbiano potuto in ciò esprimersi con minore esattezza; mentre ancor non avean ricevuto in tal materia dalla esperienza quelle terribili lezioni, che essa dettò sì chiaramente alla età nostra con voce di tuono e con luce di fulmini. La meraviglia è che tanti dopo tal magistero ancor possano essere sordi a tal voce o ciechi a tal lampo, e continuino a vantare la sovranità del popolo e i dritti inalienabili dell'uomo a governarsi da sè medesimo.
Saggio, Note LXXIX.
99. *Saggio,* §§483–85.

Society has as its purpose the perfection of the individuals who compose it, a purpose that is the common good of all associations, from the family to the state. Each particular society has limited ends or common goods that are "good" to the extent that they are useful for the pursuit of the ultimate common good of universal human society, which tends toward infinite happiness, and for that reason the authorities of those particular societies are subject to higher authorities.[100] Taparelli also uses the term "common good" to refer to care for and promotion of growth in the material supports, or means, for the pursuit of a true idea of happiness.[101] This care for the material progress of the whole of society is measured by the increase and protection of individual capital and of individual labor and the fruits thereof.[102] The primary duty of civil authorities is to support the common good of all persons in their individual and associational capacities so that they can pursue their perfection; this duty consists of the "protection and expansion of their *true* rights."[103]

> To facilitate the pursuit of natural felicity to men with external order, assuring to each one his rights and increasing for him the *means* [thereof] with social cooperation: this is in short the *civic* social duty. ...Society owes *protection* to the rights of individuals: now what are these rights of man? The right to *live*, to *have the means* thereof, to make use of them *freely*, or in other words, the rights of *conservation*, of *dominion*, of *independence*; these are the primary rights that [civic] society must protect in man. Society must increase the perfection of the individual, cooperating there *positively* in those things to which private forces cannot reach. The forces of man are of mind, will, [and] body: therefore society should positively use its activity for amplifying the *intellectual, moral, and physical* strengths of the individual with social cooperation.[104]

100. *Saggio*, §452.
101. *Saggio*, §§739, 744.
102. *Saggio*, §740.
103. *Saggio*, §1066.
104. Agevolare agli uomini coll'ordine esterno il conseguimento di naturale felicità, assicurando a ciascuno I suoi dritti e crescendogli con social cooperazione i *mezzi*: ecco in breve il dovere sociale *civico*... La società dee *tutela* ai dritti degli'individui: or quali sono i dritti dell'uomo? Drit-

We can conclude therefore that the common good is nothing other if not the highest degree possible of *justice* that protects, and the *equity* that promotes with the exertions of all, the good of each.[105]

The authority thus established, particularly in the sovereign government of a state having responsibility for the good of the whole of society, is constrained by the same limits of social purpose that ground all association. Taparelli calls that part of any "complete society" (protarchy) charged with understanding and advancing the political good, the "deliberative power." This arm of government must not confuse national wealth or power with the good of individuals.[106] "The true good of each being is its *end*, therefore the true political good is to do the good of the citizens. The first moral duty of the deliberative power is thus to intend the good of the individuals; the good of whom consists, as has been seen, in the security and facilitation of their *living* rights."[107] The deliberative power is obliged to know the facts, and the legislative power is charged with exercising political prudence.[108] The legislative power takes its direction from the deliberative power, and for law to have the force of law it must be *"just, useful, convenient, from the highest competent* authority, *clear, possible, public,* and *effective."*[109]

---

to a *vivere,* ad *averne i mezzi,* ad adoprarli *liberamente* o in altri termini dritti di *conservazione,* di *dominio,* di *indipendenza*; sono questi I dritti precipui che nell'uomo la società dee *proteggere*. La società dee crescere la perfezione dell'individuo cooperandovi *positivamente* in quelle cose a cui le forze private non giungono: le forze dell'uomo sono di mente, di volontà, di corpo: dunque la società dovrà adoprare positivamente la sua attività nell'ampliare le forze *intellettuale, morali, e fisiche* nello individuo colla cooperazione sociale." *Saggio,* §739.

105. "Concludiamo pur dunque che il ben pubblico altro non è se non il più alto grado possibiile della *giustizia* che protegge e della *equità* che promuove colle forze di tutti il bene di ciascuno." *Saggio,* §745.

106. *Saggio,* §1066.

107. Ibid.

108. *Saggio,* §1049.

109. *Saggio,* §1078. Cf. Aquinas's definition of law, *ST,* I-II, q. 90, a. 4 "Thus from the four preceding articles, the definition of law may be gathered; and it is nothing else than an ordinance of reason for the common good, made by him who has care of the community, and promulgated." Details of Taparelli's theoretical and practical arguments on the nature and exercise of the legislative and executive powers, including elaboration of his classical liberal fiscal and taxation theories (*Saggio,* §§1155–85), are beyond the scope of this study. See, Angelo Perego, *Forma statale e politica finanziaria nel pensiero di Luigi Taparelli d'Azeglio* (Milano: A. Giuffrè, 1956).

Principles of Subsidiarity in Practice

The "living" rights of individuals—"to live, to have the means thereof, to make use of them freely"—pertain to all of the associations formed out of human necessity in the furtherance of man's universal end. The complex society of intermediary associations adds an additional dimension to the conflict of rights between individuals, however, which is where the social rights of hypotactical association come into play. As Taparelli sees it, the individual or the smaller society, in joining together with other individuals or other societies, gives up some abstract independence in order to share in the increased concrete "social liberty" of the larger society.[110] Taparelli deduces the following social duties and rights: "Every consortium must conserve its own unity in a way to not lose the unity of the whole; and every larger society must provide for the unity of the whole without destroying the unity of the consortia."[111] Which is to say, he continues, "Given the facts of the association, it would be as against nature for the consortia to reject the unity of the social whole as it would be for the whole to abolish the consortium, except in exceptional cases where some intervening cause might arise."[112]

Taparelli surely lamented the elimination of the guilds and charitable associations by the French revolutionaries and other liberal regimes. But additionally, he criticized the abolition of the lower and more local administrative and political structures of civil society in the drive toward centralization that characterized not only the "mania of the revolutionary spirit,"[113] but also the rise of the absolutist, centralizing, bureaucratizing modern state. Taparelli had seen the pernicious effects of this aspect of

---

110. *Saggio*, §693.

111. "Ogni consorzio dee conservare la propria unità in modo di non perdere la unità del tutto; ed ogni società maggiore provvede alla unità del tutto senza distruggere la unità dei consorzii." *Saggio*, §694. Because the principle of subsidiarity as stated in *Quadragesimo Anno*, particularly at 78–80, is understood as the product of Taparelli's reasoning on the "universal law" of association, it can be seen now that there are important theoretical and practical implications in Taparelli's full elaboration that would benefit from further consideration.

112. *Saggio*, §694.

113. "Livellare e cancellare ogni antica memoria delle province, delle città, degli Stati: ecco qual fu la smania dello spirito rivoluzionario ovunque allignò." [To level and cancel out every ancient memory of the provinces, the cities, the states: here is what was the mania of the revolutionary spirit everywhere it took root.] *Saggio*, §695, note 'f.'

modernization particularly in France and areas brought under French control during the Revolutionary and Napoleonic era—where Restoration governments took advantage of, and national unification movements in Italy and Germany accentuated, new governmental authority and power.

As is the case with individual rights and duties vis-à-vis others in society, the constitutive facts giving rise to the various associations determine their social rights and duties. Every complex society is formed either by a synthesis of preexisting societies or by the analytical division of larger societies. The original facts related to the association (the concrete circumstances of social formation) affect each type of society differently. Synthetically formed societies maintain the original rights of their members most completely; the members making up the society sacrifice some alienable part of their liberty in support of the more perfect end of the larger society. In analytically formed societies (i.e., units established by the protarch to aid in administration), the rights of the smaller member units are more directly determined and mutable by the higher authority. In cases of the dissolution of the social whole, the subsisting unity and authority of the smaller societies remains in order to reassert control over their proper purpose. In the gravest political crisis, the authorities of these smaller groupings resume (in synthetically formed societies) or assume (in analytically formed societies) political and not merely civil authority. Where all higher unity is lost, the heads of families, that is, the authority of the most elemental society, assume general political authority in all but the most exceptional cases.[114]

The principles and consequences of subsidiarity ("*dritto ipotattico*") are elaborated in Chapter VI, Article II, "Laws of the Mutual Relations Between the Parts of Hypotactical Association" ("*Leggi delle mutue relazioni fra le parti dell'associazione ipotattica*"), of Book III of the *Saggio*, "On Human Action in the Formation of Society."[115] The first consequence is that the larger society must protect the liberty of association within and among the consortia, interfering only to the extent necessary to orient them toward the larger common good, which the larger society is obliged

---

114. *Saggio*, §§698–700.
115. The full text of this Article and related sections is included in the Appendix.

to know and make known.[116] When the protarchy is compelled to direct the individuals at more distant, elemental levels, it should, as previously noted, be guided by "efficiency and gentleness" to effect such direction via the authorities who are closest physically to the pertinent individuals and who know them best. Thus the exercise of authority by a protarch is subject not only to the natural rights of members but also to the requirements of prudence. The state— the protarchy—has a regulative, not a creative, function with respect to the social virtues, a point Rommen takes from the Taparellian teaching evident in *Rerum Novarum*.[117]

Respect for the proper sphere of liberty of subordinate authorities, in their particular pursuit of the common good, is required for the effectiveness of the social whole itself. In addition to following from the metaphysical unity of authority prescribed by eternal reason, lower authorities are the necessary means for the superior authority to fulfill its task: "To discourage and weaken the inferior is to discourage and weaken even the superior."[118] The protarchy has license to interfere even in the nearly inviolable "domestic sanctuary" to the extent serious dangers or ruin to persons is at stake, but even then, its right to do so for the common good is not necessary or useful if appropriate lower authorities, who are potentially in a better position to know and avoid the dangers and repair any damage, are willing and able to do so—the right can be present even if the duty is not. Malfeasance or incompetence by lower authorities, unable or unwilling to protect the association or individuals in question, would, however, impose a duty in addition to the right held by the protarchy to directly intervene.[119]

In fact, in such a case, malfeasance will have virtually deprived the relevant consortium of its being and liberty, leaving the members a "mass of individuals closed in certain limits of space,"[120] and its authority—which, it should be recalled, is nothing other than the right to direct a society to its proper end—no authority at all. A higher deutarchy or

---

116. *Saggio*, §§701–4.
117. Rommen, *The State in Catholic Thought*, 354–58.
118. "Avvilire ed indebolir la inferiore è avvilir e indebolir anche la superiore." *Saggio*, § 705. Cf. *Quadragesimo Anno*, 79–80.
119. *Saggio*, §§705–7.
120. *Saggio*, §708.

the protarchy intervenes in this case under the "law of correction."[121] An obvious example would be of neglect or abuse of children in a family—the offending parent's authority is lost, and correction could be sought through an ascending scale of competencies, including broader family relations, church associations, or family dispute resolution courts before reaching for more distant political intervention. But there could also be a case where a consortium's rights are being neglected or abused—this consortium might itself be a family, the most elemental society—where the fulfillment of its duties may be blocked and its rights infringed by some governing deutarchy. In this situation, even where the right of the protarch to intervene exists, the duty should proceed by steps from the next most proximate consortium or deutarchy, where the injury, the disorder within the affected consortium, is most clearly felt.

The liberty that is lost when a deutarchy or the protarchy intervenes is not that of the consortium members (down to and including the family) itself, since liberty—which for Taparelli means the ability of self-regulation in pursuit of the good—has already been impaired by the disorder of its governing authority (superior).[122] It is the government of the disordered consortium that has had its liberty diminished, whereas the liberty of the consortium becomes restored with intervention. In general, the liberty of the lower association is enhanced by regulatory corrections available from the larger, more perfect society in an appropriate case using appropriate means aimed at restoring the just autonomy of the consortium and of its members.[123] This is the significance of the "law of correction" as a remedy against the tyranny of a corrupt father, mayor, power-mad corporate leader, or any other dysfunctional social, economic, cultural, political, or ecclesial authority. The more perfect and global the society, the greater the potential liberty of all the lower associations and individuals, especially those saved from the grips of perverse and

121. Ibid.
122. *Saggio*, §617. Taparelli offers a long proof on the meaning of liberty as free will within concrete reality and the nature of moral reasoning, ibid., §§47–76 and Notes XIII-XVIII. Social or political liberty is the concrete condition of moral obligation, involving action for which the person is solely responsible—liberty therefore is the power to will one's happiness with knowledge of true ends (the intent of the creator) and to act through just and honest means. Ibid., §76.
123. *Saggio*, §709.

tyrannical deutarchs that impair the fulfillment of duties and exercise of rights of those under their purview or of other consortia—this would apply even to a protarchy as a whole were there an ethnarchy, a brotherhood of nations, able to offer gentle and effective correction globally.

The government of the consortium is thus subject to the following restrictions: (1) it cannot interfere with the pursuit of the common good of the associates, which is also a good of the consortium; (2) it must accept correction when it has failed in its own particular authority; (3) it must permit appeals from its own to a higher authority; (4) it must not take steps that might irreparably harm the common good without the consent, tacit or explicit, of the higher authority; and (5) even if the consortium's actions might result in reparable harm, the consent of the higher authority is required if the actions would affect other consortia.[124]

Taparelli considered a wide variety of actual associations that human beings necessarily form—for example, civil associations including family, charitable organizations, schools, and religious organizations, economic associations such as partnerships, professional associations, guilds, and unions—which make up a whole range of intermediary associations from the hearth and village up to the national state and potentially to the fraternal order of nations. These associations or consortia span the range of deutarchies, which are established in hierarchical levels, and culminate in a protarchy, which is simply an independent consortia, comprehending and directing the deutarchies of which it is composed to the common good, unanswerable to any higher protarchy, and therefore having sovereign authority. All are formed and operate according to principles of natural right, but they are always embodied in concrete entities based on historical contingencies, which always include conflicts of rights and prudential factors. For Taparelli, these associations, as we have seen, are formed and activated at every step by human persons, some intentionally, some involuntarily, but always personally. They find their unity, purpose, and authority as extensions of human sociality/solidarity in the pursuit of social happiness. The consortia can be compared with Edmund Burke's "little platoons," where our first public affections and awareness of our participation in

---

124. *Saggio*, §710.

the human family are formed. They are Tocqueville's and Acton's preconditions for ordered liberty, the surest buttress against any despotic tendency of centralized government. Taparelli recognized these intermediary associations as the heart and soul of personal identity and as crucial to the pursuit of human fulfillment—from the bottom up, so to speak. He set himself the project of demonstrating the natural rights of these associations, especially the family and religious associations—the church at all levels, religious schools, and charitable organizations—against the claims of radical individualists and collectivists alike, those whose competing ideologies formed the poles of modern political discourse.

Taparelli saw the assault on the rights of associations coming from two directions—egoistic individualism and grasping statism. These two currents, only in conflict as a matter of tactics, were founded on shared metaphysical and anthropological axioms.[125] Economic naturalists, as Taparelli calls them, both laissez-faire liberal and socialist, start by assuming the radical autonomy of the individual and that the subjective pursuit of pleasure is "the supreme law of nature, guiding men to their

---

125. These shared axioms are apparent in the works of Hobbes, Hume, and Rousseau. Consider, for example, Hobbes's view of an egoistic individualism that justifies the absolute sovereignty of Leviathan, the "mortal god," and his related attitude toward the "divisive" influence of intermediary associations on the unity of the body politic.

> Another infirmity of a Commonwealth is the immoderate greatness of a town, when it is able to furnish out of its own circuit the number and expense of a great army; as also the great number of corporations, which are as it were many lesser Commonwealths in the bowels of a greater, like worms in the entrails of a natural man. To which may be added, liberty of disputing against absolute power by pretenders to political prudence; which though bred for the most part in the lees of the people, yet animated by false doctrines are perpetually meddling with the fundamental laws, to the molestation of the Commonwealth, like the little worms which physicians call ascarides.

Thomas Hobbes, *Hobbes's Leviathan: Reprinted from the Edition of 1651* (Oxford: Clarendon Press, 1965), chap. XXIX, 256–57. Taparelli claimed that Hobbes's error was rooted in his false premise that the natural state of man is war. Hobbes saw the reciprocal behavior of men as being dependent solely on self-love and the passions of the appetites—but the appetites, including self-preservation, are not what make us distinctly human among animals. Taparelli accuses this "misanthrope" of ignoring man's rational and social nature:

> If [Hobbes] had understood nature, he would have seen that the reasons that make one prefer one society to another are an *individuating* circumstance, a principle from which is reduced to the concrete that general *rational* social tendency, which leads to loving man because to not love him would be *disorder* contrary to the intent of the creator, who wishes this love since he gave to everyone the same nature. *Saggio*, Note XLII.

happiness."¹²⁶ Their shared vision of the "just" society is tied to the ever-greater satisfaction of material interests. The one major difference is that while laissez-faire liberals rely on greater liberty supposedly allowing the poor to enrich themselves and defend their own interests, socialists insist on the use of state power to redistribute wealth in pursuit of an ideal of equality. Taparelli saw that the failure of the promises of laissez-faire liberalism led, already historically speaking but also theoretically, to expansion of state power. The mistaken anthropology of both poles and their fractured conception of human nature renders naturalist social science congenitally defective, Taparelli argues. False premises lead to distorted diagnoses and pernicious prescriptions. Taparelli reasoned that public policy based on what he calls "Epicurean utilitarianism" would result in ever-greater alienation and social conflict. He shared this conclusion with Karl Marx, but whereas Marx predicted the advent of a proletarian revolution and an eventual classless utopia, Taparelli foresaw a descent into anomie and consumerism, a dysfunctional, ego-driven society, and an ever-expanding state.¹²⁷ In an Epicurean world,

> while everyone wants to enjoy much without sacrificing anything, the nature of society is such than it cannot subsist if not by the sacrifice of the individual for the common good. Remove this concept and society perishes. Therefore the independence of the individual

---

126. Luigi Taparelli, "Le due economie" [The two economies], CC ser. III, vol. 2 (1856): 617. Also available in French, in Robert Jacquin, trans. and ed., *Essai sur les Principes Philosophiques de L'Économie Politique* (Paris: Lethielleux, 1943), 17–69, as part of a translation with original footnotes plus commentary on three Taparelli articles from *Civiltà Cattolica* on economics. In addition to "Le due Economie," this work includes translations of "Analisi critica dei primi concetti dell'Economia sociale," 1857, and "Indirizzo di future trattazioni economiche," 1862.

127. It is striking how close Taparelli's prophetic warnings are to Tocqueville's in the chapter of *Democracy in America* titled, "What Kind Of Despotism Democratic Nations Have To Fear," which included the following:
> If despotism came to be established in the democratic nations of our day… it would be more extensive and milder, and it would degrade men without tormenting them. …I do not fear that in their chiefs they will find tyrants, but rather schoolmasters. …I see an innumerable crowd of like and equal men who revolve on themselves without repose, procuring the small and vulgar pleasures with which they fill their souls. Each of them, withdrawn and apart…he exists only in himself and for himself alone, and if a family still remains for him, one can at least say that he no longer has a native country. …Above these an immense tutelary power is elevated, which alone takes charge of assuring their enjoyments and watching over their fate."

Tocqueville, *Democracy in America*, 661–63.

and the mania of enjoyment while on one side need society for the protection against the egoism of others, on the other side they combat society as restrictive of their own egoism. Here therefore is man in society condemned to a perpetual contradiction, preaching to others the duty to sacrifice themselves for the common good and practicing for himself the right to sacrifice nothing if not constrained by force.[128]

Driven by the logic of a disordered conception of liberty and of social utility, intermediary associations of all sorts are the first casualties of the centralizing state. Such associations are the first to be regulated, instrumentalized, or absorbed into state functions. Seen as competitors for authority and allegiance, such entities are obliterated or insidiously obliged to recede into the private realm, and while they are allowed to maintain outward appearances, they are deprived of any public influence or power. Taparelli feared that alongside religious associations, the family in particular would be seen as the other great threat to the utopian aspirations of socialist statist and laissez-faire liberal alike, viewed as the source of divided affections or of irrational restrictions on personal liberty.[129] Disor-

---

128. Taparelli, "Le due Economie," part IV, "Economia eterodossa," para. 11. CC, ser. III, vol. 3 (August 21, 1856): 263.
129. Following his treatment of the natural law's application to the near "per se inviolability of the domestic sanctuary," Taparelli takes the opportunity in Note LXXXIV to refute the utilitarian criticism of the traditional family held by the philosophe Cesare Beccaria and radically extended by romantic socialists like Giuseppe Mazzini and other "egalitarian communists." Taparelli relates Beccaria's argument (from *Crimes and Punishments*, 1764) that if the family were the foundation of society, the monarchical principle of government would infect popular thinking. Beccaria declares "the love of family" a "vain idol" that breeds selfishness. Taparelli finds it no surprise then that the "egalitarian communists" proclaim that "la famiglia individuale debbe essere abolita, conciossiachè essa diparte gli affetti, rompe l'armonia della fratellanza la quale dee collegare gli uomini, ed è cagione di tutti i mali che possono gettarli nella ruina," [The individual family must be abolished, since that divides the affections, breaks the harmony of the brotherhood which must unite men, and is the cause of all the evils that can throw it into ruin.] citing "Dottrina della setta comunistica equalitaria," in *La scienza e la Fede*, v. II, 12 (December 1811), 436, and the important reference work of Augustin Barruel, *Mémoires pour servir à l'Hist. du Jacobinisme*, 5 vols., (Hamburg, 1798–99). Taparelli would have done well to cite Rousseau in this Note, from the "Discourse on Political Economy," dealing with the dissolution of the family in favor of the love of the State, as set forth above in note 73.
    Taparelli continues with a reprimand, unlikely to persuade: "Così la discorrono coloro che hanno perduto colla fede nella rivelazione anche i sensi dell'umanità. Se il Beccaria, il Mazzini e i comunisti equalitarii avesser serbato memoria del quarto precetto del decalogo sul quale si

dered ideas of personal freedom and equality contribute to the flourishing of depersonalized exchanges of emotional and sexual services, the sort of freedom that is conducive to authoritarian rule.[130] Rousseau advocated for the elimination of the family as a source of competing affections, so that every citizen would come to regard the state as his *alma mater*.[131] Marx also longed for the end of the "bourgeois family" as the final vestige of the alienated exchange of services typical of capitalist societies.[132]

As opposed to this anarchic ideology of ill-conceived self-interest, ending in a "social paralysis" of governmental regulation, Taparelli argued from an anthropology that recognizes the complex motives of human psychology. According to him, the Epicurean utilitarian view adopted by theorists like Hobbes and Rousseau, which posited the cornerstone of the relentless egoistic pursuit of pleasure, ultimately requires the abstraction called "society" or the "state" to impose order. Such a view contains

---

fonda l'ordine della carità verso il prossimo, ne avrebbero inferito con l'Angelico: 'ergo illi sunt nobis coniuncti secundum carnis originem, sunt a nobis specialius diligendi.'" *ST*, II-II. q. 26, a. 8, o. [Thus they speak who have lost with their faith in revelation even the consciousness of humanity. If Beccaria, Mazzini, and egalitarian communists had preserved memory of the fourth precept of the Decalogue on which is founded the order of charity towards ones neighbor, they would have inferred with the Angelic Doctor: 'Therefore according as they are related to us by origin of the flesh, they are especially loved by us.']

130. Montesquieu also saw this threat of moral and political degeneration in democratic regimes: "The members of the commonwealth riot on the public spoils, and its strength is only the power of a few, and the license of many." Charles Louis de Secondat, Baron de Montesquieu, *The Spirit of the Laws*, vol. 1, *The Complete Works of M. de Montesquieu* (London: T. Evans, 1777), 27; or, in the same vein, Tocqueville, "The first, and in a way the only, necessary condition for arriving at centralizing public power in a democratic society is to love equality or to make it believed [that one does]. Thus the science of despotism, formerly so complicated, is simplified: it is reduced, so to speak, to a single principle." Tocqueville, *Democracy in America*, 650. And again, "Despotism, which in its nature is fearful, sees the most certain guarantee of its own duration in the isolation of men, and it ordinarily puts all its care into isolating them. There is no vice of the human heart that agrees with it as much as selfishness: a despot readily pardons the governed for not loving him, provided that they do not love each other." Ibid., 485.

131. See note 73 above.

132. "Abolition of the family! Even the most radical flare up at this infamous proposal of the Communists. On what foundation is the present family, the bourgeois family, based? On capital, on private gain. In its completely developed form, this family exists only among the bourgeoisie. But this state of things finds its complement in the practical absence of the family among the proletarians, and in public prostitution. The bourgeois family will vanish as a matter of course when its complement vanishes, and both will vanish with the vanishing of capital."
Karl Marx and Friedrich Engels, *Manifesto of the Communist Party*, trans. Samuel Moore, (Chicago: Charles H. Kerr & Company, 1906), 39–40.

flawed assumptions regarding both individuals and society. It presents a false dichotomy presuming that order and liberty are mutually opposed. Taparelli argued instead that liberty is only possible through order. But order can come from one of two sources: either from a moral sense of obligation that arises from the intellectual recognition of the duties and respective rights of persons in society, grasped by speculative reason as true and by practical reason as good; or from the fear of superior physical force. In the first of these alternatives, education in the virtues and formation of conscience is paramount for developing the capability of individuals to live as free and self-regulating persons.

Taparelli offers a true science of association, whereas Tocqueville had left only many keen empirical observations and a few suggestive hypotheses. Realist social science, according to Taparelli, will be in a position to correctly understand sources of conflict, among other things, and to prescribe the most gentle, efficient, and effective means of overcoming dysfunctions—the sine qua non of which is a cultural formation that promotes respect of the duties to oneself and to others, which is to say, social justice rightly understood. Specific economic and political measures also apply to promote the advancement of social perfection, but cultural and moral formation remains fundamental. As Taparelli was wont to pose the basic problem: people will be governed either by conscience or by bayonets.[133]

---

133. This is a dichotomy that Taparelli not infrequently draws between morality and force; for example, in *Esame critico*, part II, 158.

CHAPTER IV

SOCIAL JUSTICE AND SUBSIDIARITY AS COMPLEMENTARY PRINCIPLES

As the previous chapter explained, for Taparelli subsidiarity—which he calls "hypotactical right"—means that *"every consortium must conserve its own unity in such a way that does not damage the unity of the whole; and every larger society must provide for the unity of the whole without destroying the unity of the consortia."*[1] Given the necessity of association, and the inevitability that any large society be composed of lessor associations, "the duty of the *consortium* is to tend towards the unity of the *Whole*, [while] the duty of the *Whole* is to not destroy the being of the *consortia*."[2] With Taparelli's concept of subsidiarity in mind, one is in a better position to understand the extension of his theory of social duties and rights to the theory of "social justice"; that is, the respect for and promotion of the free and full exercise of duties and rights of all persons in the social context. Social justice for Taparelli, who coined the term, is not a nineteenth-century-fashionable way of referring to commutative or distributive justice.

A Coherent Account of Social Justice

Reviewing Taparelli's argument, he asserts that humans are born with natural needs that pertain to the specificity of the species. Rather than being born free, as in the view of the social contract theorists, Taparelli sees the human person as being born in a totally dependent condition (witness the

---

1. *Saggio*, §694,
2. *Saggio*, §695.

infant). As has been seen, he calls this innate need "physiological" sociality, immediately present in the infant before he is capable of any kind of reasoning. The infant needs social support to meet all of his needs, including physical ones—in the order of right reason, the infant's "pursuit" of these goods is entirely programmed into his DNA. The developing child naturally learns a normative sociality early on by a growing experience of his need for help from others for the basic goods, but also for higher goods like knowledge and pleasurable enjoyment. At some point in childhood development, a knowledge and understanding of sociality extends, by means of experience, education, and cultural formation, to the recognition that others are characterized by the same dependence and have the same social requirements; that is, to the discovery of an identity with others in their being.

From the consciousness of physiological sociality then develops a psychological context, increasingly apparent over time, in which the requirements for the pursuit of sensible and intellectual goods beyond those needed for mere subsistence become more complex. Sociality at this point is understood in right reason as a duty to ourselves, a fact of our nature, the satisfaction of which requires a certain freedom in choice of means and an ability to evaluate according to the principles of justice trade-offs in the pursuit of knowledge and true enjoyment.

Finally, the honorable, reasoning individual recognizes that the situation of our "replicated selves" (i.e., other people), signifies in the abstract that others, who are our equals, have the same duty to themselves and therefore deserve to have our help in the same way as we wish for them to help us. This recognition of identity of condition and duties presents sociality in a new light—as a moral duty to others, it is right to treat them as we ourselves would want to be treated. This aspect of sociality involving moral duty to others, including self-sacrifice, is generally discussed in later CST under the umbrella of the term "solidarity."

Without negating the requirements of self-interest, moral reasoning dictates that it is right to protect others' claims of noninterference in their pursuit of the goods of human existence, just as we claim noninterference for ourselves. It is right to recognize in abstractly identical others the same freedom to fulfill their duties that we assert for ourselves. Subjective rights, therefore, are the extension of a power that has moral force in the human conscience due to intersubjectivity with other consciences, and they involve, at a minimum, noninterference applicable in the abstract to universal humanity. Perfecting the force of this respect for the interests of others in conscience reciprocally in a society is the sine qua non for ordered liberty, that is, for allowing self-regulating persons to freely pursue fulfillment of their fundamental human needs: material prosperity, social cooperation, and intellectual/spiritual truth.

Thus, in the recognition of the identity of equals, the duty to do the good—the first precept of the natural law—translates into the corresponding duty to protect and promote the good of others. But this understanding is not a calculation of self-interest based on (consciously or unconsciously) expected gains that are sought in an exchange of services, even emotional services, as Adam Smith suggests. Rather, it comes from a connatural apprehension of being, composite human nature, and goodness. Taparelli claims to have overcome the materialist and idealist divorcing of self-interest from virtue: "Our theory which reconciles virtue and interest in a single principle, combines the advantages of the two extreme systems, and gives birth to an undeniable fact, that is the insatiable love of happiness."[3] His theory thus reconciles virtue with self-interest *rightly understood*, and in the context of abstract humanity, this reconciliation involves willing for others the same honorable happiness one wills for oneself. In the concrete circumstances of individual existence, to will the ultimate good of others means to will also the protection and facilitation of their pursuit of happiness—which is the concern of social justice.

The term "social justice" has been so broadly used in political rhetoric to support almost any demand made on larger society and government, including demands for freedom from traditional conceptions of right and justice, that it has understandably lost almost any coherence. It will be our purpose here to elaborate Taparelli's original meaning.[4]

---

3. *Saggio*, Note XXII. See Adam Smith's alternative phenomenological assessment of ethical reasoning based on the psychology of imagination in the feeling of sympathy and the urge for approval in his 1759 *Theory of Moral Sentiments*, Knud Haakonssen, ed. (Cambridge: Cambridge University Press, 2002), 11–24.

4. The term social justice took on a life of its own, so to speak, almost immediately after Taparelli's theoretical formulation. The superior general of the Jesuits, Jan Roothaan, encouraged the diffusion in Germany of Taparelli's work among members of the Society. Already in August of 1842, Roothan was discussing the need to find a translator into German. Pirri, *Carteggi del*

Natural Right to Subjective Rights

The topics of natural right and subjective rights, and of social rights and social justice, are treated in Book II, Chapter III, "Notions of Right and of Social Justice" (*Nozioni del diritto e della giustizia sociale*) of the *Saggio*.[5] For Taparelli, society is a necessary consequence of nature, and based on extending the moral principle applicable to each individual to all people in the aggregate, united in their respect of reciprocal duties, it can be understood that apprehending the order of those duties is a moral function binding individuals together by their duties to each other. For Taparelli, human beings' connatural apprehension of order and of its laws as true and good is the basis of the "opposing power," in conscience, of noninterference in the rightly ordered actions (thoughts and deeds) of others. The power of this recognition "opposes" one's own passions and material interests. "The intellect is essentially made for order, for number, for proportion: it does not have need therefore of other interest to love it [order] in itself in others, even against their own passions."[6]

Subjective rights, then, are created and draw their moral power from the intersubjective ordering of intellects to natural right, to truth and

---

Padre Taparelli, 130; cf. Jacquin, *Taparelli*, 176n112. In fact, the work was first translated into German in 1845 at Ratisbonne. Calvez and Perrin, in discussing the origin of the term "social justice," trace the concept back to the Germans and the French, particularly Heinrich Pesch and Charles Antoine, both Jesuits who certainly influenced the thought of those who had a hand in writing *Quadragesimo Anno*, primarily Nell-Breuning. Calvez and Perrin refer back to Taparelli but without providing any details of Taparelli's ideas whatsoever, not on social justice, and certainly not on subsidiarity. Calvez and Perrin, *The Church and Social Justice*, 145–46. Antonio Rosmini was using the term "social justice" extensively in his 1848 work, *The Constitution under Social Justice*, trans. Alberto Mingardi (Lanham: Lexington Books, 2007), just a few years after Taparelli had published the first editions of the *Saggio*, with which he was familiar. Taparelli had great respect for and was in corrrespondence with Rosmini. Many of Rosmini's thoughts were substantially in harmony with many of Taparelli's—particularly on the articulation of theory in fact and the need for a complete understanding of human nature in any political theory—but a comparison of the concepts of social justice in the two is beyond the scope of the current work. See Robert P. Kraynak, "The Origins of 'Social Justice' in the Natural Law Philosophy of Antonio Rosmini," *The Review of Politics* 80, no. 1 (Winter 2018): 3–29.

5. *Saggio*, §§341–64.

6. "L'intelletto è fatto essenzialmente per l'ordine, pel numero, per la proporzione: non ha dunque bisogno di altro interesse per amarlo in sè e negli altri, a dispetto ancora delle proprie passioni." *Saggio*, Note XLIII. See also ibid., §341: "One must not suppose that what seems the relative opposition of duties and rights constitutes a contradiction. They are both terms born from the cognition and natural love of order in oneself and then in others."

goodness, in well-formed consciences.[7] The entitlement to a right in any given case, and the proper exercise of the power granted by a right, resides in the presentation and logical demonstration of the clarity and utility of a chosen action in relation to the pursuit of the highest good.

> If society is a *necessary* consequence of human nature, if it is born from the application of the moral principle to the natural aggregation of human individuals, bound among them by reciprocal *duties*; it is clear that its basis is *moral order*, since in moral order resulting from the natural order, is founded every duty. Now the idea of order binds naturally every intellect, since order is *truth*; it binds equally every will, because order is *good*; therefore one cannot consider society without right away raising before [oneself] the idea of *duty* that ties the one to act for the good of the other: and the idea of *opposed power* with which this second person moves the first to act in his favor, on the strength of that law that *order* manifests to both. This power is usually indicated by the word *right*.[8]
>
> The first idea of *right* (*dritto*), namely of the *right* (*retto*—[meaning straight or correct]), sprouts in the moral awareness of order in action aimed at the essential end of human nature. ...*right* (*dritto*) is a term on the level of morality, and therefore has no place except among intelligent beings. ...But what do we mean with the words – *to have a right?* We mean to have a *power*. ...And meanwhile every *power* supposes a *force*. [And as there are only two forces in nature that we know, physical on bodies, and moral on minds,] to have a right therefore means to have a moral power, a power over minds. ...Truth acts on the intelligence, the good acts on the will, a right therefore indicates a power based on the true and on the good.[9]

---

7. *Saggio*, §342.
8. *Saggio*, §341.
9. *Saggio*, §§ 341–43. See also, ibid., Note XXVIII, on why "rights" strictly speaking are only relevant to intelligent rational creatures who make moral judgments and who can be moved in conscience by the presentation of a truth. This understanding is contrary to the use of the term to include "animal rights," a use Taparelli was already aware of. Any rights possessed by animals cannot be "inalienable" as part of their nature, but rather must be derived from some other moral principle applicable to humans, the intelligent beings who could accord some protective principle of noninterference to animals, on their behalf, based on some duty inhering in men.

The more directly related it is to the highest good, the stronger the claim of right. That is why certain rights are "inalienable"—they are ineluctable requirements of order, of the orientation of the intellect to truth, and of the striving of persons within society for the ultimate good.[10]

A social right, as Taparelli refers to these subjective rights that obtain in human society, is defined as an "indisputable power according to reason": "according to reason" identifies the moral relation; "power" distinguishes the right from the duty that is imposed on others thereby; and "indisputable" specifies that the force of a subjective right is strictly related to its ability to bind the will of others.[11] That is why the subjective right of a person is called a social right, because it creates a duty in the consciences of others—and obviously the right carries a reciprocal duty in each claimant of right. The binding force of the claimed right must not be debatable; in other words, it must be present in the rightly formed consciences of rational persons. Here can be seen again just how important the moral education and cultural formation of persons is, beginning with subjects like Aristotelian logic. The efficacy of a subjective right is contingent upon fact and conflict of rights; it remains binding on conscience so long as there is nothing materially lacking to sustain the carrying out of the corresponding duty and no countervailing, more fundamental, conflicting right of another.[12]

Social duties and social (or subjective) rights are deductions from the application of the first precept of right reason—to do the good—extended to our "replicated selves": to do good to others. But these duties, and the rights created thereby, concern abstract being—"humanity"—and can only be practically considered in the factual concrete contexts presented by the individuals and the circumstances in which we find them. "To do the good of other men is to say that we must will others that good that we will for ourselves. Now what good must I will

10. *Saggio*, §349.
11. L'analisi da noi fatta del *dritto sociale* ci conduce a definirlo – *un irrefragabile potere secondo ragione*. – Le parole *secondo ragione* lo dimostrano relazione morale; la voce *potere* lo contradistingue dall'opposto termine della relazion che è il dovere; l'aggiunto *irrefragabile* restringe l'idea di potere secondo ragione che potrebbe estendersi a tutto il *lecito*, e caratterizza il dritto che abbiam chiamato *sociale*: determinando la forza che egli ha di vincolare l'altrui volontà. *Saggio*, §350.
12. *Saggio*, §§352, 359, 361.

for myself? I must will myself perfection first of mind; second of will; third of life."[13]

Perfection of mind for Taparelli means the acquisition of knowledge—not just any knowledge, beliefs, or opinions, but knowledge of the true order of things. As intellectual rational animals, our reasoning depends on data taken as true; truth is a guide to our actions. No one wants to conduct themselves based on falsehoods. The virtue of honesty, or of honor ("*onestà*"), is a requisite for the operation of our reason, for we seek true happiness as the object of our actions, not illusions or lies. Since society is a "cooperation of intelligences harmonized in judgments" and is dependent on "reciprocal communication of thoughts,"[14] honesty is a fundamental duty and requirement of social existence. Perfection of will deals with developing and strengthening the tendency toward seeking what the intellect has demonstrated to it as good, and to cooperate with others in pursuit of that good.[15] And finally, perfection of life begins with its preservation. Since life is threatened by both violence and natural events, this includes the duties and rights of (justified) self-defense;[16] and the particularly weighty considerations of rights over property (or dominion), for the purpose of securing access to the necessary means of survival.[17]

The right of "dominion," itself based on the duty of self-preservation, is the right to some particular means of fulfilling that duty. As has been already briefly described, Taparelli makes the argument that this right, also understood as the right to private property, is a fundamental natural right of humanity—a right of every individual, in the abstract—but this must be distinguished from the idea of the ancient theory of the universal destination of goods. Against the idea that a right of private property is strictly the product of positive law, Taparelli contends that natural law theorists like Aquinas and Suarez, and "law of nature" social contract theorists like Hobbes, Locke, and Rousseau, confuse the abstract reasoning

13. *Saggio*, §365–72.
14. *Saggio*, §366.
15. *Saggio*, §373.
16. *Saggio*, §§380–97.
17. *Saggio*, §§398–420.

of natural law with the inevitable variability of its forms in concrete, historical reality. The abstract right of universal dominion, or the universal community of goods, corresponds to abstract humanity, whereas the actual working of property and restrictions on dominion over lands or personal property have always varied according to time and place. There was never a universal community of goods except as an abstraction, just as there was never an asocial state of nature prior to civil society.

Taparelli connects mistaken reasoning about the abstract right of dominion, which he thought led natural law thinkers astray, to the creation of an (imaginary) primitive community of goods that was abandoned in some way in the transition from an (imaginary) state of nature to civil society. The development of positive laws relating to private property was certainly useful for the reasons Aquinas cites[18]—indeed, in ancient or modern societies, where dominion, or the meaningful application of it, concretely belongs only to the tribe or to "the people," the lack of productivity and peaceful civilizational development is noteworthy.[19] Humanity has a natural right of dominion in the abstract; however, the exercise of this right in fact, in the concrete, has always been embodied in myriad customary or positive law arrangements, often including the absence of or serious restrictions on private property rights. But, and this is not a technicality, Taparelli points out that there was never a period before the "division" of land. Land everywhere was always being worked by someone, or some collectivity, for his or their own benefit, as well as, and it is crucial to note, for the good of others in society, either directly or through economic exchange. Locke's theory of property rights based on mixing one's labor with nature depends for its morality on a corollary that there remained "as much and as good" land for latecomers, which no doubt made sense to him in the seventeenth century with his experience of the expanses of the New World. However, Locke's theory of property rights also implied a duty to make property productive for the common good, which, in theory, made private property subject to regulation or even to being taken via eminent domain. Taparelli agreed that the right

18. *ST*, II-II, q. 66, a. 2.
19. See, F. A. Hayek, *The Fatal Conceit: the Errors of Socialism*, ed. W. W. Bartley, III (New York: Routledge, 1990).

of property, coming as it does in the form of a delegation or agency on behalf of nonpossessors in society, includes the duty to make land and capital productive for the common good.[20] For Taparelli, the variations in and successive transformations of property rights with the development of civilization are not additions to the natural law, as Aquinas saw them, but are instead simply articulations of the abstract natural law right of every person manifested in variable concrete circumstances. Property laws as historically developed in Western societies may well have distinct utilitarian advantages, but that is a different argument. Private property for Taparelli is a natural right, but not "sacred and inviolable,"[21] because the abstract right to the means of self-preservation is also vested in all nonpossessors, and the rules governing conflicts of rights apply.[22]

These then are the goods that Taparelli concludes each person has a duty to pursue: self-preservation, rational exercise of the will, and knowledge of truth. The necessary formation of society creates a duty to will the good of others, and so rights are reciprocally recognized and extended to all as social rights, which are the foundation for a proper understanding of social justice.

Social Justice Rightly Understood

Why "social" justice, when obviously justice always relates to interactions between persons and hence is social, strictly speaking? Social justice is different from fairness between individuals in exchanges of equal quantities based on subjective valuations and perceived benefits (commutative justice). It is also different from the fair distribution of the benefits of public goods or offices proportionally based on merit (distributive justice). Nor is social justice the same as legal justice; that is, acting in accordance with duly enacted laws. Social justice is first and foremost a personal virtue with regard to the disposition to protect and promote the exercise of the rights and the fulfillment of the duties of others in society. Secondarily, the term can be

---

20. Cf. Taparelli, "Agenti di produzione" [Agents of production], CC, ser. IV, vol. 3 (1859): 401–13, 529–38.

21. In terms Fortin raises concerning Leo XIII's emphasis in CST on private property and subjective rights, see "Sacred and Inviolable: *Rerum Novarum* and Natural Rights," in *Human Rights, Virtue, and the Common Good*, 191–222.

22. *Saggio*, §419.

meaningfully used as a characterization of a socioeconomic and political order, the actual arrangement of institutions, laws, and policies that operate to protect and promote the same exercise of rights and duties of individuals who make up that society. Socially just acts or, in a derivative sense, laws and institutions operate in such a way that persons and associations who possess equal rights to pursue happiness in the abstract are empowered in their concrete and natural yet unequal strengths, means, and abilities to fulfill their natural duties and freely exercise their natural rights for the good of each and for the common good of the whole. Socially just acts or measures (of persons or of their governmental authorities) will seek appropriate means, respecting the principles of subsidiarity, for individuals and associations to more fully pursue their material, moral, and spiritual perfection.

Social right, in the abstract natural law of society, and subjective, human rights in the concrete as a basis for talking about social justice, must first be distinguished:

> Therefore *if one considers only humanity* all men have equal right to do that which seems best to them for obtaining one's own good, and no one can obstruct or contradict *the right of others* without sinning against the *order* of justice from which this right depends. This unquestionable power to act upon one's own good according to one's own judgment without being [un]reasonably blocked, is that called the right of *independence*; and has full vigor in man to the extent he is considered solely in his abstract humanity.[23]

Conflicting rights and variations in the power of actual persons to exercise their abstract rights in society are facts of concrete existence. The duty and right to pursue one's own good—including self-preservation, freedom of association, and the pursuit of happiness—are among the inalienable duties and rights of man because, derived as they are (like all social, or subjective rights) from the raison d'être of society itself, they cannot be diminished without the natural order of society itself being

---

23. *Saggio*, §360.

distorted.[24] Subjective rights act on the conscience of another person who might otherwise be opposed to the fulfillment of your particular duty in the way you see fit. And from this understanding of "right," Taparelli draws the conclusion that "social" justice describes the habitual inclination of right-reasoning minds to foster the exercise of the rights and fulfillment of the duties inhering in others.

> From the idea of [social or subjective] right springs spontaneously the idea of social *justice*. A right mind admires order and loves it in itself and in others, and by consequence makes efforts to preserve it, acting such that to the *right* corresponds the fulfillment of the *duty*. This habitual inclination to equalize the parties is customarily called *justice*: but for establishing this equalization it must have bases on which to form its judgments: what will these bases be?[25]

But what can it mean, Taparelli asks, to equalize the parties in the exercise of their duties and rights in a concrete reality made up of individuals who are manifestly unequal in many different ways?

> *Social* justice is for us justice *between man and man*. . . . Between man and man considered under this [abstract] aspect it is clear that there exist relations of perfect *equality*, since *man and man* signify nothing here if not *humanity replicated two times*. . . I can therefore conclude that social justice must equalize *in fact* all men in that which belongs to *the rights of humanity*, since the Creator equalized them *in nature*; and that man operating on the norm of such *justice* accomplishes the intent of who created him.[26]

24. *Saggio*, §349.
25. "Dalla idea del dritto nasce la idea di *giustizia* sociale. Un animo retto ammira l'ordine e lo ama in sè e negli altri, e per conseguenza inchina a custodirlo, facendo sì che al *dritto* corrisponda esattamente l'adempimento del *dovere*. Quest'abituale inclinazione a ragguagliare le partite suol dirsi *giustizia*: ma per istabilire questo ragguaglio ella dee aver delle basi sopra cui formare i suoi giudizi: quali saranno queste basi?" *Saggio*, §353.
26. "La giustizia *sociale* è per noi giustizia *fra uomo e uomo*. ...Fra uomo e uomo considerato sotto tale aspetto egli è chiaro che passano relazioni di perfettissima *ugualianza*, perocchè *uomo e uomo* altro qui non significa se non la umanità replicata due volte... Posso dunque conchiudere

...

But go slowly: where is this *abstract man*, this *replicated humanity* the notion of which suggested to me the first elements of social justice? If there exist men associated with other men, they exist always *concretely*, always individuated, always gifted with determinate strengths and properties. Now when I consider men under this new aspect, where is the equality? Comparing age with age, intelligence with intelligence, robustness with robustness, etc. everything here is disparity among men, and disparity, take note, that derives from nature, since nature is that which forms individuals ... I will conclude therefore correctly that all human individuals are among themselves *naturally unequal* with respect to their *individuality*, as they are naturally *equal* with respect to the *species*; and for that, the action of man will be *just* when it will be appropriate to the diverse individual rights of those with whom one is dealing.[27]

The idea of social justice, in Taparelli's conception, aims at equalizing individual persons, and the intermediary associations they form, in their concrete capacities of exercising their abstract rights to life, liberty, and the pursuit of happiness. In other words, social justice seeks to equalize actual persons, as well as their various associations, with respect to the freedom to fulfill their duties of self-preservation, social order, and pursuit of the truth and happiness, in light of the natural, finite, temporal goods available in society. Taparelli reasons from the absolute equality of men considered in their abstract humanity as rational animals. And

---

che la giusizia sociale debbe ragguagliare *nel fatto* tutti gli uomini in ciò che spetta *i dritti di umanità*, siccome il Creatore li ragguagliò *nella natura*; e che l'uomo operando a norma di tal *giustizia* compie gl'intenti di chi lo creò." *Saggio*, §354.

27. "Ma adagio; dov'è questo *uomo astratto*, questa *umanità replicata* la cui nozione mi ha suggerito i primi lineameti della giustizia sociale? se esistono uomini associati ad altri uomini, esistono sempre *in concreto*, sempre individuati, sempre dotati di forze di proprietà determinate. Or quando io considero gli uomini sotto questo nuovo aspetto dove è la uguaglianza? Paragonate età con età, ingegno con ingegno, robustezza con robustezza ecc. tuto è qui disparità fra gli uomini, e disparità, notatelo, che deriva dalla *natura*, giacchè è quella che forma gl'individui... Concluderò dunque rettamente che tutti gl'individui umani sono fra loro *naturalmente* dissuguali per ciò che s'aspetta alla individualità, come sono *uguali* naturalmente per ciò che s'aspetta alla *specie*, e però l'operar dell'uomo allora sarà *giusto* quando sarà appropriato ai dritti individuali diversi di quelli con cui tratta." *Saggio*, §355.

so the first law of social justice is to equalize all men in practical terms in the way they are related abstractly: social justice would be the principle and measure of authentically progressive society made up of flourishing persons and of flourishing intermediary associations. This is the virtue of social justice looked at another way: man acting according to social justice seeks to enact the intentions of the creator who made all men equal in nature.[28] In any case, it is clear that an evaluation of social justice—the protection of rights favoring the material, moral, and intellectual perfection of individuals—involves rational argumentation within specific contexts and an understanding of the limited and intermediate goods achievable in society. This is especially true in the context of a pluralistic society.[29]

The individuality of concrete circumstances extends beyond characteristics imposed by genetic inheritance to the conditions into which one is born, social relations in the family, and the array of historical, socioeconomic, and cultural conditions within which one is raised and lives out life. The duties and rights of humanity considered in the abstract are equal, but the fulfillment of those duties and the exercise of those rights of individuated human persons are bound to concrete heterogeneous reality with its "thousand other accidental causes."[30]

---

28. *Saggio*, §354.

29. *Saggio*, §§868–901 deals with the intellectual perfection of individuals under the ideal of confessionally Catholic states versus the possibilities in non-Catholic (rationalist or heterodox, for example) states that lack the presence of an infallible authority, where there may be Catholic associations and no rational argument opposing religious practice or imposing conformity of beliefs. In such cases society as a whole is not in a position to perfect individual intelligences with regard to the greatest good and can only concern itself with perfecting them with regard to particular and temporal goods (§§903–19). This is to be accomplished primarily through liberal, technical, and scientific education, carried out with respect for parental rights (§919). The perfection of the will of individuals is treated in §§920–47. Of course, Taparelli was a zealous defender of freedom of association with regard to Catholic institutions under non-Catholic governments and of the rights of Catholic education at a time when freedom of education was a political flash point. He wrote a blistering essay in the first issue of *Civiltà Cattolica* on all aspects of these issues. See "Teorie sociali sull'insegnamento," [Social theories of education] CC, ser. I, vol. 1 (1850): 25–51, 129–57, 257–74, 369–84. These topics are of great interest but beyond the scope of this present work.

30. *Saggio*, §356. On the confused idea of individual equality in the concrete as a natural law, see Note XLVI.

With these ideas of *right* and of *justice*, based on the fact of the natural identity in nature and of the equally natural inequality of the individual, we can now enter into considering partially the social *rights* and *duties*, with the certainty to see them arise from nature itself and from the facts. And since the first moral principle [to do the good] applied to social being obliges us to seek the good of others, and by consequence to abstain from impeding others from it, it is clear that there arises in others the correlative right to act for their own good without being impeded, so long as they do not create an obstacle to ours."[31]

Social Justice and Subsidiarity Applied: Social Economics

What does the virtue of social justice look like in practice? The question is particularly relevant, as Taparelli well understood, to the practice of economic science and to the formulation of socioeconomic policy. In the last six years of his life, Taparelli turned his attention to a fundamental overview of economic science as it then stood, given the importance of economic development as the material foundation of the whole of individual and social perfection. He offered an analysis of the failures of "naturalistic" economics and indicated the work that needed to be done to craft an alternative based on Aristotelian and neoscholastic anthropology. The essay "Analisi critica dei primi concetti dell'economia sociale" (1857),[32] along with his earlier essay, "Le due Economie" (1856),[33] and the later "Indirizzo di future trattazioni economiche" (1862),[34] together form the basis of Taparelli's realist social theory as it relates to economic science and policy.

---

31. *Saggio*, §359.
32. CC ser. III, vol. 8 (1857): 546–59; ser. III, vol. 9 (1858): 17–34. See also, Luigi Taparelli, "Critical Analysis of the First Principles of Political Economy," trans. Thomas C. Behr, *Journal of Markets and Morality*, vol. 14, no. 2 (Fall 2011): 613–38; for a discussion of "Critical Analysis" see, Thomas C. Behr, "Luigi Taparelli and Catholic Economics," *Journal of Markets and Morality*, 14, no. 2 (Fall 2011): 607–11. See also, *Saggio*, §§458, 1155–85, dealing with economic policy.
33. CC, ser. III, vol. 2 (1856): 609–20; ser. III, vol. 3 (1856): 257–72, 465–85, 611–24; ser. III, vol. 4 (1856): 397–417.
34. "Indirizzo di future trattazioni economiche" [Direction of future economic treatments], CC ser. V, vol. 1 (1862): 146–57.

Taparelli held the conviction that the logic of classical liberal economics, shared with socialist economics, was founded on a distorted economic naturalism and false anthropology. He recognized that among economists there were "honest" thinkers who in practice sought to mitigate the conclusions deriving from the logic of their premises, but this came at the cost of coherence and the risk of imposing arbitrary hierarchies of value. Moreover, Taparelli believed that ignoring the moral-cultural sphere could only lead to irrational economic behavior, social conflict, worship of the state, and dictatorship. Taparelli believed that such defects rendered economic science as it then stood incomplete in its diagnoses and dangerous in its policy prescriptions.[35]

Compared with Naturalistic Economic Thought

To review, Taparelli identified two sets of fundamentally opposed anthropological premises concerning human psychology and the teleological ends of human action. One of these is based on the Aristotelian conception of hylomorphic, composite human nature, and as Aquinas and Taparelli see it, confirmed in (*not* proven by) the conception of God as creator and author of the laws of nature, knowable from natural reason, though known more completely through revelation. The other, that of the economic naturalists, both classical liberal and socialist, begin with an assumption of the radical independence of conscience and the subjective pursuit of pleasure as "the supreme law of nature, guiding men to their happiness."[36] Whereas socialists insisted on the use of political power to achieve positive equality between unequal classes in society, and liberals—Taparelli has Bastiat specifically in mind—rely on greater liberty to enable the poor to defend themselves against the rich, both agree that

---

35. Taparelli, "Le due economie," CC, ser. III, vol. 2: 609–12. To those naturalists who find the satisfaction of primary instincts for self-preservation, social standing, power, or sex to be the "purpose" of life, Taparelli might well have pointed out with C.S. Lewis that there seems not to be any additional instinct that specifies which of the instincts to pursue at any given time, in any given way, with any given person, etc., without positing the submission of instincts to intellect and reason and with true happiness as the universal end and aim. See, C. S. Lewis, *The Abolition of Man*, 18–20.

36. *Saggio*, §617.

satisfying the desire for pleasure is the proper end of human action.[37] From false premises come false analyses and perverse policies: Taparelli argued that a laissez-faire liberal economic policy founded on Epicurean morality and materialist metaphysics had only one tool in its bag: the stimulation of egoism, which can only lead to mindless consumerism, alienation, and social conflict.[38]

This "perpetual contradiction"—each individual wanting to give as little and get as much as possible—is the effect, Taparelli implies, of an education and cultural formation that distorts truth and morality, teaching that man acts only out of material self-interest, primarily manifested as the enjoyment of physical pleasure and avoidance of physical pain, taking the arguments of Bentham as the last word on human action. The correlative growth of the need for "social force," and consequently of the power of the state that wields it, would entail, Taparelli argued, an unlimited increase in government exactions and spending: "The limit on taxation will no longer be that which is *necessary* for the society to spend, but rather whatever is possible to get individuals to surrender."[39] Over time the public would look more and more to the state to satisfy its appetites and to supply various kinds of benefits, with everyone trying to "direct water to his own mill" without regard to distributive justice and leading to the enrichment of the most powerful private interests,[40] whether bosses or mobs. Driven by the logic of a distorted conception of liberty and social efficiency, intermediary associations—the network of subsidiary initiatives in any complex society, including families, churches, schools, businesses, professional and benevolent associations, and so on—would become viewed with suspicion and risk marginalization, abolition, or

---

37. Taparelli is sympathetic to what he perceives to be Bastiat's motives and to many of the practical conclusions of "honest" classical economists, despite the occasional ideological interpretations of their popularizers. Cf. Thomas Sowell, "Social Philosophy," chap. 1 in *Classical Economics Reconsidered* (Princeton: Princeton University Press, 1974).

38. Taparelli, "Le due Economie," CC, ser. III, vol. 3: 264. Taparelli finds confirmation for this point in Bastiat's repeated assertions to the effect that "every producer is inherently antisocial" and that the "social sciences would not have an object if citizens did not tend toward mutual exploitation," and from Bastiat's correspondence with the socialist-anarchist Proudhon, from which Taparelli observes the strong similarity of their premises.

39. Taparelli, "Le due Economie," 265–66.

40. Taparelli, "Le due Economie," 262.

being tightly controlled, as had in fact tended to be the case where radical liberal regimes had come to power since 1789. "Once these associations [*i corpi morali*, "moral bodies" or legal entities] that form the organic parts of the larger society are destroyed, society finds itself essentially altered, and reduced to a dust cloud of plucked atoms, lacking all cohesion, all special function, and chained to a total dependence on the supreme force [of the state] as a heap of purely passive and inorganic molecules."[41]

Indeed, as has been seen, Taparelli echoes Marx's theory of pauperization and class struggle, but Taparelli saw communism as the consequence of a society founded on what he identified as the deceptively liberating principle of the "independent man."[42] Taparelli explained and predicted, therefore, how laissez-faire liberal economic thinking, by its mistaken anthropology and morality, leads to big government liberalism, and how that new "liberalism" would be theoretically impotent against the egalitarian allurements of communistic socialism. For the *coherent* utilitarian, persons themselves tend to become reduced by "logical consequence" to objects of utility like any other good, and woe to the person who is not seen as socially useful: his very right to exist is called into question.[43]

It was Taparelli's intention to develop what he called "social economics" as an antidote to, or rather a supplement to, classical economics founded essentially on material self-interest and faith in the invisible hand of the market. This correction required understanding the additional principles that naturally guide calculations of "self-interest" for right-reasoning persons: order and justice, truth and charity (love). Taparelli suggested that self-interest properly understood includes our interest in social order and in the fullness of truth, interests that are part and parcel of our natural inclinations. Material self-interest (physical perfection), order and justice (social perfection), and truth and charity (intellectual perfection), are together the three motors of human action, and each needs to be given due weight in social analysis and policy—as these ends taken together are in fact the "common good" of each individual human person, with

---

41. Luigi Taparelli, "La libertà in economia: Conclusione," [Liberty in economy: Conclusion] CC, ser. IV, vol. 11 (1861): 547.

42. Taparelli, "La libertà in economia," 266–69.

43. Taparelli, "Le due Economie," CC, ser. III, vol. 3: 269.

intellect and reason informing the pursuit of the flourishing of the whole person as much as for the whole society. Healthy life is the good, material prosperity is the means; social order is the good, justice is the means; truth is the good, piety (or at least honesty or humility) and charity (love) are the means.

Therefore an economic science and policy based on a realist theory of human nature and human society would look to understand social justice in the way Taparelli describes, fostering the conditions (material and otherwise) of human flourishing. Taparelli recommends that those in governing positions research the "true causes and effects" of people's economic behavior, and the various means that might be available to encourage an increase in the production of wealth without detracting from concerns for justice or from pursuit of the higher ends of human action, the ultimate goods, to which the expansion of prosperity is only a means.

Taparelli criticized naturalistic social theorists for neglecting the study of human psychology and motivations that do not fit into their reductionist paradigm based on material self-interest. Following Aristotle and Aquinas, he sees material self-interest as merely the first, animal level of human motivation and action—the most basic, egoistic, and subjective. The other two motors of human action, justice and charity, are developments that flow from man's social and intellectual nature and from his first reflective acts of practical reason, acts that reveal in the developing individual person the presence of these higher inclinations or interests that are crucial for human flourishing, and that social scientists must not ignore.

Taking these three motors of human action fully into account was for Taparelli the key not only for reaching comprehensive explanations of economic phenomena but also for formulating public policies that would not ignore the necessary connections between material progress and moral progress in the service of an authentic progress of civilization. Disordered conceptions of progress that seem aimed at realizing the absolute freedom of individuals, with absolute security from adverse consequences, are rife with self-destructive contradictions. The focus on narrow, materialistic self-interest controls only for the most ubiquitous, least specifically human, of the motivations of self-interest rightly understood. Fully accounting for all these motivations, from the least to the most human, should be the starting point of a realist social science and the basis of an approach to all areas of social scientific research generally.

Principles and Objectives

Taparelli proposes an alternative Christian social economics, not a throwback to caricatured medieval theories, which had been described by Bastiat as founded merely on asceticism and charity (as alms).[44] For Taparelli, the starting point in economics, as it is in ethics generally, is the first question of the Catholic catechism: Why did God make us? A morally-ordered economy is governed by clearly defined standards and a hierarchy of values that depend on the answer to that question.[45] According to Taparelli, as well as Aquinas, one cannot separate natural law virtue ethics from theistic teleology and faith in a "supreme Artisan."[46] The "social paralysis" of governmental regulation identified by Taparelli leads to the creation of a very different society than one founded on an anthropology that posits man as dependent on a created natural order. It is a false dichotomy to think that order and liberty are in opposition to each other when they actually rise and fall together.[47] What social economics wants to add to the classical economics founded on material self-interest and competition are the two additional principles of human nature and action we have identified: justice and charity. One must be careful, therefore,

---

44. See Taparelli, "Le due economie," CC, ser. III, vol. 3: 617. For a more complete account of the evolution of medieval Scholastic economics as it would have been understood by Taparelli, see Odd Langholm, *The Legacy of Scholasticism in Economic Thought* (Cambridge: Cambridge University Press, 1998). See also, Chafuen, *Faith and Liberty*; and Joseph Schumpeter, *History of Economic Analysis* (New York: Oxford University Press, 1994).

45. Taparelli believed, along with Aquinas, that the existence of a provident God was knowable by natural reason. Even if that supposition—that God created and rules the universe—were to be pragmatically bracketed in a pluralistic society, and the ultimate end or purpose of human existence similarly bracketed, the empirical basis and falsifiability of natural law reasoning, tracking with eudemonistic ethics, presents a far from moot challenge to one-dimensional or relativistic social scientific paradigms.

46. Taparelli, "Le due economie," CC, ser. III, vol. 3: 467.

47. Taparelli, "La libertà in economia," CC, ser. IV, vol. 11 (1861): 551.

not to deceive oneself in imagining that Catholic doctrine denies or repudiates absolutely all of the economic laws that one has been able to deduce from antagonism and competition. . . . the passion of [material] interest retains a greater or lesser vitality; and consequently the practice of asking *more* and *offering less* and engaging in honest rivalry, within the limits of justice, applies equally to Catholic workers and businessmen."[48]

Classical economists had acknowledged the beneficial effects of religion in mitigating the potentially destructive tendencies of a system erected on material self-interest. Taparelli devotes a long passage in "Le due economie" to refuting the claims of Bastiat that philosophical or religious morality functions merely, albeit usefully, as a secondary support to economics, a sort of emergency brake in practice on the natural tendencies assumed to govern the behavior of both capitalists and the oppressed classes.[49] Taparelli suggests rather that interests in justice and fraternity are equally as inherent in our natural inclinations as our animal nature, and they need be given due weight in both the analytical methods of and political proposals emanating from the social sciences.[50] Taparelli is not persuaded by Bastiat's faith that the antagonisms in society will tend on their own toward the creation of harmony; Bastiat suggests that they will do so "as liquid seeks its own level."[51] Taparelli points out just how inapt a metaphor that is, to compare society to a body of homogenous molecules operating in a closed system, implying a social system characterized by complete equality of knowledge and identity of circumstances as between its members. Human interests are never so simplistically opposed or in harmony.[52]

Realist social science proposes policies and regulations that promote social justice and maximize the free exercise of the duties and

48. Taparelli, "Le due economie," CC, ser. III, vol. 3: 474.
49. Ibid., 264.
50. Cf. *ST*, I-II, q. 94, a. 2.
51. Taparelli, "Le due economie," CC, ser. III, vol. 3: 622.
52. Ibid. 621–23.

rights of individuals and of the associations they form in their reasoned pursuit of happiness: this is dramatically different from the centralization then being proposed by both wings of the ideological spectrum, the bureaucratic administration that Taparelli calls "the great wound of modern society."

> These considerations lead us to touch and uncover the great wound of modern society, *centralism*; which we carefully distinguish from social unity. Social unity joins the parts without destroying them, and it joins them for their common good, to which is sacrificed some part of their private independence. Centralism oppositely, formed of itself an idol of the ideal unity that is called the STATE, to this is sacrificed not only administrative liberty, but the very existence of the organic parts, transforming, altering and morally destroying the state itself, reduced to an instrument of private advantage for the good of its bosses.[53]

Taparelli concludes his essay with what he sees as the consequences of radical independence as a social doctrine, using even harsher language—but also with a reminder of the cure.

> Here finally is the true corrective of that vicious centralism that, claiming to gather in the fist of one alone all the powers, interests, and means of a society, has formed an army of bureaucrats to contain an army of slaves. To hope for a true economic liberty as long as this vicious centralization lasts would be a deplorable illusion. But a thousand times more deadly the illusion would be if it claimed

---

53. Queste considerazioni ci condussero a toccare e scoprire la gran piaga delle moderne società, il *Centralismo*; cui distinguemmo accuratamente dalla unità sociale. L'unità sociale congiunge le parti senza distruggerle, e le congiunge pel loro bene comune, al quale si sacrifica una qualche parte della privata indipendenza. Il centralismo all'opposto, formatosi un idolo di quella unità ideale che appella STATO, a questo sacrifica, non solo la libertà amministrativa , ma l'esistenza medesima delle parti organiche, trasformando, alterando e moralmente distruggendo lo Stato medesimo, ridotto a stromento di privati vantaggi pel bene dei suoi padroni.
Taparelli, "La libertà in economia," CC, ser. IV, vol. 11: 548.

true liberty by removing every rule on private covetousnesses in the hope that, moderating each other in exchange, [competing private interests] would be forced to run the ways of equity and of justice. A law, certainly, would establish itself; but it would be the law of the monopoly of the strongest, of the oppression of the weakest, and of liberty abolished for all; there being no liberty if not where every living right can, without encountering [just] obstacles, obtain a just satisfaction, and every violent opposition receive an efficacious repression.[54]

And so, Taparelli argues, principles and anthropology must be revisited. Social economics claims to offer guidance to governments on how to properly care for the public good—the good of individuals in society—but Taparelli highlights the then-existing widespread disagreements about such "good." One point of moral clarity that Taparelli draws from Christian belief is that "human persons" and "things" are absolutely distinct, with the former destined for God and the latter intended to serve as means. "The human person is the end of all things not endowed with reason."[55]

Taparelli sums up his psychology of human action in "Analisi critica." Economics based on a "true anthropology" takes man as a union of body and soul, with each "part" having its proper good and its own specific "reason" and will, such that production of valuable goods and services—directly for the material support of the body, in service to the soul, or for the support of one's peers—is not merely legitimate but necessary, and therefore constitutes a duty associated with economic rights. That is

---

54. Ecco finalmente il vero correttivo di quel vizioso centralismo che, pretendendo raccogliere in pugno di un solo tutti i poteri, gi' interessi, i mezzi di una società , vi ha formato un esercito di burocratici per contenere un esercito di schiavi. Sperare una vera libertà economica finché dura questo vizioso incentramento, sarebbe illusione deplorabile. Ma mille volte più funesta sarebbe l'illusione, se pretendesse vera libertà col sottrarre da ogni regola le private cupidigie, per la speranza che temperandosi scambievolmente, esse saranno forzate a correre le vie d'equità e di giustizia. Una legge, sì, verrebbe a stabilirsi; ma sarebbe la legge del monopolio dei più forti, della oppressione dei più deboli e della libertà abolita per tutti; non essendo libertà se non colà dove ogni diritto vivo può, senza incontrare ostacoli, ottenere un giusto appagamento, ogni violenza opposta incontrare un'efficace repressione.
Taparelli, "La libertà in economia," CC, ser. IV, vol. 11: 548.
55. Taparelli, "Le due economie," CC, ser. III, vol. 4: 400.

because, for Taparelli, as we have seen, first in the order of rational apprehension in the developing person is an appreciation of human identity, specifically in the conditions of sociality, which gives rise to an interest in order and an inclination to justice. Second, beyond the recognition of abstract equality and concrete inequality, the grounds for the moral obligations of social justice, there comes the recognition of suffering, which gives rise to compassion and an inclination to charity, the moral perfection of sociality—therefore persons have "interests" even in solidarity and sacrificial love.[56] These latter interests or inclinations are cultivated particularly by religious piety or at least by public honesty.

Other features of economic rights, as has been seen, include the right to property and the right to the fruits of one's labor, which further imply a right to protection from theft and excessive taxes, and the exercise of both the right to work and to a just wage; exercise of these rights can be facilitated by the formation of various kinds of associations. Taparelli's support for worker associations was radical in mid-century, predating their endorsement in *Rerum Novarum* by four decades.

> In order to support individual efforts in associations of common protection, there are two social duties: encourage their activity, regulate their management.
>
> Encourage their activity, 1st because modest associations are a faithful fulfillment of the first social principle; 2nd because they are a very tight link of social unity; 3rd because they correspond to the right that everyone has to have help in their calamity; 4th because they are one of the most effective ways of obtaining the public good, giving an organism to the popular classes the more effective in operation as the participation in it is more gentle and spontaneous in the people. And this is the reason for which the Catholic Church favored in all times, as was well noted by Balmes, this principle of association among workers most worthy of Catholic charity.

---

56. "The feeling of need and the desire to satisfy it (which as an economic engine has been called, and we will call it that again, interest) essentially includes an egoistic tendency." Taparelli, "Critical Analysis," 625.

But the same effectiveness of these associations could render them dangerous, if, diverting from the right (correct purpose), no longer for helping but for harming, it turns on the larger society: [the larger society] would therefore have to direct their management in such a way that, without losing anything of its activity, they participate in the common good, to which they are directed by nature, as every part is by nature inclined to the good of the whole.[57]

Taking the three motors of human action described above fully into account was for Taparelli the key to reaching a coherent, comprehensive explanation of economic phenomena and, moreover, to formulating public policy that had as its goal maximum human flourishing with maximum personal liberty.[58] The specifics of his economic analysis and policies must be read in the context of realist social theory generally, with the principles of social justice and subsidiarity as the rule and measure of personal and social perfection.

Scope and Limits of State Intervention

How does this work in practice? Taparelli would gladly have endorsed Thoreau's maxim from "Civil Disobedience" (1849) that "government is best which governs least," or certainly no more than necessary to keep the wheels of civil society spinning in tune with the common good, and subject to what Taparelli calls "just economic liberty."[59] Recognizing that

---

57. In quanto a secondare gli sforzi individuali nelle associazioni di comune sicurezza, due sono i doveri sociali: fomentare l'attività, regolarne la direzione. Fomentare l'attività, 1. perchè modeste associazioni sono un fedele adempimento del primo principio sociale: 2. perchè sono un vincolo strettissimo di sociale unità: 3. perchè soddisfano al diritto che ha ciascuno di avere aiuto nelle sue calamità: 4. perchè sono uno dei mezzi più efficaci ad ottenere il be pubblico, dando un organismo alle classi del popolo tanto più efficace nell'operare, quanto è più soave e spontaneo nel popolo l'aggregarvisi. Ed ecco la cause per cui la Chiesa cattolica favorì in ogni tempo come ben nota il Balmes questo principio di associazione fra gle operai degnissima della carità cattolica. Ma la stessa efficacia di queste associazioni potrebbe renderle pericolose, se, divertendo dal retto, non più ad aiutare ma a ferir si vogessero la società maggiore: dovrà questa dunque reggere in tal modo la lor direzione che, senza nulla perdere di attività, concorrano al ben commune, a cui sono per natura indireizzae, come ogni parte è per natura inclinata al ben del tutto. *Saggio*, §771.
58. Taparelli, "Critical Analysis," 637–38.
59. Taparelli, "Indirizzo di future," 147.

protecting the rights of the weak from abuse by the powerful is one of the first economic duties of government,[60] he viewed the most just and efficient means for accomplishing this to consist in the protection of rights and private interests.

Social economy teaches these various influences of cause and of the economic effects of administrative systems, studying the means of growing utility without losing anything of justice. Governing *persons* in such a way that, with all *rights* protected, their *interests* are advanced in the public order; here therefore in substance is the premise of all social economics, here are the three supreme concerns [persons, rights, and interests] that must predominate every particular question.

Please note that "*all rights protected*" means in substance to say each one protected in his reasonable liberty, there being no liberty if not in rights that are reasonably determined. (A liberty not intended by right would be license.) When therefore the interests of the state, of the public, of the people, are advanced, and offend the rights of a citizen or of a class of citizens, all the reasons of public good can be nothing more than palliative hypocrisy or ignorant excuses. There is no public good when right comes to be sacrificed to material interests.[61]

While it is necessary to coordinate the actions taken by private initiative in the pursuit of personal prosperity and the prosperity of the society as

---

60. Taparelli, "Indirizzo di future," 156.

61. L'economia sociale insegna queste varie influenze della cause e degli effetti economici negli ordinamenti amministrativi, studiando i modi di crescerne l'utilità senza nulla perdere nella giustizia. Ordinare le *persone*, in modo che, salvi tutti i *diritti*, se ne vantaggino gl'*interessi* nell'ordine pubblico; ecco dunque in sostanza l'assunto di tutta l'economia sociale, ecco i tre riguardi supremi che debbono predominare ogni quistione speciale.

Notate di grazia quel *salvi tutti i diritti*, che equivale in sostanza a dire salva a ciascuno la ragionevole sua libertà, non essendo libertà se non nei diritti ragionevolmente determinati. (Una libertà non voluta dal diritto sarebbe licenza). Quando dunque si vantaggiano gl'interessi dello *Stato*, del *Pubblico*, del *Popolo*, offendendo i diritti di un citadino o di un ceto di cittadini, tutte le ragioni di bene pubblico non possono essere che paliativi d'ipocrisia o scuse d'ignoranza. Non vi è bene pubblico quando al materiale interesse viene sacrificato il diritto.

Taparelli, "Indirizzo di future," 148.

a whole, this must be done with maximum respect for people's liberty, because every regulation imposed without a true necessity is a violation of right and an attack on justice. Assuming, superficially, the approximately equal effectiveness of an interventionist solution and a private solution to a social or economic problem, the private solution is always preferable. Even in the case of personal hardships or a natural disaster, rather than turning first to governmental action to provide for the emergency, charitable efforts may often provide the most efficient and effective solution. On the other hand, in other imaginable cases of hardship, public benefits, first distributed on the local level, could provide what is lacking in private charity. Support for charitable and local efforts is in accordance with the principle of subsidiarity and advances liberty by promoting a proper understanding and application of "the three driving powers of the human heart."[62]

By this analysis, Taparelli connects his natural law concepts of social justice, solidarity, and subsidiarity to principles of economic science and limited government. Government has this dual responsibility—it should ensure for each individual the liberty to pursue his material needs in association with others and the right to keep the fruits of his work; it must also harmonize the cooperation of individuals and intermediary associations directed toward the common good. Social economics researches the combined influences of material interest, interest in justice, and interest in truth and charity (love), all of which governments must take into account in the formation and execution of policy. And to reiterate: even social justice rigorously pursued may not by itself be enough to solve the situation of the poorest—social charity, or solidarity, is also needed: "If society does not manage to give due consideration and influence to [charity] and to say: 'we give to him who gives us nothing in return,' the economic problem will never be solved."[63]

All of the foregoing considerations lend clarity to Taparelli's recommendations as to how government can best remedy individual poverty and the conflicts in society by a proper understanding of human action and with recourse to indirect means, according to subsidiarity, whenever possible. Government fulfills its one essential duty when it works to

---

62. Taparelli, "Indirizzo di future," 150.
63. Taparelli, "Critical Analysis," 630.

order society according to justice, including social justice, and by ensuring that all rights are secure and all duties fulfilled, especially the duties and rights of the weakest. But government can achieve this fundamental duty of protecting the weak in one of two ways: either by defending their interests directly as administratees, or alternatively by furnishing them with the means to strengthen their own abilities to pursue their interests and to resist violations of justice: "The first means would lead to centralization, the injustice, inefficiency, and tyranny of which we have demonstrated at length."[64]

Taparelli was convinced of the dangers if economics remained a disordered, positivistic science. He argues that it should be recognized as a practical science that must also be concerned with the moral implications of economic choices, as well as with the economic implications of moral choices—which is not the same as insisting that economic science and policy be conducted from the viewpoint of a predetermined morality.[65] Taparelli strips the ideological facade off political economy, stating that as a practical science, it is inevitably based on an anthropology and a philosophy of nature or metaphysics. He sees the choice of paradigm as between two battle cries: "SUPREMACY OF SELF-INTEREST" or "SUPREMACY OF ORDER."[66] In other words, the choice is between two opposing views of man: man merely as a complex of material passions or man viewed also as a social and rational animal.

Studying and encouraging market solutions to social and economic problems is always preferable to promoting regulation, given the benefits that trade, exchange, and communication between and among individuals and groups can have for promoting material as well as moral progress. Commercial activity has a socializing effect that is also a good in itself, as it "becomes a most efficacious principle of universal association, and

---

64. Taparelli, "Indirizzo di future," 150.

65. The latter approach to a "Christian economics"— whether of a Liberatore, Pesch, Antoine, or Nell-Breuning— simply could not compete as a scientific model of economic behavior with the twentieth-century positivistic economic schools of thought. See Luca Sandonà, "Once Upon a Time: The Neo-Thomist Natural Law Approach to Social Economics," *International Journal of Social Economics* 40, no. 9 (2013): 797–808. Taparelli's paradigm of realist social scientific research has yet to be fully studied or tested by experiment. Neoclassical and rational choice economic researchers could well put "realist choice theory" to the test.

66. "Le due economie," CC, ser. III, vol. 2: 619 (capitalized in original).

produces among nations an exchange of good offices, that could well be called the application of the principle of universal human charity [as fraternal benevolence]."[67] Taparelli calls for the kind of research that needs to be done in any particular case to evaluate the most effective way of confronting a given social problem so that maximum respect can be accorded to individual liberty. When individual persons or authorities at any level of hypotactical association seek to empower weaker individuals and groups with the means to protect their own rights and to advance their own interests, that is an act of social justice in accordance with the principle of subsidiarity, and it is even an act of solidarity, an expression of love of neighbor in their dignity as persons. Individual persons and associations, coordinated ultimately by the protarchy government, must address the four sources of an individual's or group's inability to accomplish their own perfection: 1) lack of knowledge, 2) lack of will, 3) lack of personal strength, and 4) lack of external support.[68]

As to the first of these "lacks," Taparelli argued that government must assure education in four areas: literary culture, technical knowledge, morality, and law or civics. Taparelli thought this can best be accomplished by relying on private educational associations, at least through secondary school. Government's role in education is first of all to promote private associations in meeting this need. In pluralistic societies, where there is no consensus on the ultimate good, Taparelli underscored the importance of freedom of religion in education, including in higher education, though he acknowledged the probable utility of public universities for technical and scientific disciplines.[69]

On the question of stimulating the will of people to work and to persevere, Catholic education and spiritual formation counsel a rational approach to goods and a chaste detachment from them, reminding persons that material goods are merely means to an end, necessary and proper for the support of one's family, community, charitable works, and personal perfection. Cultivating right reason and public honesty

---

67. *Saggio*, §967.
68. Taparelli, "Indirizzi di future," 151–54.
69. Taparelli, "Indirizzi di future," 151.

would contribute to this understanding of material goods and leave freedom to the individual as to the choice of the practical means.[70] Taparelli thought the key to cultivating private initiative is in empowering persons to defend themselves morally; it is not in stimulating people's appetites but rather in teaching people how to reason well. Taparelli suggests that there are two requirements especially conducive to stimulating private initiative: the first is the freedom to dispose of one's property and energies as one sees fit, and the second is the assurance that the fruits of one's labors will be protected. As a result, the role of government in this question of "will" should be directed primarily at easing the availability of credit, protecting property from crime and excessive taxes, and facilitating savings.[71]

There remain the two physical sources of the impediments to the practical fulfillment of duties and exercise of rights: (1) lack of personal, physical strength, and (2) isolation, that is, the lack of external support. Since government has the common good of the whole to coordinate, it may have the duty of addressing questions of public hygiene, healthcare, pollution, food supply, and commerce, for instance, but it should always operate with regard for the principles of subsidiarity. The socially just redress for these deficits of personal health is first of all to promote associations with particular ends related to the health and well-being of persons—private insurance of various kinds, including those that defray the costs of fitness and wellness plans, readily come to mind today.

70. "Tutta questa varietà di sentimenti e d'opere, nasce dal retto uso di ragione commisurante i mezzi al fine, e lascia piena libertà a ciascuno nel determinare il proprio andamento economico." [All this variety of sentiments and works, born from the right use of reason, adapting means to the end, leaves full liberty to each one in determining his own economic course.] Taparelli, "Indirizzi di future," 152.

71. Taparelli, "Indirizzi di future," 151–54; see also *Saggio*, §§948–79. With regard to the crucial issues relating to the circulation of capital and overcoming the Aristotelian-Thomist position on the sterility of money and the problem of usury, that is, that usury is a vice that must be tolerated, Taparelli recognizes that money is dynamic and productive: a loan includes the capital as well as its future fruits. The lender gives up use but not dominion— that is, the right to benefit from its possession—over the lent capital, which justifies the taking of interest on principles of commutative justice. Government, while it should discourage actual usury, has an interest in promoting the practice of lending at interest in order to facilitate entrepreneurship. With the principles of subsidiarity in mind, Taparelli advocated for rural credit cooperatives and would no doubt endorse the microcredit movement of today.

If in the absence or malfeasance of any other part of civil society to adequately protect the common good, government must regulate directly, but these regulations should be managed with the principles of subsidiarity in mind (having recourse to those closest to the problem, those most able to know the details of and gently, effectively correct the problem, etc.). Given the justice of the laws, government has a singular duty to enforce the rule of law equally and to facilitate access to legal redress of grievances—also according to the principles of subsidiarity.[72] Taparelli saw that the individual power of the weakest will always amount to relatively little when confronted with the powerful if they cannot find help by exercising their fundamental right of association, and so he offers a clear endorsement for worker's associations, describing them as "one of the most efficient means of assuring their just economic liberty."[73]

To sum up this chapter, Taparelli would say that the paradigm of the naturalist social scientists assumes a one-dimensional, disordered human will, which ushers in prescriptions that give birth to a host of unintended consequences. Policies based on radical conceptions of autonomy and of materialist morality undermine the character of people and cloud their ability to reason rightly about their own pursuit of happiness, let alone about the common good of society.

Taparelli concludes:

> The reader sees therefore that, if we research how social economics can be baptized sincerely catholic and renounce filthy *utilitarianism*, by which it becomes a blind adorer of the penny god; not by this do we renounce the value of the beautiful and ample observations with which modern economics has spread so much light on the way of usefully administering public wealth. The vice of this science is not in the truths it studies, since the truth is always divine: it is in the end to which it is directed, that presupposes disorder of the will; and in the exclusion of those more noble ends and of those more honest, even obligatory, means, the absence of which in economic

---

72. Taparelli, "Indirizzo di future," 154.
73. Taparelli, "Indirizzo di future," 154, and see note 186 above.

tracts renders them theoretically crippled, practically ineffective, morally and religiously deadly.[74]

Taparelli finishes his "Indirizzo" with a review of the topics needing study, as these relate to the three motors of human action, to human flourishing and to authentic progress, the perfection of which would see the protection and promotion of the fulfillment of all duties and the free exercise of all of rights in accordance with the principles of social justice, subsidiarity, and solidarity.

> Wanting to make it such that all *know* equally how to reach their own good, one must discuss public education, free [education], popular [technical], elementary, [and] higher [education], etc., and then also the influence of the press and the propagation of doctrines. Wanting to make it that all *will* their own good, one must treat questions of obligatory work, of salary and subsistence of the workers, of the security for the fruits of their labors, of the capital they have access to for their work, and by consequence, of the various freedoms of commerce. Wanting, finally, to make it such that all *can*, [by] lending aid to the weak against violence, three major remedies present themselves: the assistance of the courts, freedom of association, and public beneficence.[75]

---

74. Vede dunque il lettore che, se da noi si ricerca che l'economia sociale si battezzi sinceramente cattolica e rinunzi al turpe *utilismo*, per cui diviene cieca adoratrice del dio quattrino; non per questo rinunziamo a far tesoro delle belle ed ampie osservazioni, con cui la moderna economia tanto lume ha sparso sul modo di utilmente amministrare la pubblica ricchezza. Il vizio di cotesa scienza non istà nelle verità che studia, giacchè la verità è sempre divina: sta nel fine a cui le rivolge, che presuppone disordine della volontà; e nella esclusione di quei fini più nobili e di quei mezzi più onesti, anzi doverosi, la cui mancanza nei trattati economici li rende teoricamente monchi, practicamente inefficaci, moralment e religiosamente funesti.
Taparelli, "Indirizzo di future," 155–56.

75. Volendo far sì che tutti *sappiano* ugualmente giungere al proprio bene, dee discorrere intorno all'istruzione pubblica, alla gratuita, alla popolare, alla elementare, alla sublime, ecc. e poi intorno alle influenze della stampa e all propagazione delle dottrine. Volendo fare che tutti *vogliano* il proprio bene, dee trattare del lavoro obbligatorio, del salario e sostentamento degli operai, della sicurezza pei frutti di loro fatica, dei capitali intorno ai quali essa dee esercitarsi, e per conseguenza delle varie libertà del commercio. Volendo finalmente far sì che tutti *possano*, apprestando sussidio alla debolezza contro la violenza, si presentano tre grandi trattazioni: dell'assistenza dei tribunali, della libera associazione, della pubblica beneficenza.
Taparelli, "Indirizzo di future," 156–57.

Note well the order of these remedies offered by "public society" through the coordination of government: access to the courts for the vindication of rights, private initiative (commercial ventures, nonprofit and charitable undertakings), and lastly, to meet remaining charitable needs, public welfare—which it must be noted, should also be administered according to the principles of subsidiarity.

There can be no doubt concerning Taparelli's overall political views with regard to the modern state—his warnings concerning centralized power have already been seen. Taparelli concludes that the ultimate end of universal humanity must always be kept in mind as the foundation for any moral order—and again, he argues that this belief is reasonable and accessible to all. Yet, "the essence itself of man limits social operation to the external, and therefore the immediate social end is of the temporal and external order."[76] Society exists for the good of men, not the other way around, for their natural felicity, even though the perfection of the internal order of spirit is the ultimate good that society must foster. But, especially in a pluralistic society, how? His answer is summed up again in the *Saggio*.

> To facilitate in the external order the attainment of natural felicity to individual humans: here therefore is the natural end of every *complete* particular society.... From which one sees that society is a *means* to help individuals, not at all an *end in itself* intended by the Creator: it is, Romagnosi would say, a *helpful machinery*. When therefore it is said that the *good of the* INDIVIDUAL *must subordinate itself to the social good, we are speaking of* ONE *individual set against the others* [in other words, in a concrete context, and not as an abstract principle]. [Therefore] it would be most opportune to immediately add: *and the social good must measure itself by the good that results in the whole of individuals*, in order to avoid the Platonic *utopias* of certain politicians that form an idol of their *State*, a Moloch devouring its own adorers. They do not care about rendering the peoples miserable so long as they obtain the good of the *State*. To this school belongs, with a thousand others who call themselves liberals, the

---

76. *Saggio*, §§721–25.

too famous Michelet [as] in his little book *Le Peuple*: [citing *Univers*, 14 août 1846] "M. Michelet, like the school calling itself liberal, declares that man belongs body and soul to the state." But to this inhuman and servile doctrine Guizot has already responded long ago, with Royer-Collard: [citing Guizot, *Civ. franç.*, l. I, pag. 14] "Is society made to serve the individual or the individual to serve the society? ... M. Royer-Collard has resolved this question. Human societies are born, live, and die on the earth: there their destinies are accomplished. But they do not contain the whole man. After he has engaged himself with Society, the noblest part of himself remains to him, these high faculties by which he raises himself to a future life... We, individual persons, beings endowed with immortality, we have a different destiny than states." ... And what part in such facilitation does public society have? Act such that the rights of each [person] are preserved: here is the first duty of society, and with this, even by itself, it acts well enough in favor of each one; since, for the rest, man is *obliged* and *inclined* to provide for himself.[77]

---

77. *Agevolare agl'individui umani coll'ordine esterno il conseguimento di natural felicità*: ecco dunque il fine naturale di ogni particular società *completa* della quale parliamo ordinariamente, quando altro non ispieghiamo. Dal che si vede che la società è *mezzo* ad aiutar gl'individui, non già *fine per sè* inteso dal Creatore: ella è, direbbe il Romagnosi, una *macchina di aiuto*. Quando dunque si dice che il *bene della* INDIVIDUO *dee subordinarsi al bene sociale*, si parla di UN *individuo* contrapposto *agli altri*. E sarebbe opportunissimo il soggiungere tosto: *e il bene sociale dee misurarsi al bene che ridonda nell tutto degli'individui*: affine di evitare le platoniche *utopie* di certi politici che formano del loro *Stato* un idolo, un Moloch divorantesi i suoi adoratori; e non badano a rendere sventurati i popoli purchè ottengano il bene dello *Stato*. [Vedi in al proposito, Haller, *Restaur. de la sc. polit.*] A questa scuola appartiene con mille altri che si dicono liberali il troppo famoso Michelet nel suo libercolo *Le Peuple*: "M. Michelet comme l'école soi-disant libérale déclare que l'homme appartient corps et âme à l'état." [vedi *Univers*, 14 août 1846] Ma questa dottrina inumana e servile rispondea già da lungo tempo col Royer-Collard il Guizot:"La société est-elle faite pour servir l'individu ou l'individu pour servir la société? ...M. Royer-Collard a résolu cette question. Les sociétés humaines naissent, vivent et meurent sur la terre: là s'accomplissent leurs destinées. Mais elles ne contiennent pas l'homme tout entier. Après qu'il s'est engagé a la Société, il lui reste la plus noble partie de lui même, ces hautes facultés par lesquelles il s'élève à une vie future... Nous, personnes individuelles, êtres doué de l'immortalité, nous avons une autre destinée que les états. [Guizot, *Civ. franç.*, l. I, pag. 14]
... E la pubblica società qual parte ha in tal provvedimento? Far sì che sieno salvi a ciascuno I suoi dritti: ecco il primo dovere della società, e con questo, anche solo, ella opera assai in favore di ciascuno; giacchè del rimanente l'uomo è *obbligato* ed *inclinato* a provvedere per sè.
Saggio, §§726–27.

CONCLUSION:

TAPARELLI'S REALIST SOCIAL SCIENCE

THIS BOOK HAS OFFERED AN unprecedented account of Luigi Taparelli's natural law social scientific thought. His normative social science, built on Aristotelian-Thomist foundations, had a profound influence on the theoretical and practical framework of modern Catholic Social Teaching (CST). Two of the fundamental principles of CST, social justice and subsidiarity, were first fully conceptualized by him, and for this reason it is very good that Taparelli's full elaboration of these principles can now be known in English.

Taparelli's ideas developed in an historical and intellectual context that help with understanding his motivation and genius. The time frame largely corresponds to the search for a new political order in the wake of the murderous excesses of the French Revolution and Napoleonic Empire, through the European Restoration (1815–30), the Revolutions of 1848, and the consolidation over the next decades of more or less authoritarian centralized states in France, Germany, Italy, Austria, and Russia. Economically and socially, the background is the ascendancy of European industrialization (which was already advanced in Great Britain) and the pressure of what was called the "social question," with the growing influence of the worker's movements and revolutionary socialism. Culturally and intellectually the background revolves around the crisis of Enlightenment rationalism engendered by the failure of the French Revolution, spawning a philosophical and cultural interregnum that followed the death of Old Régime paradigms and which led to a plethora of idealist, materialist, eclectic, and romantic notions in a period often referred to as the Age of Ideology. In this maelstrom, the Catholic church as an institution and the Catholic faithful struggled to maintain religious freedoms and to find an adequate response to the poverty, violence, and oppression of those revolutionary times.

We introduced Taparelli's main work, the *Saggio teoretico di dritto naturale appoggiato sul fatto* [Theoretical treatise of natural right based on fact], 1840–43, and considered his arguments, focusing on the aspects of his social theory that contributed to the development of modern CST. Taparelli played a central role in reviving the study of the philosophy of St. Thomas Aquinas and the later Scholastics. From those philosophical foundations, Taparelli sought to baptize modern social scientific theories and methods with a holistic understanding of human nature and to create a neoscholastic natural law framework through which the Catholic Church could come to terms with modernity. Chapters Three and Four thoroughly explained Taparelli's two most innovative ideas, namely social justice and subsidiarity, and how these relate to a personalist and moderate classical liberal view of the purposes and limits of government. Taparelli's realist social theory advances our comprehension of the connections between economics, politics, and culture, all of which he grounds in an integral conception of the human person as a social animal and intellectual truth-seeker endowed with reason.

Taparelli only rarely uses the word "state" without reservation or irony, but it is not out of an affectation or nostalgia for medieval models that he maintains such ambivalence toward the modern conception of the state—he saw the terrible power and insatiable appetite of Leviathan. Against the modern *raison d'état*, the confusion of public interests with the interests of the government and the governors, Taparelli steadfastly maintains the traditional Catholic conception of government as the necessary means for advancing the common good—rendering unto Caesar what is actually Caesar's. And, taking a further position that assured his infamy among European liberals, he steadfastly maintained the traditional Catholic indifference as to regime form, rejecting as unhistorical and theoretically suspect the modern faith in liberal institutions founded on representative democracy as the summit or end of human history. He rejected as a matter of principle the arguments of liberal Catholics that the Church itself had to be liberalized and "modernized." Taparelli's rejection of these modern liberal shibboleths (garnering him both notoriety and ridicule) was directly reflected in the "Syllabus of Errors" attached to Pius IX's 1864 encyclical *Quanta Cura*. Taparelli's realist natural law social theory elaborated a dialectical methodology of applying theoretically reasoned truths to inductively ascertained facts, hence the title of his treatise. What was being asserted by political leaders and popularizers about liberal political institutions might even, for Taparelli, be acceptable as a matter of political prudence under the circumstances of a specific historical context, but such an "hypothesis" must not be mistaken for a universally true "thesis," not if one were committed to the pursuit of authentic human flourishing and progress. Taparelli's unabashed contestation of these points must be the chief reason Pope Leo XIII (1870–1903), a former student of Taparelli's who surrounded himself with Taparellian protégés, one of whom was a main author of *Rerum Novarum*, ceased making reference to Taparelli's work, particularly after it became Vatican policy to embark on rapprochement with republican regimes such as the Third Republic in France. Taparelli's great influence over the development of modern CST was strategically buried by Leo.

Summary of the Argument

Taparelli developed his ideas in the first half of the nineteenth century, an age of seemingly ceaseless social and political instability in the European world, the rhythm of which was largely dominated by the political and ideological situation in post-revolutionary France. The Old Regime had been decapitated, and parties and ideologies competed for power. The Catholic Church struggled to come to terms with the radically new political situation. Survival of the Church itself was at stake. Catholics engaged in society in any capacity were often divided along party and ideological lines.

Throne and Altar arrangements were no longer viable in this new reality. After the Napoleonic enterprise, the church was struggling to recover its autonomy and was forced to arrive at an understanding of the nature and proper spheres of both the church and the modern state. It did so with an urgency not felt since the Investiture Controversy.

Misunderstandings, missteps, and conflicts that shook the Church hierarchy inevitably occurred also between and among various influential Catholic socio-economic and political groupings.

In the midst of such instability and paradigm interregnum, Taparelli elaborated his natural law social theory, including its political and economic components. Eschewing Enlightenment materialist and idealist abstractions, Taparelli's theories derive from the hylomorphic realism of Aristotle and the Christian development of Aristotle's system by Aquinas and others in the Scholastic philosophical tradition. According to this classical conception of human nature, no man is born free, as Hobbes, Locke, and Rousseau mistakenly argued. Quite the opposite: man is totally conditioned by the facts of nature, biology, history, and individual circumstances. From this realist viewpoint, Taparelli developed his neoscholastic theory of social order, which yielded new perspectives on subjective rights, including the concepts of social justice, subsidiarity, and social economy. The *Saggio* became a standard natural law textbook in Catholic institutions (schools, universities, and Jesuit seminaries) in Italy, France, Spain, and Germany. Taparelli's ideas were later instrumental in shaping modern CST, beginning with Pius IX's and then Leo XIII's pontificates, and most notably with Leo's 1891 encyclical *Rerum Novarum*.

The ideas of Joseph de Maistre and of the Abbé Lamennais, which dominated Catholic political-religious thought in the Restoration era, had an early influence on Taparelli's thought. Traditionalists such as Maistre viewed the revolutionary spirit in Europe as the product of the moral decadence of both the ruling and popular classes, which was ultimately caused by the Enlightenment philosophes' skepticism and materialism. Traditionalists rejected the rationalistic, atheistic components of the Enlightenment and of the Encyclopedist heritage that, in their eyes, represented the *abuse* of reason and the downfall of authentically human standards of morality.

Lamennais began as a Traditionalist in the early Restoration era but his thinking evolved dramatically. In 1830, he founded the journal *L'Avenir* under the motto "*Dieu et Liberté*" ("God and Liberty") and gathered around himself a group of brilliant Catholic Liberals, including Henri

Lacordaire and Charles de Montalembert. They welcomed many of the principles of the Revolution as the secular expression of evangelical ideals, and consistently advocated for various freedoms (speech, press, association, education). Lamennais came to argue for the separation of church and state and for universal suffrage. He believed that the application of these liberal principles could lead to political stability, including the regeneration of the church and the advancement of a renewed Christian civilization. Lamennais was able to persuade Pius VIII to look benignly on the liberal revolution of 1830 in France but ended up alienating Pope Gregory XVI in 1832 with his excessive claims of a right to rebellion in principle. The sequence of events surrounding Lamennais's democratic turn was symptomatic of the hierarchy's lack of a comprehensive approach to the challenges modernization posed to the faith and to the institution of the church itself, especially in relationship to the modern state.

In addition to facing the competing worldviews of Traditionalists and Liberals in the public square, Taparelli also engaged the controversies between competing philosophical systems when he became responsible for reforms at the Collegio Romano. He had been appointed the first rector at the Jesuit seminary, which Pope Leo XII had returned to the Jesuits in 1824. There his conversion to the philosophy of Aquinas, to which he had first been introduced as a seminarian in 1816 by colleague Serafino Sordi, became complete. The philosophy of Aquinas and of the later Scholastics had been among the chief intellectual influences in the late medieval and early modern church, attaining quasi-official standing in the Catholic Reformation after the Council of Trent (1545–63). It had become a fundamental part of the educational system of the Society of Jesus. However, such was the decline of interest in Thomism, and in Scholasticism generally in the "Age of Enlightenment," in favor of Cartesian and Kantian theological and philosophical perspectives, that when Taparelli sought to reintroduce Thomist studies at the Collegio Romano in 1827, he was obliged to form a clandestine study circle. Among Taparelli's protégés there were Carlo Maria Curci, later co-founder with Taparelli of the journal *Civiltà Cattolica* in 1850, and Vincenzo Gioacchino Pecci, the future Pope Leo XIII, author of *Aeterni Patris* (*On the*

Restoration of Christian Philosophy, 1879) and *Rerum Novarum* (*On the Condition of the Working Classes*, 1891).[1]

Taparelli identified the chief cultural-ideological problem of modernity as a flawed conception of human nature and an irreconcilable confusion arising from the empiricism of the materialists and the rationalism of idealists. In his eyes, Aquinas's logical realism represented a return to a true model of human existence, thought, and action. A few Aristotelian-Thomist arguments were particularly persuasive for Taparelli: first, metaphysically, *being* as the first object known by our mind, connaturally, immediately in itself, with the evidence for it so strong as to be beyond any doubt; second, epistemologically, a distinction between speculative reason, which deals with the universal and necessarily true, and practical reason, which deals with the good achievable by action; third, ethically, man's fulfillment and happiness consisting in the flourishing (perfection) of his hylomorphic nature (material, social, intellectual); and fourth, theologically, harmony between faith and reason, both instantiated by God as the author of revelation and as the creator of the world and the human mind. Taparelli accordingly saw revealed knowledge and natural knowledge as independent from each other yet existing in harmony, and he also understood that the fact that man has an eternal destiny means that moral theology and moral philosophy or natural law deal with different but complementary subjects; respectively, with man's ultimate end (as an intellectual/spiritual being) and with man's life in society under concrete circumstances (as a material and social being). Taparelli built his system of natural law moral reasoning in economics, society, and politics on these premises.

Taparelli appreciated that Thomist natural law leaves open to evaluation practical conclusions with respect to concrete circumstances and the acquisition of new experience. Natural law reasoning is open to the materially progressive potential of civilization, as well as to subjective cultural-historical contexts. This point was essential to Taparelli's conception of natural law and its applications. In fact, his theory of human action relies

---

1. Gerald McCool, *Nineteenth-Century Scholasticism*, 81–87; Boyle, "A Remembrance," 7–22; Romanus Cessario, OP, *A Short History of Thomism* (Washington, D.C.: The Catholic University of America Press, 2003), 82–86.

on the difference between abstract principles of natural law and concrete circumstances, thesis and hypothesis, a difference that requires an evaluation of the concrete application of natural law principles in the abstract. Taparelli follows Aquinas on the need for the exercise of judgment and prudence in the practical sphere.

In his "Treatise on Law,"[2] Aquinas describes his idea of natural law and its related political applications. Natural law is the product of the rational creature's participation in the eternal law, the law that governs everything in the universe, on the supposition that "God's providence rules the world."[3] The natural law is simply the dictate of reason in the rational animal that must choose how to provide for itself and others based on the immutable arrangement of things stamped on the world and on us.[4] This practical reasoning working in concrete circumstances and involving the employment of prudence shaped the methodology of Taparelli's realist social science "based on fact."

Taparelli's debt to the philosophy and natural law theories of Aquinas is clear, yet he was far from slavish to them in his method of reasoning and even with respect to certain conclusions. So much was his method and overall approach sui generis that some commentators have found his lack of direct sourcing to Aquinas as a sign of inadequate or even defective knowledge of the philosopher. This is an understandable mistake, founded as it seems to be on, first, a failure to appreciate Taparelli's exaggerated humility in describing his own intellectual development, and second, on a failure to appreciate the low standing of Thomism in the 1840s and 1850s; there was little to be gained at the time by explicitly relying on the authority of Aquinas. Taparelli had been studying and teaching the works of Aquinas, although we do not know how intensely, for twenty-four years when he wrote the first edition of his treatise. Indeed, Taparelli had incurred opprobrium and demotions within the Society of Jesus twice in that period of time precisely because of his activism on behalf of Thomist studies; he was first demoted from the position of rector of

---

2. *ST*, I-II, qq. 90–105. The section of Aquinas's *Summa Theologiae* comprising the so-called Treatise on Law is sometimes considered to cover only qq. 90–97.
3. *ST*, I-II, q. 91, a.1, and q. 93, a.1.
4. *ST*, I-II, q. 91, a.2, and q. 94, aa.1, 2.

the Collegio Romano to directing the Jesuit seminary at Naples (where he brought together the neo-Thomist brothers Serafino and Domenico Sordi and began the process of converting Matteo Liberatore to Thomism), and then was practically exiled to a teaching post in Palermo, Sicily—where, as a result of being assigned a course on natural law, he wrote the first edition of the *Saggio*. Even when Pius IX granted his approval to Taparelli and his neo-Thomist protégés, Curci and Liberatore, to launch the intellectual journal *Civiltà Cattolica*, the influence of Aquinas and the other Scholastics was still highly problematic and was therefore rarely invoked in any authoritative way. For strategic and rhetorical reasons, Taparelli preferred citing a point of agreement from Montesquieu or some other antagonist over citing an obvious inspiration or confirmation from an argument in Aquinas.

A prominent example of how Aquinas was the point of reference for Taparelli (without, however, dispositively controlling his conclusions) can be noted in Taparelli's assessment of private property. For Aquinas, the institution of private property evolved out of an original community of goods as the result of the inventiveness of reason. Private ownership as an addition to the natural law is useful for temporal utilitarian reasons, and this is reflected in positive law. Taparelli took a different view, different also from the positions of Suarez and Locke based on his overall method of reasoning: he held that the natural law contains within its duty of self-preservation an abstract right of universal dominion, but that this abstract right of humanity to the means of self-preservation has always been concretely embodied in some form of personal dominion, exercised by some individuals or groups on behalf of others. Because concrete persons exercise this abstract right of universal dominion on behalf of even non-possessors, their actual right in practice is subject to regulation according to the common good. A further example is found in Taparelli's careful exegesis of Aquinas and Suarez on the topic of legitimate political authority in his refutation of the axiomatic claims of the age on behalf of popular sovereignty. Taparelli's arguments and clarifications used in these two cases demonstrate his familiarity with Aquinas and other Scholastics. A thorough study of Taparelli's cited and un-cited references to Thomist arguments would reveal a profound debt to them throughout his work.

Taparelli's *Saggio* is divided into seven books ranging over the following subjects: (1) a metaphysical and anthropological inquiry into principles concerning the nature of man, human agency, and individual moral action; (2) society as a requirement of human nature and agency; (3) the theoretical and actual historical conditions for the formation of intermediate associations and of society at large as the foundation of human rights; (4) the natural law basis of positive lawmaking in terms of its ends (i.e., for the perfecting of human associations); (5) the forms of political authority organically resulting from associations of persons and associations; (6) the relationship between and among human societies, including questions of international law and global integration; and (7) the application of the principles of realist social theory to specific topics of law and historical development. This introduction to Taparelli's realist social science has focused on Book III.

In the *Saggio*, Taparelli expounds a normative social theory as the basis of his realist social science. He emphasizes the dichotomy between Scholastic and what he generally refers to as "heterodox" philosophy, namely the rationalistic schools that he claims have their roots in Protestant "independence of reason." The contrast between the epistemologies in the two philosophies is telling: the demonstrative way of the Scholastics versus the inquisitive way of the moderns, and the distinction between practical reason and speculative reason in the classical thinkers versus the conflation of the two modes in the moderns. The differences are strikingly evident to him as seen in his statements that (1) classical thinkers proceed from certainty, moderns from doubt; (2) the proper standard of the former is evidence, of the latter, certainty; (3) the former in arriving at its judgments relies on any rational element whatsoever, while the latter accepts only one, ratiocination; and (4) the former produces in souls a disposition that is catholic, social, and practical, the latter a disposition that is heterodox, antisocial, and impractical.

For Taparelli, the abstract reasoning of natural law must be derived from and confirmed in its concrete articulation by facts. The mass and vast variety of the facts of experience, personal and social, must be organized and understood theoretically as instantiations of abstract laws. In other words, universals exist as abstractions only in the human mind, while in the actual, historical world they exist only in specific matrices of facts in which truth, moral obligation, and the exercise of prudence meet.

Taparelli's political, social and economic views follow from this. Like Aristotle and Aquinas, he believes that the human person is by nature social and political; that is, characterized by unavoidable sociality. Even more than other animals, humans naturally live in and require extended groups. Taparelli develops a natural law theory of society based on a realist appreciation of the phenomenon of human association from the family to the state, a phenomenon that gives rise to the requirements of social justice, solidarity, and social charity, all governed by the principles of subsidiarity, all aimed at the flourishing of human persons and of civilization. It is a demonstration of his philosophy that during the Revolution of 1848, in Palermo, Taparelli claimed protection for church offices based on the human right of association. He penned a manifesto arguing that the church as an association asks only for its just liberty. He explained that the right of association was an inalienable right, and that its violation even in one case would undermine the reason for the existence of society itself.

Immediately after the revolutions of 1848 and the brief establishment of a Roman Republic, together with the exile of the pope, Pius IX decided to publish a journal with an aggressive mandate to respond to the fractious claims of liberal and socialist alike, enlisting the help of a group of scholars who would quickly become the "think tank" of the Vatican. The pope turned to the Jesuits and to Taparelli in particular, along with the more formally philosophically trained Liberatore and also the energetic Curci, who became the journal's first director. Taparelli wrote a bi-weekly article of dozens of pages for twelve years on topics related to politics, economy, and culture. His articles on political regimes were published as a two-volume work, *Esame Critico degli Ordini Reppresentativi nella società moderna* (Critical examination of the representative orders in modern society), in 1854. That work earned him a wider reputation, but also sealed his lasting infamy among liberal Catholics and not a little miscomprehension among Catholic Liberals. None of these have left behind signs of having seriously studied the work, but they believed they knew enough about its arguments on popular sovereignty—namely against the axiomatic claims that popular will is the source of all legitimate political authority—to be outraged. There was no appreciation or tolerance of Taparelli's "thesis and hypothesis" distinction, a keystone of his method: that what could not be accepted as a thesis (universally true) could be considered as an "hypothesis," and even embraced as a relative good as a prudential matter in particular circumstances.[5] Ten years later, the same widespread incomprehension and condemnation by liberal Catholics would greet Pius IX's Syllabus of Errors (1864), which, having been called for already in 1849 by Cardinal Pecci and then in the 1850's by the *Civiltà Cattolica*,[6] cleared the deck of falsely axiomatic liberal claims concerning politics, faith, and the church. Pius declared which of these claims could not be taken as "true" (meaning universally and axiomatically true). The Syllabus very much reflected that aspect of Taparelli's project aimed at restoring clarity on first principles for the sake of coherence going forward. At that time, Msgr. Dupanloup of Lyons offered a widely read apologetic for the Syllabus, highlighting the pope's reasoning along the lines of Taparelli's thesis and hypothesis methodology—of course without referencing Taparelli, whose memory (he had died in 1862) was already a lightning rod.[7] Dupanloup's explanation met with overwhelming acceptance in ecclesial circles (630 bishops wrote him personal expressions of gratitude), but he also faced a great deal of criticism from liberal Catholics who resented what they called his medieval (meaning deceptive) semantics.[8]

---

5. One study traces the emergence of the thesis and hypothesis distinction, or rather, according to the author, reemergence (from *ST*, II-II, q. 10, a. 11 on the toleration of infidels—with which Taparelli was well familiar), to the response of *Civiltà Cattolica* (ser. V, vol. 8, October 2, 1863, p. 149) to Montalembert's controversial 1863 speech in Malines on the "free Church in a free state," but all the while the author is completely ignorant of Taparelli's considerable use of the methodology in the *Saggio* from the 1840's and Taparelli's *Civiltà Cattolica* articles from 1850 to 1862. Joseph Lecler, "A propos de la distinction de la 'thèse' et de la 'hypothèse,'" *Recherches de Science Réligieuse* 41 (1953): 530–34.

6. Roger Aubert, "Internal Catholic Controversies in Connection with Liberalism," chap. 20 in *The Church in the Age of Liberalism*, ed. Roger Aubert, Johannes Beckmann, Patrick J. Corish, and Rudolf Lill (New York: Crossroad Publishing, 1981), 293–94.

7. It is worth noting that Pope Leo XIII used Taparelli's thesis and hypothesis reasoning concerning religious toleration in the encyclical *Immortale Dei* (1885), and it has been taken to be the first expression of this kind of dialectical reasoning by a pope. Owen Chadwick, *A History of the Popes, 1830–1914* (Oxford: Clarendon Press, 1998), 293.

8. Marvin R. O'Connell, "Ultramontanism and Dupanloup: The Compromise of 1865," *Church*

Liberatore became a very influential member of Leo XIII's circle of philosophical advisors and he collaborated on the drafting of *Aeterni Patris* (1879). Leo himself would later refer to the encyclical as "the restoration in Catholic schools of Christian philosophy according to the mind of St. Thomas Aquinas, the Angelic Doctor."[9] Taparelli's project begun in 1824 at the Collegio Romano was complete. Formed in Taparelli's natural law social science, Liberatore went on together with neo-Thomist Cardinal Zigliara to co-edit the final drafts of *Rerum Novarum* (1891). Thus modern CST, beginning with Leo XIII's first encyclicals and *Aeterni Patris*, culminating in *Rerum Novarum*, was shaped by Taparelli's advocacy for the restoration of Thomist philosophy, and specifically of Aquinas's natural law reasoning, which he developed as a normative social science capable of addressing the needs of modern social, economic, and political life.

"Subsidiarity" and "social justice" are among the most important normative sociological principles set forth in Taparelli's *Saggio*. Both concepts are clearly elaborated in *Rerum Novarum* but only make their formal appearance in Pius XI's social encyclical *Quadragesimo Anno* in 1931, forty years later.[10] To Taparelli, these ideas are simple: social justice is both a personal virtue, the personal habit of will to protect and to promote the fulfillment of duties and exercise of rights by all persons, and by extension also the proper goal of any sound government, following the principle of subsidiarity.

Social justice is what is due to other persons based on their common membership in society and their common origin in the plan of creation. The total social dependence characterizing every individual of the human species at birth is the first manifestation of sociality. Sociality arises as a duty with the growth and moral development of the person from the first precept of natural reason—to do the good—first with reference to oneself and then extended to others in society in whom we see our replicated

---

History 53, no. 2 (June 1984): 215; Chadwick, *A History of the Popes*, 178; Josef Altholz, *The Liberal Catholic Movement in England: The "Rambler" and its Contributors, 1848–1864* (London: Burns & Oates, 1962), 232–33.

9. Boyle, "A Remembrance," 7n1.

10. The "subsidiary function" of intermediate associations was referred to in *Quadragesimo Anno*, 80, and "social justice" at 57, 58, 71, 74, 88, 101, 110, 126.

selves. Growth and moral development also teaches that we need to associate with others for virtually every satisfaction, from the most base to the most sublime requirements of life. Thus sociality, as a need of human nature first, becomes the duty to do the good of others—"solidarity," as it comes to be called in CST. Social justice then is what is due in order to facilitate the fulfillment of duties and the exercise of rights of all persons, our replicated selves, in society. This is the basis of the natural law of just interpersonal relations and social organization, the flourishing of which would characterize the just society. The duties to do the good and to do the good of others are understood simultaneously from the apprehension in speculative reason of order as true and in practical reason as good. In other words, the understanding of both 1) the duties to oneself and 2) human identity exercises an indisputable power in one's conscience and in the conscience of others, dictating at first a principle of noninterference in the fulfillment of those duties *in* others: this amounts to a right to noninterference *from* others. Subsequently, in the morally developing person, facilitating that exercise of rights and fulfillment of duties by others reflects the hoped-for social cooperation we ourselves must seek, and the way we ourselves want to be treated. These norms of social justice and solidarity are none other than the natural law expression of the evangelical commandment to love one's neighbor as oneself.[11]

Taparelli understood that every society of more than the most modest size is composed of multiple intermediary associations, both horizontal and vertical.[12] He described a series of corollaries for evaluating the proper balance between authority and liberty (order and freedom) as that balance is related to the inalienable human rights of life, liberty, and the rational pursuit of happiness, the exercise of which is the end or purpose of the social order itself. And because he was charting new territory, he coined a host of new technical terms: "consortia" is the generic term for all kinds and levels of associations composed either of individuals or of other less comprehensive (or less complete or "perfect") associations; "deutarchies" are associations established for limited practical ends and

---

11. Refer to Chart 3, "From Natural Right to Subjective Rights to Social Justice." Also see *Saggio*, Book II, chap. 3, "Notions of Right and of Social Justice."
12. Refer to Chart 2, "Subsidiarity: Sociality and Hypotactical Society."

stand in relationships of subsidiarity to other more comprehensive (more "perfect") consortia (which may be other deutarchies), or in relationship to independent and sovereign ("perfect") political societies or states, called "protarchies." Among intermediary consortia standing between individual persons and the protarchy, then, there will normally be overlapping horizontal and vertical associations. Association being necessary due to innate human sociality, associations have their proper ends and proper authority, and they are themselves social persons endowed with particular duties and rights. With this realist analysis, Taparelli demystified prevailing ideologies of state and society as being either a contractual association of free and independent individuals or a mass of appetite-driven individuals requiring subjugation to a General Will or Leviathan state.

Taparelli was the first Catholic theorist to explore the relationship between natural right and subjective rights, identifying the origin of the latter in the moral compunction resulting from the former, as applied in concrete social reality. The principle that higher levels of authority, particularly protarchies, must respect the rights of the lower deutarchies, is the principle that Taparelli calls "hypotactical right," which he translates from an ancient Greek term applicable to rules of grammar and military organization, that is, rules governing subordinate elements in sentences and the martial endeavors of military units. In the course of standardizing Taparelli's natural law theory of social order as CST developed, his Italian term, "*dritto ipotattico*," was Latinized into "subsidiarity," which refers to the subsidiary functions and rights of associations. The term subsidiarity was first formally employed as the "principle of 'subsidiary function,'" in *Quadragesimo Anno*. This change of language has had its downsides—first because the actual theoretical background of subsidiarity has almost totally escaped the attention of scholars, and second because subsidiarity has at times been conceived of as dealing essentially with "subsidies," that is, something coming from the top down, when in fact it primarily deals with the cooperative support of relatively autonomous intermediary associations from the bottom up in order to further the common good (the protection and promotion of life, liberty, and the pursuit of happiness) as it applies to each person.

With this natural law theory of social right, Taparelli intended to demonstrate the due independence of intermediary societies, cooperation with which fulfills the common good, or end, of the state. Thus, social "subsidy" (Taparelli does use this term, "*sussidio sociale*") is what people seek as a result of the fact of sociality by associating themselves with others in particular societies or what smaller societies seek in associating themselves with larger societies—but in seeking and receiving greater social protection and promotion of their interests, no association or person gives up their own authority or freedom, though some theoretical freedom may be traded for some expansion of concrete freedom. Taparelli specifies the types of associations: natural (e.g., the family), voluntary (relationships with others for the common pursuit of some limited good, e.g., any of the whole host of associations of civil society), and dutiful (those exceptional cases where a disproportionate balance between duty and right pertain, such as compulsory military service, compulsory schooling, or incarceration).[13]

It is important to remark that Taparelli recognized these intermediary associations as the heart of personal identity and liberty and as crucial to the pursuit of human fulfillment in the concrete circumstances of every individual, based on the fact of sociality. Therefore, he was strongly motivated to protect the rights of these associations (especially domestic, religious, and charitable associations) against the claims, pulling in opposite directions, of radical individualists and collectivists, who then and today exercise a certain hegemony over the competing discourses of political morality.

Because Taparelli's theory of social justice has not been studied except through secondhand, even thirdhand sources, it has been widely misunderstood. It is important to point out that Taparelli's idea of social justice is not just legal, commutative, or distributive justice dressed up in progressive-sounding words. His virtue of social justice is founded on the personal dictate of conscience, the "constant and perpetual will to render to each his right,"[14] and on a developed habit of acting[15] with an understanding of our common origins, natures, duties, and rights despite the ubiquitous inequality of actual abilities and circumstances. Social justice is the disposition to protect and promote the fulfillment

---

13. Refer to Chart 2, "Subsidiarity: Sociality and Hypotactical Society."
14. *ST*, II-II, q. 58, a. 1.
15. *ST*, I, q. 79, a. 13.

of all duties and exercise of all inalienable rights. Therefore, it can refer as well, metaphorically, to the structural facilitation of that habit of "rendering to each his right" in the actual arrangement of institutions, laws, and policies within any and every association. Thus, this would apply to the governmental authorities of associations of individuals in particular cooperative ventures, from the family up to and including the sovereign association of the state. Social justice is advanced by governmental arrangements that foster the ability (the power) of individuals, and of the associations they form, to pursue the fundamental (indisputable) good, the common good of persons and of associations in fulfilling their moral obligations according to the dictates of reason (of each proper authority).[16] Social justice, whether as personal virtue or as a principle of just government, could well seem an unattainable disposition of character or rule of government were it not for the ordering principle of Taparelli's natural law social theory, subsidiarity.

The relationship between the duties of social justice and the respect due to the just liberty of persons (and of the range of associations they necessarily form) finds fuller development in Taparelli's writing on economy. His economic views are based strictly on his ideas of the composite nature of human persons, on the conditions of sociality, and on the principles of subsidiarity. He consistently holds that governmental intervention in economic activity is allowed only if strictly necessary. Government should ensure for each individual the liberty to pursue his material needs in association with others. Its main goal must be to promote the cooperation of individuals and intermediary associations directed toward the common good—which is above all the protection and promotion of the fulfillment of duties and exercise of rights. Social economics, Taparelli contends, certainly deals with the science of the production and distribution of wealth, and it also certainly must include the science of government policies to coordinate that production and distribution to maximize the public good, but these sciences should be based on a proper understanding of the human person—which, Taparelli asserts, both laissez-faire liberalism and socialist economics ignore.

---

16. Refer to Charts 3 and 4, "From Natural Right to Subjective Right to Social Justice," and "Social Justice, Subsidiarity, and Social Economy."

Taparelli set a social scientific research agenda crucial to his entire project: study is required of the operation of the "three motors of human action," of effective means of empowering their harmonious operation, and of the social, economic, cultural, and political policies that can empower the flourishing of fully human persons. These three "motors" amount to interests or fundamental motivations of human action that are derived from the hierarchy of needs of composite human nature. Beyond material self-interest, there is also the natural motivation toward, or "interest" of the rational person in, ordered liberty. And beyond material and social interests, there are the "interests" (though Taparelli admits it is an unusual use of the word) pertaining to the ultimate orientation that thinking, reasoning persons have toward the created order and the creator revealed therein—"interests" in truth, brotherly love, and piety.[17]

Taparelli offers a thorough philosophical account of these psychological/moral motivations and social behaviors, offering normative sociological principles that make sense of the astute empirical observations of Tocqueville.[18] Tocqueville claims to find the development of fraternal benevolence among the Americans in their habit of professing to be interested in others in order to obtain their support, which eventually leads to their becoming habituated (near to a virtue) to "self-interest rightly understood." This would seem to be an outcome, essentially, of sublimated hedonism. No doubt associations are the places where benevolence can flourish in practice, and experience in improving ("perfecting" in Taparelli's lexicon) benevolence is valuable in itself. But Taparelli's "self-interest rightly understood" is a result of the same series of intellectual apprehensions, dictates of reason, and duties in conscience that constitute the natural law, moral obligation, and personal responsibility. There is a development of rightly understood self-interest that tracks the right understanding of the self. The development and operation of the three motors of human action tracks the development of the moral reasoning of each person, from material self-interest strictly speaking (or physiological sociality), to a recognition of abstract equality with, but also intersubjective dependence upon,

---

17. Refer to Chart 1, "Self-Interest Rightly Understood: The Three Motors of Human Will/Action."
18. There is no indication in the *Saggio* that Taparelli knew Tocqueville's work, however.

our "replicated" selves (which brings with it more complicated calculations of trade-offs in our relations with others, or what Taparelli calls psychological sociality), and, finally, to embracing the truth and goodness of a certain preference and self-sacrifice for others (what Taparelli identifies with piety or honesty, and charity or brotherly love, which comes to be called in subsequent CST solidarity or social charity). The indispensable role of cultural formation in the moral development of persons is clear. Minds and consciences are not filled with innate ideas in Taparelli's system any more than in the system of Locke. Education is crucial for the cultivation of natural reason, the formation of conscience, and the attainment of piety, or of at least what Taparelli calls public honesty.

Economic, social, cultural, and political policies matter because they affect the development of reason and conscience of human persons and can undermine the capacity even for self-preservation. Tocqueville points out that Americans combat the egoistic tendencies of individualism, the precursor of despotism, with free institutions. Persons need to be concerned with providing for themselves and only thereby can they develop the competencies (intellectual and practical) for flourishing as human persons. Dependency on an administrative state enervates people and fosters moral and physical inertia.[19] Tocqueville's analysis of the corruption of the human spirit generated by governmental centralization would have been fully endorsed by Taparelli, who well understood that failing to respect the natural law rights of persons and associations and ignoring the dictates of reason in this way has inevitable negative consequences for moral as well as for material development. Taparelli would have gone further to highlight the tendency toward corruption and endless fiscal exactions imposed by the centralizers, with a dystopian end result of the bifurcation of society into governors and an atomized, rootless, hedonistic mass of the governed. As was discussed in our introduction to this study, Tocqueville saw tendencies present in democracies as favoring the rise of despotisms. On these points, Taparelli—who was certainly thoroughly familiar with the political cycle described by Plato and Aristotle and the luxury cycle of Polybius—had seen his concerns reflected in Montesquieu, who described the final degeneration of the centralized, democratic state: "The members

---

19. Tocqueville, *Democracy in America*, 86–87, 88–89.

of the commonwealth riot on the public spoils, and its strength is only the power of a few, and the license of many."[20]

Taparelli argued that the false metaphysics and anthropology of modern materialist or idealist schools of economic, social, and political thought were the chief sources of the immorality, deracination, and conflict then reigning—at a time when science and technology were prodigiously advancing the material horizons of society. He made the case that his realist social theory explains the proper connections between economy, society, politics, and culture, all centered on the composite human person, the knowledge and application of which could make the difference between authentic flourishing of human civilization and degeneration into faceless totalitarianisms. He clearly attributes the failures and dangers of laissez-faire liberalism and its socialist heir to their flawed anthropology and metaphysics. Those social and economic theorists whom he sought to correct, whom he calls "naturalists," take no account of every person's natural understanding of the goodness of order and solidarity, nor of his natural understanding of right and justice—legal, commutative, distributive, and social (rightly understood). What is particularly deadly for the flourishing of persons and societies is that the naturalists take no account of the natural desire of all persons to understand the whole truth about themselves, and of their need for fulfillment and happiness within the order of nature. As a paradigm for personal or political reasoning, the naturalistic social sciences are incomplete from a theoretical point of view, inefficient at best, often counterproductive and as a self-fulfilling prophecy, destructive of piety, and private and public morality.

---

20. "When virtue is banished, ambition invades the minds of those who are disposed to receive it, and avarice possesses the whole community. The objects of their desires are changed; what they were fond of before has become indifferent; they were free while under the restraint of laws, but they would fain now be free to act against law; and as each citizen is like a slave who has run away from his master, that which was a maxim of equity he calls rigor; that which was a rule of action he styles constraint; and to precaution he gives the name of fear. Frugality, and not the thirst of gain, now passes for avarice. Formerly the wealth of individuals constituted the public treasure; but now this has become the patrimony of private persons. The members of the commonwealth riot on the public spoils, and its strength is only the power of a few, and the license of many." Montesquieu, *The Spirit of the Laws*, vol. 1, *On the Principle of Democracy*, 25–26.

The Development of Catholic Social Teaching

While his conception of economics involves claims concerning human nature and the functioning of society that differ from aspects of the classical economists, Taparelli was more dramatically opposed to socialist economics and any view of state interventionism that would unduly diminish the just liberty of persons, including with respect to property rights. Indeed, Taparelli did not seek to overthrow classical economic thought, but rather to supplement its economic naturalism with a holistic anthropology, and in the process properly integrate the Scholastic and late Scholastic sources relied on by classical liberal thought generally. He sought to "baptize" economic science as he found it and return it to its place as a subdiscipline of ethics without diminishing its value as a positive science of the production and distribution of wealth.

Taparelli's natural law approach to economic, social, and political issues is thus in continuity with, and not a refutation of, classical liberal political and economic thought, connected as the latter was to medieval, Aristotelian-Thomist, and late Scholastic roots. His approach provided the theoretical and practical foundation for modern CST from the pontificate of Leo XIII onward.[21] CST has been subject to diverse readings, from both an historical evolutionary perspective and from an internal, textual perspective, with respect to both its theoretical argumentation and specific conclusions. Reflections on the implications of the intellectual sources behind CST gained a certain momentum in anticipation of the hundredth anniversary of *Rerum Novarum*, culminating in the publication of John Paul II's *Centesimus Annus*, which lent itself similarly and inevitably to a variety of readings.[22]

21. Langholm, *The Legacy of Scholasticism*, 198–200; and see generally, Chafuen, *Faith and Liberty*. On the encyclical tradition since Leo XIII, see Weigel and Royal, eds., *A Century of Catholic Social Thought*; George Weigel and Robert Royal, eds., *Building the Free Society: Democracy, Capitalism, and Catholic Social Teaching* (Grand Rapids, Mich.: Eerdmans Publishing, 1993); and Kenneth Grasso, Gerard Bradley, and Robert Hunt, eds., *Catholicism, Liberalism, and Communitarianism: The Catholic Intellectual Tradition and the Moral Foundations of Democracy* (Lanham, Md.: Rowman & Littlefield, 1995).
22. Cf. Giovanni Antonazzi, "L'Enciclica 'Rerum Novarum', testo latino e autentica versione Italiana, Introduzione," in Giovanni Antonazzi and Gabriele De Rosa, *L'Encyclica 'Rerum Novarum' e il suo tempo* (Roma: Edizioni di Storia e Letteratura, 1991), 45–74; Actes du colloque international organisé par l'École française de Rome et le Greco n. 2 du CNRS, '*Rerum Novar*-

It is crucial to note in this regard that modern CST has involved a sort of two-tiered reasoning: both a natural law moral philosophical approach and a moral theological approach have been brought to bear.[23] While the unity of truth, one of the fundamental premises of Thomist thought, justifies this approach, and addressing the church's message to an increasingly pluralistic audience requires it, the relationship between these two approaches has not always been thoroughly articulated in church documents on particular points.

Despite his recognized influence, Taparelli has hardly been seen as a key to interpreting CST. This is in part because he was deliberately marginalized by his own former students and protégés, including Leo XIII himself as the pontiff moved to engage the complex problems of modernity that Taparelli, among other Catholic conservatives, had articulated. This burying of Taparelli's foundational influence was due to his status as a lightning rod for liberal Catholic condemnation across Europe, stemming from his polemical work at the *Civiltà Cattolica*, his criticisms of the assumptions of laissez-faire liberalism, his rejection of the idea of popular sovereignty as the sole principle of political legitimacy, and his realist, thesis-and-hypothesis methodology. The influence of Taparelli was overwhelming in not just promoting the revival of neo-Thomist philosophy but also in creating a particular realist social theory and methodology. The momentousness of the Church's doctrinal turn in modern CST could not be risked by open association with the notorious, however wrongly infamous, "Jesuitical" zealot of the *Civiltà Cattolica*—as he was widely regarded in by Catholic Liberals and liberal Catholics across Europe. If Taparelli's name had been associated with any part of the magna carta of CST, *Rerum Novarum*, it would have been as dead on arrival in terms of relevance, as it also would have been had the pope not been persuaded to endorse, for prudential and

---

um,' *Écriture, contenu et réception d'une encyclique* (Rome: École Français de Rome, 1991); Ernest Fortin, "From *Rerum Novarum* to *Centesimus Annus*: Continuity or Discontinuity," in Fortin, *Human Rights*, 223–29; Russell Hittinger, "The Problem of the State in Centesimus Annus," *Fordham International Law Journal* 15, no. 4 (1991–92): 952–96. For one view of the problem of reconciling market forces with social order (justice) and charity in the social encyclical tradition, see A. M. C. Waterman, "Market Social Order and Christian Organicism in *Centesimus Annus*," *Journal of Markets and Morality* 2, no. 2 (1999); 220–33.

23. Cf. Calvez and Perrin, *The Church and Social Justice*, 36–53.

"hypothetical" reasons, the idea of worker's unions—something Taparelli himself had advocated four decades earlier.

Taparelli's natural law, realist, social scientific enterprise should not only be of interest to scholars and students of modern CST. His work can be appreciated apart from a particular religious belief or idea—even though Taparelli certainly considered Catholic piety and the Catholic confessional state as ideals in the abstract. His *Saggio* is a work based on natural reason, invoking the providential role and intent of the creator, the grand architect, only to the extent that access to knowledge of the existence of God was available to natural reason. As polemical as his writing frequently seems, the *Saggio* offered a basis for authentic dialogue with the liberal and progressive spirit of his age, calling for reflection on the true pursuit of happiness in a vision of fully human progress. His work invites a reconsideration in the *ressourcement* of the ideas of social justice and subsidiarity that would contribute to authentic dialogue.

CHART 1—Self-Interest Rightly Understood: The Three Motors of Human Will/Action (in Social Economy)[1]

Composite Human Nature	Motor	Inclination
Rational	Abstract Reasoning (awareness of higher order, fraternal benevolence, solidarity)	Piety, Charity, Truth, Honesty
Social	Practical Reasoning (sense of natural order, "do the good," sociality)	Justice
Material	Appetites and Passions (individual feeling of need and desire to satisfy it)	Egoistic self-interest

1. "We have therefore three forces [or inclinations] that we can call productive and regulative of wealth: *interest* that thinks about *Me, justice* that equalizes it with regard to others, and *piety* that gives to others a certain preference. Researching in this way, a governor may obtain, with the use in various proportions [of] these three motor forces, the ordered advancement of public goods; this is, in our opinion, the main assumption of social economy." "Analisi critica dei primi concetti dell'economia sociale," CC ser. III, vol. 8 (1857): 546–59; ser. III, vol. 9 (1858): 17–34. See also, Luigi Taparelli, "Critical Analysis of the First Principles of Political Economy," trans. Thomas C. Behr, *Journal of Markets and Morality* 14, no. 2 (Fall 2011): 613–38.

Chart 2 — Subsidiarity: Sociality and Hypotactical Society[2]

Ethnarchy (society of *independent* national protarchies)
- → protect and promote exercise of national rights and liberties
- → tend to polyarchical form, consensus among equals

Protarchy (responsible for direction of social Whole)
- → promote common good, protect and promote fulfillment of duties and exercise of rights (thesis)
- → *sovereign* – having a superior *independent* of other superiors
- → governmental form indifferent, result of antecedent facts (hypothesis)

Deutarchy (*intermediate consortia*, synthetic or analytical formation)
- → greater or lesser comprehensiveness with regard to other deutarchies
- → selection and form of *superior* based on *facts* of formation, including prevailing right

Note 1. Requirements for *any* Society, sovereign or intermediate (between the individual and the state)
  a. proper end - legitimate extrinsic principle of unity, e.g. security, material needs, reproduction
  b. proper authority - legitimate intrinsic principle of unity, vested in a superior, required for the direction of plural intelligences
  c. proper being and legitimate liberty

Note 2. Association is the first effect of physiological sociality, persons need social help (*sussidio sociale*), whereas formation of particular consortiums → persons *subordinate* themselves, ceding some *abstract* private liberty for liberty *in fact* by associating

Note 3. TYPES of associations: Natural (persistent or accidental), Voluntary (of equals or unequals), Dutiful (prevailing right or violent); all associations are ultimately voluntary, or unstable conditions of tyranny pertain (obligation of conscience or by bayonets)

---

2. "In every large society there must be found a system of *deutarchies*, it being necessary that there be diverse *ends* subordinated to the end of the *protarchy*: and diverse *superiors* that guide to *deutarchic* ends. We have called *hypotactical right* the complex of the laws resulting from such relations." *Epilogo Ragionato*, §70. Prop. XIX. Coroll. 3.

Chart 3 — From Natural Right to Subjective Rights to Social Justice[3]

Social Rights and Social Justice = equalize in fact unequal individuals with respect to their ability to exercise their rights and fulfill their duties

Abstract Human Equality exists only in Concrete Individual Inequality

Power = ability to do, as opposed to duty to do
Indisputable = the force that it has to bind the will of others
According to Reason = moral obligation

Right = Indisputable Power According to Reason

Duties and Correlative Subjective Rights in Society
Moral Obligation to Others from Recognition of Truth and Goodness of Social Order,
Natural Order [Eternal Order] NOT result of exchange, contract, or interdependence
(i.e. the duty does not *create* the right, nor the right the duty)

Moral Sociality and Abstract Human Identity: *Do the Good of Others*

Natural Aggregation of Individuals, physiological to psychological sociality

First Precept of Practical Reason: *Do the Good*

Human Nature: materiality, sociality, rationality

Natural Order [for believers, Created Order]

---

3. *Saggio*, Book II, chap. 3, "Notions of Right and of Social Justice," §§341–64.

Chart 4 — Social Justice, Subsidiarity, and Social Economy

Equalizing *in fact* = improving ("perfecting") opportunity for protection of rights and fulfillment of duties of human persons[4]

Sources of de facto "inequality"	Remedies	Means – Indirect whenever possible
Lack of knowledge	Promote education: literary, cultural, moral, legal/civic, scientific, and vocational training	Private consortia (mainly); free through secondary education; private (mainly) liberal arts higher education; likely public subsidized for science/technology
Lack of will	Promote reasoning well Promote "social honesty" Protect property rights Protect personal liberty	Education (see above) Freedom of association Appropriate libel, censorship, and anti-corruption laws Low taxes Work requirements Facilitate credit and savings
Personal strength and external support	Promoting/protecting health Aid to workers and small capital Public infrastructure and security Aid to handicapped and infirm	Laws on hygiene, food, commerce, safety, etc. Associations of workers, trades unions Reasonable taxes for public works (for which no private interest is sufficiently able or motivated), security, public benevolence, etc. Economic associations (partnerships, corporations, etc.) Private charity (nonprofit associations) Appropriate law enforcement Access to courts Public benevolence

---

4 "To invigorate these rights [of the weak], two means can be adopted by the governor; which is to say, either to assume himself the administration of the interests of the weak that he governs, or, to add to their forces supports (*sussidii*) that invigorate them and render [their rights] more difficult to violate. But the first means, as everyone sees, would lead to that centralism, the injustice, ineptitude, and tyranny of which has been demonstrated by us at length." "Indirizzo di future trattazioni economiche," *Civiltà Cattolica*, ser. V, vol. 1 (1862): 146–57.

APPENDIX

Luigi Taparelli, SJ, "Treatise on Subsidiarity"

From *Saggio teoretico di dritto naturale appoggiato sul fatto* [Theoretical treatise of natural right based on fact]. Rome: Civiltà Cattolica, 1949 (first edition, 1840–43).

Book III, "On Human Action in the Formation of Society," Chapter VI, "Degrees of Subordination Among Diverse Societies, or Rather, Hypotactical Right." (§§685–720)

Note: Significant infra-textual cross references, in brackets, to other parts of the treatise, are additionally translated below the main text. Parenthetical remarks are Taparelli's, my own clarifications are in brackets. Footnotes are from significant notes in the 1949 text, with Taparelli's abbreviated citations expanded and corrected where necessary, listed with continuous numbering here, but present in non-sequential alphabetical signs in the 1949 text. Italics all as in original.

Article I. "Observations on the Nature of Such Association."

Summary
685. Necessity of treating this new matter. – 686. Problem to be resolved. – 687. principles established elsewhere. – 688. every consortium has its being, distinct from the communal – 689. therefore must have its own end, authority, and action. – 690. The hypotactical system is from nature, factual proof – 691. rational proof – 692. necessity of other subdivisions – 693. every consortium is a society – 694. 1st hypotactical law: the part serves the whole, the whole the part – 695. this law supposes the association already formed – 696. by means of composition, or

division, or mixed. – 697. Bonds of individuals in the various hypotactical forms – 698. 2nd law: on social organization in the case of dissolution of the whole – 699. its demonstration – 700. consequences of hypotactical theory and its importance.

685. We have spoken so far of the formation of society considering only the associating *force*, that could call itself the *nisus formaticus* of the social order. But the fact of association and the laws that result therefrom can receive great light from the consideration of the *subject* in which this [force] exercises its influence: whence it is important to apply ourselves to such consideration. It is all the more so important considering that I know of no author that has made the kind of theoretical study that the matter requires; thus Romagnosi was right to lament that the doctrines around municipal right are still obscure and poorly founded. But unless some mistake has betrayed me, it seems to me that I can affirm that the obscurity and vacillation of those doctrines is not exclusively a problem of right properly called *municipal*, but concerns generally all of the theory of right of *subordinate* societies that form part of another higher society, where united they seek a common good. The laws of their *subordination* have not ever been contemplated, that I know, with a bit of a metaphysical eye, from which is born great confusion of ideas, and dangerous enough doctrines around the formation and dissolution of society, around citizenship and foreigners, around civil and public rights, etc.

686. The fact which we must clarify and explain the laws of, is this. – Every large society is composed not only of individuals, but also of other minor societies (we will call them *consortia*) which have their own rights; but [rights] such as must often recuse themselves for public advantage. One wonders how such an association is born, in what relations the minor societies find themselves with the higher one? And what laws are deducible from the nature of their relations? – The reader will soon recognize that in this problem, considered with such generality, are included the germs of many special doctrines concerning important associations, both civil and religious: such that the correct solution of the problem can give greater light and consistency not only to *public* but also *canonical* law.

687. To proceed in an orderly way, let us remind ourselves of principles planted elsewhere. 1st: Two individuals cannot meet each other without

finding themselves in reciprocal relation of natural love, and then as conspirators to the common good, which is to say *associated* [314]. 2nd: This universal association, when it comes to be limited in certain ways, for some particular ends (means of happiness), determines the fundamental laws of the particular society that results from it [442]. 3rd: Every society has its *being* and *unity* from the *end*, an extrinsic principle, determining its species, and from the *authority*, an intrinsic principle, the efficient cause of its work [424]. 4th: Every particular society as such subsists to the extent that it has its particular end, its authority, its operation [442 and 446].

688. With these fundamental notions, the fact that we observe everywhere of the subordination of various societies (that we will call *hypotactical association*[1]) presents us a notable consequence at first sight: if every *higher society* is composed of *consortia*, and if these consortia are something, in other words have *a being*; this *being* is different from the *being* of the higher, otherwise there would not be any difference between the society composed of *consortia*, and the society composed of individuals; furthermore who does not see one [species of] being in a multitude of two thousand men, and another [species] in a legion composed of twenty centuries? Who does not see one [species of] being in a heap of meat at the butchers, another in an organized body of an animal? In the centuries you recognize a proper unity and a proper organization, tending rather toward better obtaining the common end, but forming, precisely toward that end, a system unto itself. In the parts of the animal, beyond the form and the strengths, you see a unity of *end*, [the end of each part is] subordinated to the totality but, precisely to better cooperate toward the whole end, concentrated in that particular part. To the advantage of the whole animal, the eye sees, the foot walks, the ear hears; but not for this is the eye foot, or the foot ear, or is the ear the animal: every member has its end, the end determines the work, the work necessitates the organization, which then, animated and moved by the *one* vital principle, executes for the good of the whole animal, its own proper action. Therefore every consortium has a *being* of its own.

---

1. We should not be faulted for the novelty of the word: it is necessary to determine this species of social relations, since the term *subordination* is used indistinctly for every ordinary dependence; the addition of *social* would not clearly determine the subject since *social subordination* expresses equally the dependence of societies between themselves and of the individuals of the society.

689. But the consortium is [a] *society* even itself, and a particular society: thus it must necessarily have an *end*, include an *authority*, execute certain *actions* proper to itself following the 3rd and 4th principles enunciated above, and which things if they were taken from it, it would cease to have a particular being and it would transfuse into the only common being. Thus a family that would lose its name, its memories, its rights, its affections, its mode of thinking, etc., would become a heap of citizens in the city, or of equal men in the state of independence. Every corporation, every academy, every business would cease if would cease its *end*, its own *direction*, [its] *operation*. We are thus compelled either to not recognize consortia or to grant them particular authority and end and operation distinct from the social operation of the whole.

690. Let us ask now in fact if this division of society into consortia is natural or positive; it will be posited to us as natural, since which is ever the somewhat extended society that has existed without subdivisions? The consortium could have an existence subsequent or prior to the [higher] society, since sometimes it happens that the division forms itself in the whole, sometimes the whole composes itself of elements at first separate; in one mode and the other it comes to be used that way by nature in the moral as well as in the physical order: but a vast society not organized in *diverse bodies* (in *consortia*), this is never seen.

691. And the argument shows us that this fact is born by necessity of nature. Since every man has multiple individual needs, for which he seeks aid when he associates himself [444] according to the 2nd principle, this social help must be obtained through the participation of partners directed by authority [305]. Now it is impossible that all of the partners might have will and capacity and place and time and opportunity to occupy themselves for all, it is impossible that the limited mind of any man whatever, in whom supreme authority resides, could know[2] all the individual needs: therefore, for the material division

---

2. "The civil authority can do nothing better than to trust the prudence of individuals for the conduct of their personal interests, that they will always understand better than the Magistrate. But the head of family must continuously supplement the inexperience [Taparelli comments:] (and one could add a thousand other needs for order) of those who are under his care." (Bentham, *Oeuvres de J. Bentham*, t. 1 (Brussels: Société Belge de Librairie, 1840) 209. "Usage de la puissance de l'éducation")

of space, time, capacity, etc., men must necessarily group themselves in various consortia when the society is vast; and for the limited strength of mind and body in he who holds supreme authority, it is a necessity that every consortium have of its own particular authority, a particular possessor and administrator, who can know the individual needs of his own [members of the consortium], and apply the strengths of the consortium in support thereof.

692. Therefore the organic division of large societies into lesser consortia[3] appears to be a necessity of nature: and with the same reasoning it could be demonstrated that if the lesser consortia were to contain such a number of partners, who were to exceed with needs to be satisfied the strengths of one single supervisor, these too would have to divide themselves in other groups, ever decreasing until arriving at a [a consortium of] sufficiently limited number such that its needs can be known totally by a single intelligence, and [can] easily provide for itself with those *external* aids to which human society is destined [305]. *External* I said, because the internal [aids] coming to us directly from the beneficent hand of the Creator whose infinite intelligence knows all, from him [these internal aids] can come exactly provided without needing helpers; and yet he alone is sufficient authority over the purely internal order, and only by revelation do we know that also in this order he wished to distribute hierarchically the workings of angelic intelligences; a subject that goes beyond the limits of our science.

693. To each of these *consortia* and subordinate *groups*, as you well see, we must apply all that which we have said concerning *society generically*, since each of these is one, small yes, but true society. Each one thus has its end, authority, operation; each one may be either natural, voluntary,

---

3. The factual examples could multiply themselves as much as large associations multiply themselves, but the two following examples from Rome and from Athens suffice: "The empire attempted to bring unity to this spread-out society...this vast system of administrative despotism extended over the Roman world a vast network of functionaries hierarchically distributed, dedicated to bringing about in society the will of the [central] power, and in the [central] power the tributes and strengths of the society." François Guizot, *Cours d'histoire moderne: histoire générale de la civilisation en Europe* (Paris: Pichon et Didier Editeurs, 1828), Leçon II (25 April 1828), pag. 16). [As for Athens:] Some minor societies were subject to greater ones like limbs to the body, they even had each one separately their own rights, and administration of common things more or less separate from the republic in general (Cesare Cantù, *Documenti alla storia universale: legislazione* (Torino: Editori Giuseppe Pomba E C., 1839), pag. 73).

or dutiful; each one considered in itself would be naturally independent, but in society, in becoming part of a larger whole, it loses its own proper independence, and participates in social liberty . . . in conclusion, every *consortium* is [a] *society*: this said, all is said.

694. Up until here we have explained the first idea of *hypotactical* association [688], the nature of which can now express itself in the form of general principle stating that *every* LARGE *association is composed, by necessity of nature, of other smaller societies*. One might ask what I mean by *large* society, and what number is sought to take that title. This question seems satisfied to me, even though indeterminately, by the proof derived from our proposition: *large* is that society the administration of which exceeds the strength of one organizing mind. From which descends a universal law, the beginning of all hypotactical right, born from the essence of these relations – *Every consortium must conserve its own unity in such a way that does not damage the unity of the whole; and every higher society must provide for the unity of the whole without destroying the unity of the consortia.* – It seems to me nearly useless to demonstrate this law, since it flows spontaneously from that which so far has been said. Since it is the will of nature [690–91] attested to by fact and from [logical] argument, that a vast society [must] be composed of lesser societies; now the will of nature imposes obligation manifesting to us the intentions of the Creator; therefore posited the [inevitability of] association, it is against nature both in the consortium to separate itself from the social whole and in the whole to annul the consortium, so long as some exceptional cause not intervene.

695. No one, I hope, would want to believe me so senseless that I would want to *obligate* by this law every society to make itself a part of another larger whole, or to divide itself in various consortia; let us leave to *nature*, to *needs*, to *right* [599] the task of associating *consortia* and forming from them the social *Whole*: *given this formation*, we say that the duty of the *consortium* is to tend towards the unity of the *Whole*, [while] the duty of the *Whole* is to not destroy the being of the *consortia*.[4]

696. This hypotactical system of association can form itself in various ways, happening at times that consortia groups themselves gathered

---

4. To level and cancel out every ancient memory of provinces, of cities, of States: here you see what was the mania of the revolutionary spirit everywhere it took root.

together give existence by such *fact* to the higher society (that which usually happens in the *voluntary* association produced by need): at times the larger society dividing itself gives rise to the smaller ones (that which usually happens in *dutiful* societies, produced by prevailing right, in which the supreme authority shares a part of its right with subordinate officials, and designates them heads of lesser societies), at times both of these forms of subordination combine themselves, such that a same social Whole finds itself composed of a hypotactical system produced, so to speak, by way of *division*, and another system produced by way of *composition*. And this would be the state of societies thus derived, in which the Government, whatever it might be, adopts for the convenience of its administration a system of subordinate authorities directing artificial consortia; while the society finds itself originally composed of other consortia organized under circumstances existing prior to the most recent hypotactical [administrative] division.[5]

697. This observation is, in practical terms, of much importance in cases of birth and cessation of authority. In the birth of the hypotactical order, if the association forms itself by way of composition, this composition may be the work of either individuals, or of particular authorities [of particular consortia]: if all of the individuals have with their personal *will* or *duty* or *necessity* formed the bond, it is clear that they are obliged by their doing and in proportion to it.[6] But if the union was done by the action of the respective authorities (as happens, e.g., in the turning over of a city, in the confederation of several provinces, etc.) what is the bond that obligates the individuals to form part of the higher society? Everyone sees that they are obliged to the greater one by the same bond that ties them to the lesser one: such that if to the minor one they were bound by revocable *voluntary consensus* or by residence in the territory, they will be able to separate from the greater one, separating themselves from

---

5. Gian Domenico Romagnosi, *Istituzioni di civile filosofia ossia di giurisprudenza teorica* (2 vols., 1839), vol. I, pag. 546, showed how problematic *confusing* these two orders is, *transforming the head of the municipal family into a royal commissioner.*

6. Cyrus elected by his republic as head of the expedition selected two hundred of his peers, each one of which selected four others; and each one of the thousand chose from the people ten shield bearers, ten rock launchers, ten archers. Cesare Cantù, *Storia Universale* (Torino: Editori Giuseppe Pomba e C., 1839) vol. 2, pag. 69.

the minor one or emigrating from its territory; if to the minor one they were tied by *duty* of obedience, they will not be able to not enter into the greater one so long as such consociation had been legitimately commanded.[7] In short, the link that *binds* individuals to the permanence of the social Whole is the same one that tied them to the consortium, such that if the authority of the consortium separates itself legitimately from the Whole, the individuals would be left equally unbound [from the Whole].

But, please, be warned not to confuse the duty of *permanence* with the duty of *obedience*. The duty of permanence arises from a concrete fact [442, 597] and constrains [one] by accidental bond to live in relation with certain determinant individuals; but the duty of obedience is born from the essence of society, and so, *given that by fact you must* live in that social Whole, you must obey the supreme authority from which the order of the Whole arises; and you must obey it as an immediate duty, as to [the] *principle* of social order, not already as [a] *participant* [under] the authority of the consortium. The consortium binds you to remain, nature obliges you to obey.

If then the association had been formed by the *Whole* which divides itself for convenience of administration, then it is clear that the dependence of individuals is originally upon the Whole, and then derivatively upon the consortia; wherefore [if] the consortium be dissolved they return to blend themselves in with the Whole, and they are obligated to remain there.

698. From this same observation arises another most important law for the social order; and it is that if sometime the social Whole itself might dissolve for any reason, all the authorities (except the supreme authority which falls, and those established by it) remain in possession and in duty to provide for public order;[8] nor by this [fall of the Whole]

---

7. "A man comes to place himself under the faith of the king, to declare himself his vassal; he comes *cum harimannia sua* which is to say followed by his warriors. See thus the Ahrimans who are already followers, the vassals of a man, and come to become the undervassals of the king." F. Guizot, *Essais sur l'histoire de France* (Paris: J. L. J. Brière, 1823), 240.

8. The case which is noted by two most serious historians, in the fall of the Roman empire, during which, notes Cantù: "It was not known how to spread the action of a central Government to all the parts of a vast empire. There prevailed therefore in the lands subject to Rome two powers, one supreme, not inclined to extend its intervention any more than what was believed required to the public well-being, another official, etc., to the cities it left, etc. If the oppressive

does every individual enter into possession of *natural* independence, as delirious, demagogic liberty would claim. This is not the place to examine the related doctrines surrounding the downfall of the supreme authority; since without those doctrines we know from other [experience] it can happen that a supreme authority falls and leaves the consortia that depended on it in independence. Now in such a case what is the law of social order? If the hypotactical association were *entirely* dependent by reason of division of the fallen authority (as happened with the *armed retainers* of the middle ages, that subsisted [as a group] only by their captain) then certainly every individual would acquire if not a true independence, certainly at least a real equality *with respect to the dissolved society* (I except now other ties). But when the social Whole is composed of other lesser associations having their own unity and end and authority, etc., then the dissolution of the supreme bond produces nothing other than to lower the rank of primacy, putting in first rank that authority that held the second. In that way, if for example the confederation of the United States of America were to dissolve, each province would remain with its proper Government, which at that time would be supreme: and if this further were to cease, the civic Government would enter into primacy; and after the fall of this, the domestic or patriarchal [society], step by step is advanced to the supreme.[9]

699. The reason for such law seems evident to me. Every *social Whole* brings together consortia but does not destroy their *natural* unity; thus subsists in them their ordering principle (authority), the cause of that

---

supreme direction lets up, or perhaps as entities [these lesser authorities] aspire to independence... uniting themselves in a type of federative regiment, etc." Cantù, *Storia Universale*, op cit, vol.. IV, pag. 22-23.

Guizot speaks the same way: "As the empire became disorganized each province became disorganized the same...the city, the primitive element of the Roman world, survived nearly alone out of the ruin." *Cours d'histoire moderne: histoire de la civilisation en France* (Paris: Pichon et Didier, 1829), vol. I, Leçon VIII, pag. 302. "The world returned to its first state: cities had formed it, cities remained." *Cours d'histoire moderne: histoire générale de la civilisation en Europe*, op. cit., Leçon. II, pag. 21).

9. G. D. Romagnosi in his *Istituzioni*, bk. VII, sec. 1, note 1, concedes to *individuals all the right to propose and to act* in case of revolution. Does he not know therefore domestic authority? And yet at page 541 ff. he tells us that *"the family binds itself to the father*: in the congress of fathers consists *the true principle* of the tribe." How then does he abandon the overthrown State to the individual, he that in less serious disruptions would secure the state in the well-ordered municipality? (pag. 551).

unity; and it subsists by virtue of the association of the [particular] consortium [466], and not by virtue of the total association; therefore if the association of the consortium lasts, after the fall of the *social Whole* and of the total *authority*, the authority which gives unity and vigor to the consortium lasts as well. Therefore the individuals and the *groups* that compose it are, as before, bound by all those duties that bind the subject to the superior. So, as unusual as it is that a physical composite decompose into its smallest elements, so rare is the case that a numerous society dissolve itself into individuals, detached and free.

700. If this doctrine will merit examination of the experts, they will perhaps discover in it the germ of social theories with which many political problems are resolved, in a manner diverse from that used so far. Thus, e.g., the principle that determines *political* rights in social crises will be seen; so long as there subsist many secondary authorities these are naturally invested with those rights. And here is why this right ofttimes devolves to the heads of families (of which the *social contract* never knew how to explain the *why*); because it is nearly impossible that a political society crumble into individuals, the family is the most elementary part into which society [465] dissolves itself; thus the heads of families are the natural superiors in a dissolved society and have the Government of it. It will be seen how nature tends to conserve the social order even where there are *electoral colleges* and *assemblies* saddling secondary authorities with the duty to reestablish the legitimate order. It will be seen that when in a *mixed* hypotactical association the supreme power ceases, cease with that the subordinate series of powers that from it receive their power and right, but the surviving consortia, that have [power and right] from nature, do not cease. ... But let us leave deducing corollaries to greater experts and pass on to examine the relations of the parts in hypotactical association.

Article II. Laws of the Mutual Relations Between the Parts of Hypotactical Association

Summary
701. First law of mutual relations: private liberty – 702. second law: subordination – 703. third law for the collision of the preceding – 704. the

authority can limit the liberty of the consortia directing them to the common good – 705. fourth law: and yet reserving supreme influence to particular [inferior] authorities; the fifth [law] and [particular] reverence due to [that influence] – 706. sixth law: the common authority can insert itself at times in the consortia – 707. to prevent disorder of particular authorities – 708. this is not an offense against particular authority – 709. neither against the liberty of the consortium – 710. Relations between the lesser authorities and the greater – 711. Epilogue. Cause of hypotactical society – 712. forms; composition or division. – 713. Relations – 714. laws.

701. Applying to the parts of the hypotactical association and to their whole the first principle of humanity *Do the good of others*, we have deduced just previously from the consideration of the *being* of such society the 1st law of its action – that the Whole should benefit the part, the part the Whole; – or in other form – the part should not withdraw itself from the unity of the Whole, the Whole should not absorb into its own unity the unity of the part. Let us give some explanation to this law.

In what consists and where from is born the unity of the consortium? It is born from the necessity of subsidy and immediate direction, and from the impossibility that an extended authority can reach to the most minute particulars; it consists in the direction given to members of the consortium toward its particular end from a proportionate authority. If the Whole must take care of the unity of the consortium, it must therefore operate in a manner that this may obtain its special end under the direction of its particular authority. The operation of a *being* not necessitated by an extrinsic cause is called *liberty* [617]; the first perfection therefore of hypotactical association is the *liberty* of the consortia.

702. But this liberty can never be total; since if the consortium wishes to share in the good of the whole it must make itself part of it; now every part shares from the action of the whole, and yet depends on the whole in action; that which in operation is moved by external cause, is not free; therefore when the consortium operates as *part* of the higher society it definitely shares in the *liberty* of that, but diminishes somewhat of its own [619, VI]. Neither is this a loss, since, [considering these things in] the concrete, who does not see the advantage that a smaller society derives from participation in a greater one, if the [higher one] can be satisfied

with its due, leaving to [the smaller society] a proper existence, neither claiming to swallow [the smaller society] up by stripping it of every property? By how many goods is the patriarchal estate diminished with respect to the civic [estate], [and the civic] with respect to the political! Liberty left by the Whole to the part, willing participation of the part in the common workings, here is a first development of the fundamental law.

703. But this *duty* of participation collides with, as everyone sees, the *right* of private liberty: one may ask oneself what are the respective limits of that? The reply depends on that which we will say elsewhere in general concerning the laws under which every activity imprints direction upon the social body. We will reply here primarily with only general ideas, primarily that the common authority must move the *consortia* toward the common good, since it alone can make [the common good] manifest, being *solely* able to fully know it. I well understand that excellence of mind is not always among the gifts of the person who is in command: nonetheless I sustain that *ordinarily* [the common authority] *alone* knows the social good, (1) because it *alone* has the duty that obliges it to that; (2) because to it *alone* all the relations of society lead; and (3) because many social goods, even though they have a principle from the nature of the things, yet they do not *completely* acquire the aspect of social good without the authority affixing its stamp on it, because in the nature of things they would not have a precise and determinant existence. Thus the term of *minority* [as an indication of legal age] status is a good, but nature does not determine the day; *coining* money is a good, but nature does not design the emblem or weights of it; the *social* cult toward God is a good, but nature does not determine the liturgy of it. The supreme authority has therefore not only the *duty* and the *power* to know that which *precisely* suits the nature of the social relations; but also the *right* to *specify* that which nature has left indeterminate. It alone therefore which knows its own designs, can guide the consortia to the common good.

704. The authority *may* therefore *enter into the management of the consortia when it is a matter of directing [their orientation] toward the common good*.[10] Here is the 3rd law that establishes the limits of superior action

---

10. It is worth reading in this regard chap. IV of Book VIII of *The Spirit of the Laws* (Montesquieu).

on the liberty of the consortium. And it follows from that, even though the supreme organizer must not insert itself into private administration, nonetheless it could have the right, to the extent that the general good requires it, [for example] to know the revenues of it and to exact impositions from it, etc.: even though it is not its place, as Burlamacchi thought, to make itself master of dogmas and of customs, yet it may influence them in order that they do not become corrupt; even though it need not provide everyone with appropriate entertainments, yet it may prohibit those of them dangerous for the public. In sum, the supreme authority alone knows the needs of the whole, therefore it can oblige the consortia to cooperate toward them.

705. But when these [generally applicable] interventions must be applied internally in the consortium to the individuals of which it is composed, this individual application can better be done by who better knows the individuals, and by who more immediately touches them. Now the particular authority better knows and touches its private dependents. Therefore a fourth law: the action of the supreme ordinator will be more effective and agreeable if it passes into the lower [consortia] by way of the subordinate authority; now [this lower authority] must be all the more as effective and agreeable as it can; therefore. . . , the consequence is clear; and it has been deduced more or less as appropriate by all cultivated nations, among which the domestic sanctuary was always (more or less) revered and *per se* inviolable, in which consists *domestic* liberty [619, VI]. And if such a consequence has not been extended to more vast consortia, we will see the reason for that at the proper place.

From which another law follows, that is the obligation imposed on the superior authority to respect itself[11] [as represented] in the inferior; since 1st properly speaking the authority of the universe is *one*, even though represented by many, and it is the eternal Reason [428], and 2nd the inferior authority is of the superior a necessary means, and natural participation; whence to humiliate and to weaken the inferior is to dishearten and to weaken also the superior. And here is why in every wise legislation the paternal authority is an object of respect to civic [authority], and [the

---

11. To the point it is written of divine authority *cum magna reverentia disponis nos*. Wisdom 12:18.

civic authority] to the supreme [authority]; and the individuals that bear [this authority] hold a particular characteristic of dignity, which, for the common good, must be carefully considered in the correction of mistakes, saving as much as possible this characteristic even in punishing the person.

706. I called just now the domestic sanctuary *per se* inviolable, given that the cases are not rare in which the common Authority can, *for accidental reasons*, penetrate to the heart of any consortium whatever. To properly understand [this exception] consider that [the domestic sanctuary] is indeed socially *one*, but its unity is *moral*, dependent that is on the *free* action of individuals, whom abusing their liberty would be able to break, although culpably, the bonds of it. Now the supreme authority is obliged to will the good of it, to care for the unity of it, to prevent disorder in it [701]: therefore, when it apprehends ruin or grave danger, *it can have right* to rush to its protection.

707. *Can have it*, I say, but will not always have it: since does not every consortium have its own proper authority, and precisely because its own [is] more subtle and effective [705] at protecting against harm and risk? Therefore if the private authority orders with prudence and wills effectively, public intervention is neither necessary nor useful. But how many are the consortia where the ordering authority falls in the hands of either senseless or raging persons, who, the sacred text would say, are lions that put their society to confusion![12] In these cases it is evident that the supreme *ordering* reason not only has the *right* but the *obligation* to intervene. Denying this would be saying that [the supreme ordering reason] is not the ordinator of the whole society; is not the *curator* of it; is not the *guarantor* of it; in short, it would be stripping it of both the duty and the right to provide for the common good.

708. But in that guise the authority of the consortium will not any longer be *real authority*, [and] the consortium will not any longer be *free*; but deprived of its own being, it will be nothing other than a multitude of individuals enclosed in particular limits of space. As a matter of fact, in that guise, the authority of the consortium will not be able in the least to be *true authority, pure authority*. Indeed, what is *authority*? It is the *right to*

---

12. *Sicut leo in domo tua evertens domesticos tuos. Eccl.* 4:35. [note: 1855 ed. uses different Latin paraphrase, *quasi leo in domo tua subvertens domesticos tuos,* perhaps from Bonaventure.]

order a society *to the good*; therefore the less the reason of the superior be subject to disorder, the more its authority is true and *forthright*. Now this hypotactical law (that we will call of *correction*) impedes disorders of the subordinated superior: therefore it guarantees authority [that is] more *clear*, and *true* and *revered*: more *clear* because free of disorder; more *true* as the effect of reason, and not passion; more *revered* because *right reason*, natural participation in the celestial light, makes itself naturally revered.

709. At least acknowledge [one might say] that the liberty of the *consortium* is thereby lost, as it no longer governs itself by itself – No; even this *in large part* is false, and the falsity arises from confusing two fairly diverse things, *the liberty of a society*, and *the liberty of who governs it*: the liberty of a society consists in having within itself the cause of its own actions *in conformance with its proper nature* [619, VI]: now the superior authority must only check the inferior in *disordering* action, in other words [action] contrary to nature; therefore on this side nothing is diminished of the liberty of the consortium. Rather this [liberty] increases, especially in the subordinated associates, to whom the direction of the immediate *authority* gets guaranteed against the corruptions of *human weakness*. In fact, would the children of a shrewish father not be rather less free had he not above himself a moderating authority of his excesses? And in the Middle Ages under what despotism would the civilization of European society have necessarily succumbed, if those unrestrained rulers impetuous at every suggestion, one time of ambition, at another of cruelty, another of lust, had not found an embankment in the universal pontifical authority, all the more just in containing aberrations with reason, even while weaker at repressing them with force! Liberty of a society does not consist in the uncontrollability of who governs it, but in the exemption from impediments to just government of who presides wisely. Therefore, I repeat, the objection *in large part* is false.

That if the consortium inserted into the social Whole is, *as consortium*, in some part less free (and we ourselves concede this), that happens under two headings: either 1st by the direction that the consortium receives from the supreme authority toward the common good of the social Whole; and in this case the diminishment of private liberty is an addition of perfection, as was said above [619, VI], and of shared liberty;

or 2nd by the abuse of the superior power, in which case the diminution of liberty is a true calamity, a real damage; but this calamity, this damage arises not from the subordination, but from the disorder (and it would arise equally and perhaps worse if the disorder happen, without an existing supreme power, in the immediate [consortium], since this disorder wounds closer to home). Subordination can therefore diminish liberty in the consortium either in so far as it is made to serve the common good; or in so far as it can be oppressed by the common authority.

But when, leaving aside the *common direction* and abuses, one considers the *consortium* considered as such, within the higher society, that it *freely* receives from its special authority all the prudent directions toward its particular end; and this special authority does not receive from the whole other influences apart from those that impede it, in its particular government, from exceeding its bounds and departing from the order of reason; then for sure the liberty of the consortium is greatest, because not only is it regulated by its own proper authority; but this [authority] can not give other than reasonable directions to it, guided as it is by a superior principle by which the lower consortium receives a greater perfection, and the subordinate authority greater rectitude.

710. From which things it becomes clear that every time a lesser society makes itself part of another greater one, the immediate superior remains free, rather, to achieve its true good, but under conditions: 1st, to not impede thereby the common good that is a good also of the consortium, but rather to cooperate toward it; 2nd, to accept correction even on the level of the particular good whenever he [the immediate superior] disregards it; 3rd, to permit, consequently, an appeal from his own to the superior authority; 4th, and in any case, to not take, without the tacit or manifest consent of [the superior], any steps, the effect of which, if it deviate from the common good, would not be able to be annulled by the supreme authority. And here is why the death penalty that belongs in the patriarchal estate to the father, passes quasi-naturally into the civil society, where the public authority must be able to remedy even the excesses of a father: what remedy would death have? And who could make an appeal from it, since [the aggrieved] had received the blow? 5th, the supreme authority would be able to take upon itself not only these cases

where the disorder is an irreparable harm, but also others, where, if not irreparable, [the harm] might be general. And here is why in proportion as societies advance in true civilization, which is to say in *order*, inferior authorities diminish in power, with the more serious cases (major causes) being taken up to the superior authority, when, [with] the greater interweaving of social relations, disorders of the consortium can have greater influence on the public order.

All the above-indicated limitations on particular authority, and all the other effects of hypotactical association, are products of the same causes from which every association becomes formed, namely either by nature or by consensus or by binding right (save those conditions and exceptions that the nature of the associating causes can permit). So that many times the consortium will be associated by force of *nature* to a greater society, and the laws of association must be deduced from the nature of the fact and of anterior *possession* [611]; other times by *free will*, and in that case the contracting parties can determine conditions; other times by *right*, and the association will follow the disposition of the right [621ff].

711. Let us reduce now therefore in brief what we have said regarding the formation and the particular laws of hypotactical association. The *fact* of this subordination had to be explained: the final cause we have found in the limitation of human strengths that make it necessary; the efficient cause we have observed in those same causes that form every other association.

712. One inquired how hypotactical relations are born. We have seen that these can arise either with the association of individuals or else of consortium authorities, or with the division and subdivision of large social bodies. In the associating of individuals, every individual obligates himself immediately to stay there; the associating of secondary authorities obliges the individual indirectly by the link that binds him to the consortium; the connecting force in the subdivisions of the social Whole is none other than the supreme authority, the ceasing of which, cease [also] the consortia established by it.

713. One inquired what relations arise from hypotactical association. We have seen that in individuals arises the duty of obedience to the supreme authority, and the right to receive from it protection against the

disorders of the subordinate authority. In the consortia arises the relation of a part with the whole; and therefore the duty of sharing the burdens, and the right of sharing in the common good. In the higher society arises the relation of a whole with the part, and thereby the right to make use of [the parts] for common advantage, and the duty to protect their existence and felicity, even *as parts*.

714. One inquired what laws arise from such relations and it has been seen 1st that the particular authority must provide freely for the good of his *consortium*; 2nd that [the particular authority] must receive from the supreme authority, and communicate to its own dependents, directions for the common good; 3rd, that [the particular authority] must be returned to order by the supreme authority if at times [the particular authority] departs from [order]; and 4th, that it will take the place of the supreme government when it might happen to fail, in order that society not remain prey to anarchy.

Everyone sees how much these laws affect the art of governing, and how much more just a government is, how much more gentle, how much more effective, when these laws become exactly observed: so true it is that order established in society is an infallible means of unity and effectiveness, thus of happiness! [455ff] But this is not the place to make the application of them, since we speak only of social formation and of that which immediately results from it.

Article III. Epilogue of This Book

Summary

715. Necessity of a concrete principle of association – 716. where it is found. – 717. Laws and authority which derive from it – 718. superiority by right of correction – 719. authority de facto. – 720. Individual society, hypotactical society.

715. Let what we have said on the formation of society be summarized in a brief epilogue. It is the duty of associated man to cooperate toward the good of those he has conjoined to himself as companions; but who obliges him to associate himself? Nature calls him to it. Yes; but nature does not call him to these more than to those individuals; not in

these more than in those relations. And yet man finds himself there, and not rarely against his will, such that if duty did not bind him there, he would soon leave. Now whence arises such a duty in him?

716. This may arise at times by fact of nature that constrains him to live with those he has not chosen, at times of his own will that by interest he freely binds himself, at times by the right of another that justly obliged him there; at times by more than one of these principles, that together combine their operations to render the union firmer.

717. That same principle under the influence of which society forms itself, dictates the laws of it, and determines the authority of it: nature as an expression of the creative will; human will by free agreement determined by the needs of the contracting parties; prevailing right founded on those titles by which it is superior.

718. This superiority of right arises also among equals when they find themselves for whatever reason in contact, and is born when any of these leaving the paths of order must be led back to it by the others; much more then does he acquire it who in his own rights came to be offended by the crime, being able in such case not only to return the *delinquent* to order, but to expect reparation from him as *offender*.

719. It happens sometimes that, as an affront to right, a society comes to be formed by force: can it remain without a government? No: its essential authority will be then administered by the unjust possessor, but without ever having the right to possess it, neither [will] the society [ever have] the duty of ensuring that [de facto] possession; that obtained *solely* by force falls with the falling of the same force.

720. Considerations concerning the *associating principle* can become notably clarified from the contemplation of the *associated subject*: since one thing is a society of individuals, another is an association of societies. The unity of the consortia combined with the social unity [among consortia] forms both the most beautiful order of societies that exist, and the security of the parts in societies that dissolve.

Here in few lines are the principle parts of the theory with which we have managed to explain the birth of particular societies, and to clarify the essential principles of them. Let us move on now to see the laws of human action in [already] formed society.

Selected cross-references to sections of the *Saggio* cited in the foregoing text:

From Book II, "Theory of Social Being," Chapter I, "Nature of Society."

305. From which it appears how the conjunction of forces is in the present state of man a necessary consequence of the association of intentions. [Once] arrived as we will be at possession of that infinite good to which nature impels us, society will exist only for the communication of [the] end already possessed; but so long as we are aspiring, each of our societies always aims at an intention not yet obtained. [Society] aims therefore at an intention, and in order to obtain it, being necessary the means, a concord of wills induces by legitimate consequence to conjunction of means.

From Book II, "Theory of Social Being," Chapter II, "Origin of Society."

314. In finishing Book I, we had presented a treatise on the duties of man toward God and toward himself; and we had deduced them all from the first universal principle *do the good*, combined with the observation both of the facts and of the nature of things, [observations] that naturally make manifest to us the intentions of the Creator and by consequence the natural law to which we must conform ourselves. There remained for us to consider the duties of man toward other men; and these too must spring as every other [duty] from the general principle *do the good*, applied to other men.

Now what does the principle mean – *do the good* – considered in relation to others? It is to say – accomplish relative to these the intention of the Creator; an intention that I must recognize consulting the facts of nature. Here therefore I turn to ask myself: What, according to the dictates of nature, had to be the intention of the Creator with respect to [these others]? The response is evident to any, [even] the most immature, intelligence; every man has from the Creator that same nature that I have; therefore the intention of the Creator is for each one of them the same as I contemplated for myself. And by consequence my behavior relative to them will be that much more perfect to the extent that it more contributes to procuring for them that which I must procure for myself.

To determine my duties toward men I do not have, therefore, to do other than turn toward them the various forms in which the universal principle presented itself considered relatively to myself. From this material transformation I will obtain therefore by analogous reasons the following formulas, all substantially equivalent: *do the other person's good, act such that he tends toward his end,* [act] *that he conserves order, that he lives honestly and suitably, that he attains his perfection, that he becomes happy, that he tends toward God, that he manifests divine perfection, that he gives glory to his God.* – Compare, courteous reader, these formulas with those that express the duties of man [toward] himself and you will see that these are nothing but a transformation of the universal moral principle applied either to the objective or to the subjective. That if ulteriorly you wish to consider how desiring the other's good is that which is usually called *benevolence* or *love*, you will see the social principle reduced to the known formula – *love others as oneself.* – All these expressions of a same principle find themselves adopted by various moralists as the foundation of duties toward others.

From Book II, "Theory of Social Being," Chapter V, "On Authority."

424. Let us consider therefore the nature of society. Society, we ourselves have said, is the harmonious aspiring of many free intelligences toward a common end: but how can these free intelligences acquire such harmonious action? They have, this is true, in the common end a principle of social unity, but this end is not so strictly tied to this or to that means, that all of the intellects always concur *per se* in recognizing as necessary the one in preference to every other; rather reason no less than experience demonstrates to us that uniting opinions in such matters is most difficult. Now social perfection necessarily requires the coordination of means not only internal but also external; and if one does not coordinate arranging these means, either one does not arrive or arrives badly at the objective. It is useful therefore that there be a principle of unity that coordinates the members of the society in the use of means, as the unique end coordinates

them in the general volition of the social good; and this principle of unity must coordinate the external means with an internal principle, given that society is a harmony of intelligences; it must be intelligent therefore, and communicate itself to intelligences, and communicate itself in a way that impresses upon all a harmonious movement in the use of the means.

428. *Subordinately to* [divine authority] I say; since, let us recall it, every positive obligation has no force if not from natural obligation; now natural obligation is an effect of the ordination, with which God knew in his wisdom the connections of certain effects with certain causes, for example health with sobriety, felicity of children with their obedience, social harmony with dependence on an authority, etc., and imposed the duty of it with the act of his will. Natural obligation depends therefore upon divine Intelligence and will, and likewise from divine Intelligence and will derives every positive obligation. Now *authority* is the right *to oblige* the will of others; therefore every authority is subordinated to the divine will and to the supreme Intelligence from which [the divine will] moves. Wherefore when the Apostle intimates to the faithful – *It is not power if not from God* (Romans 13:1) – [and] when eternal Wisdom by the mouth of the wise King attributed to itself the principle of the authority of every Prince (Proverbs 8:15), they announced with simple forms a profound philosophical theory, that contains the most metaphysical of ideas concerning the true principle of every obligation, and that [theory] will acquire ever greater force by that which we will say afterwards concerning the concrete element of society and of authority.

From Book II, "Theory of Social Being," Chapter VI, "Of Society in Concrete, its Tendencies, its Origins."

442. What do we mean when we speak of society in the concrete? We showed another time that every fortuitous encounter of men finds society already formed by the hand of nature; now this encounter without intent to live together is very much subject to the laws of already *formed* universal society by the hand of nature, since every man must cooperate with others in tending toward the universal end of the human species; but [this encounter] cannot call itself a *forming of society*. When will man

become the author, a founder of some society? When in order to obtain the good some men unite themselves, with the intent to live together toward such end and to use some determinate means. Thus scholars form academies in order to find the good by means of study in common, shopkeepers [form] societies of commerce, hoping for the good by means of a common profit, spouses [form a] marital union searching the good by means of mutual help and of the propagation of children. In these and similar cases a *particular good* being the principle of social unity, also the society becomes *particular*, since, as we have observed elsewhere, social *unity* becomes determined by the end, and the being is proportional to the unity. The principle therefore of the particular society is the determination of some means for attaining the good, namely the universal end, and that means from which the associates receive the impulse to unite themselves becomes the good or rather the immediate and particular *end* of their society, and establishes the proper character of it, or rather the species.[13] In as much that every tendency and every action must determine itself by the object or rather the end to which it tends, the association formed by the intent or rather the *tendency* toward some objective cannot receive its own proper character if not from this same objective. And thus indeed particular societies specify themselves in common language and distinguish themselves: *of letters, of business, philharmonic, scientific*, etc.

444. And the first feature that blossoms forth from nature, or rather from the first rudiments of human nature, is that *every particular association is an effect* (since man is a contingent being), and yet [the particular association] *has its cause* upon which it must be dependent. Ponder, please, attentively this most important consequence, so simple and evident, and yet, who would believe it? so ignored by many publicists. Yes: because man is a contingent being, every moment of his existence presupposes a

---

13. "A society only dissolves because a new society ferments and forms itself in its bosom, etc." Guizot, *Cours d'histoire moderne: histoire de la civilisation en France*, op. cit., vol. I, Leçon VIII, 314. "Every lasting government must result from preexisting conditions." Vincenzo Gioberti, *Introduzione allo studio della filosofia* (Brussels: Marcello Hayez, 1840), vol. II, part I, pag. 220. "From the individual estate... powers pass to the developed one, serving always that continuity, or rather that gradual passage, that having its teething in the previous estate, assures the duration and strength of the subsequent one" (Romagnosi, *Istituzioni di civile filosofia*, op. cit., vol. I, pag. 433; vol. VI, ch.2, sec. 3, lastly).

cause upon which he has some essential or accidental dependence. True it is that man is free; but human liberty is not such that it subtracts the individual from great influences of external causes even in his moral action.[14]

446. Now these [anterior] facts can concern either the *origin* of the particular society, or the *end* to which it tends, or the *means* with which it tends there. Considered as *origin* of the particular society these anterior facts, at least logically, to the associating of the individuals, can establish between them either necessary or free relations. Thus, for example, necessary is the relation of a son with the father, of a loser to a victor, since it was not free to the son to find himself in society with the father, neither to the loser to find himself with the victor; on the other hand the groom is free in the associating himself with the bride, the religious in the entering into [a religious order]. The particular society can therefore be either necessary or free; and a fruit of the systematic spirit is the principle embraced by Burlamacchi, by Spedalieri,[15] and other authors, that the association of man, in order to be natural and legitimate, must be voluntary to him. What society is more natural, and which is less voluntary than the society of a son with the father? There are therefore societies where the will is bound by the duty, there are others where the duty becomes formed by the will: those are *necessary*, these *free*. True it is that these must then all be embraced by the will; in fact, more effectively the necessary ones because they arise from duty; but this does not mean that [these societies] should call themselves born of the will, while on the contrary the will is necessitated morally from the duty. And here perhaps may be the misunderstanding by which those authors were misled: seeing the impossibility of men associating without the binding of their wills, they believed that their obligation depends *always* upon their assent; while on the other hand, very many times, the assent depends upon the obligation: these [persons] yield with the will *because* they are associated, not are they associated *because* they yield with the will.

14. "A same idea recognized as true, such is the fundamental basis, the hidden bond, of all human society." Guizot, *Cours d'histoire moderne: histoire de la civilisation en France*, op. cit., vol. I, Leçon 12, pag. 425.
15. See Nicola Spedalieri, *Dritti dell'uomo* (Assisi: n.p., 1791), Bk. I, ch. 6, sec. 4.; ch. 12, sec. 3. – G. G. Burlamacchi (Jean Jacques Burlamaqui), *Principii del diritto politico*. Translated from French. (Venezia: Giovanni Gatti, 1780), Bk. I, Part I, Ch. III.

455. The simplicity of the *social end* depends in the particular society on the perfect subordination of the *particular* [end], which is [a] means to the *general* [end], which alone can be called genuine *end*; since if such subordination is absent, the society will have two, not one end only: one established for it by nature, the other chosen by will. It will lack therefore the *first* principle of unity, which is to say of social *being*. Now when this is lacking, can there be efficacy? I conclude that a particular society cannot have true *happiness* and *good* if it does not subordinate all of the particular intentions to honesty.[16]

But the *end* is the merely extrinsic principle [of], even though prior to, social unity; the intrinsic principle is the *authority*; therefore in so far as the authority will in itself be more simple, and with the other social person more tightly conjoined, so much more will be the unity and for that reason the perfection, the social happiness.

465. Reason is here therefore in accord with history to assure us of the true origin of domestic society. So far as political society, we cannot explain the origin with full evidence, if first we do not subject the fact [of political society] to a more careful analysis. Meanwhile however the principles established by us show clearly that, if we do not suppose it created by God in one stroke, it must arise from the domestic one: since every society must arise from anterior fact; and the first fact, whence man has existence, being domestic society; political [society] necessarily arises from this place. From the fundamental theorem we can therefore deduce that the basis of society is conjugal society; the others are secondary. But this truth receiving its total *ultimate* evidence from history, cannot call itself *pure* philosophical truth.

From Book II, "Theory of Social Being," Chapter VII, "Of Authority in Concrete."

466. If the nature itself of society carries by essential consequence the coexistence of an authority that forms it, it is clear that society in concrete

---

16. This is the great defect that renders many societies guided by the the utilitarian principle so imperfect. [See Taparelli, *Esame critico*, Part I, chaps. 8 and 9. Ed. note: "honesty" in Taparelli's usage equals public virtue in a pluralistic society, honorableness, especially honoring duties, and corresponds to piety in a confessional society.]

carries by consequence authority in concrete. That which is so evidently necessary, that not even the universal society of men can be considered by us as concretely existing without the divine, supreme Legislator being seen at its head, who promulgating his law imprints upon them unity of end, of cognition, of will, of movement. Nonetheless, having considered how society appears in the concrete, we must, and always on the track of the facts, look for how authority exists in the concrete, summoning reason as well to confirm and to generalize the facts.

From Book III, "Of Human Action in the Formation of Society," Chapter I, "Solution of the Fundamental Problem."

597. The first fundamental problem that presents itself when undertaking to determine the moral laws that must guide human action relative to society, is the problem concerning the *duty to associate oneself*. In the preceding Book, when we showed society to be born of nature, we were led to recognize that certain cases could be given in which duty obliges one to bind oneself in society, or to remain there: But when? But in which of the many concrete societies enumerated in Chapter VI? But for how much time? But with which obligations? etc. All these problems were inopportune while [our] attention was turned solely toward the *being* of society.

Now that the *being* [is] known, taking up contemplation of the *action* of [society] is necessary to resolve these things; but to proceed [in orderly fashion] it is our practice to begin with the most general, and to ask ourselves: how can it happen that man *must* form a stable association with certain other determinate men?

599. And since in the moral order I can be bound either by my free will, or independently of that: we will have three species of facts that can oblige me in the concrete to this or to that other association; first, necessity of physical nature; second, freely given consent; and third, indisputably obliging right. From the *natural need* of the son, the father is obligated to live with the son to give him assistance, the son with the father in order to receive it. By pure necessity of a physical kind a castaway is constrained to live on that island where he was thrown by the storm if

he has no vessel with which to leave there, a servant in that family, outside of which *he absolutely cannot* manage life, etc. From freely given *consent* comes to be obligated a mercenary to the master with whom he made an agreement without compulsion, a people to an elected sovereign, a religious to the Order which he joined, etc. From indisputably obliging *right*, a people conquered in a just war may be bound to society with the victor, [and] a son to live at a place of education determined by the father.[17] The first association is formed by the hand of nature, the second by free will, the third by moral necessity: the first and the last belong to that class of society that we have called *necessary*; but since necessity rooted in physical order can produce consequences diverse from that the roots of which stand fixed in the moral order, we will distinguish them calling the first *natural*, and the last *dutiful*: *voluntary* then or *free* [we call] those of which the bond arises from free assent of the will.

From Book III, "Of Human Action in the Formation of Society," Chapter II, "Theory of the Laws of Social Action in the Birth of Natural Society."

611. The 2nd law of *necessary natural* society is the law of *possession*, the spontaneous consequence of natural independence and equality abstractly considered. Whoever stands in legitimate possession cannot be dispossessed without sure right.[18] Now the two associates in our case have nothing if not the *equal* rights of humanity; therefore they cannot dispossess each other reciprocally, but remain in possession, each one of that which he had.

---

17. The historical facts confirming this theory would be infinite: but we content ourselves pointing to the historical observation of Guizot which seems to be made just for citing in support of our proposition, if in speaking of barbarian conquest he reasonably infers a despotic authority, which if produced by a just conquest should be called monarchy. "Thus in this organization of the German tribe you see appear the three great social systems, the three great origins of sovereignty: 1st association between men equal and free, where political sovereignty develops; 2nd natural primitive association where unique patriarchal sovereignty reigns; 3rd forced association resulting from conquest, given over to despotic authority." Guizot, *Cours d'histoire moderne: histoire de la civilisation en France* (Paris: Pichon et Didier, 1830), vol. IV, Leçon III, pag. 91.

18. See Gianvincenzo Bolgeni, *Il Possesso: principio fondamentale per decidere I casi morali* (Orvieto: Sperandio Pompei, 1847), part 5, n. 19, pag. 15.

From Book III, "Of Human Action in the Formation of Society," Chapter III, "Formative Laws of Voluntary Society," Article I, "General Laws."

617. Free we say is the opposite of necessary: and since an *obstacle* which we encounter in our action *arrests* us, or to be precise imposes on us such a *necessity* of nonaction, thus the exemption from obstacles enters and insinuates itself into the notion of *liberty*, but it is not, as Romagnosi would like, the first element. In fact internal necessity cannot be called an obstacle, rather it can be the natural quality of a primitive impulse; and yet it is irreconcilable with the notion of *liberty* as even in popular language every impassioned man protests when he says (though falsely) to *not be able to resist*, to be drawn along by passion. The first sense of the word *free* is therefore *autonomos* from the Greeks, REGULATOR OF SELF: and here [we find in] the root itself of the notion, the reason for its various equivocal significations. That pronoun SELF that enters into the explanation of the connected *free*, and is together regulator and regulated, can refer to a thousand diverse subjects, at times simple, others more or less complex, and change under such an appearance into a thousand forms the meaning of the connected part, [*free*]. Let us apply it to the subjects from natural right that are *individual* and *society*.

619. From these observations I conclude that:

I. The first idea of liberty is placed in the exemption from necessity in acting.

II. That this exemption should be considered in the subject agent taken in all of its extension and under the command of all the laws belonging to its nature.

III. The supremely free act will be that which has in itself alone *every* cause of acting, finding in itself alone its own existence, matter, force, idea, [and] end of every one of its operations: and such exactly is the operation of the Creative Act subsisting eternally, which is God.

IV. All inferior beings to man, acting naturally by internal necessity, then will be called free when they will be regarded as exempt from outside [necessity]. The rock therefore that from its own nature is in moving necessarily determined, will be said *free* if it not become necessitated in that [internal determination] by external causes; and in the same mode the plant will be *free* if its vegetation does not become restricted; [and] *free* the brute animal, if instinct not [be] violated. Man then who in his own nature is exempt in many of his actions from internal determining necessity, and is called *naturally free*, even though he can be subjected to many external forces, which either externally or internally diminish this autonomy and influence his self-determining, so much less will be said *free*, to the extent that he will not have within himself *alone* the total cause of his acting.

V. But as every created *being* naturally forms part of various subordinate *wholes*, thus every being can be called either *free* or dependent according to how it is being referred to a lesser or to a greater whole, because every created being must necessarily become *subjected* to more laws in proportion as it conjoins itself in more extended relations. Speaking this way of material [nature], gas that combines itself with a base whatsoever loses a part of its action subjecting itself to the laws of the compound and ceases to be *free*. The salt that emerges from it loses in part its native strengths while it enters, for example, to nourish the plant and becomes subject to the laws of vitality, etc., the plant while being in the service of man becomes transplanted by him and pruned and consumed for his needs. As much can be said for the moral order: the will which *in isolation* shows itself to us as psychologically free, entering into the composite of the moral individual becomes *subject* to the laws of reason. The individual that by his own reason alone would be guided if he were alone in the universe, being in family is subject by reason itself to the laws of domestic order, the domestic order to the civil, the civil to the public, etc. In sum in proportion as one goes participating in more extended goods, one also goes subject to more complicated laws.

VI. But notice that this subjection, which relative to the *elementary* state is a diminution of freedom, also is a *truly natural* state, and therefore *free* [in terms] of being considered in the *perfection* of its development. Wherefore the citizen is *as citizen* truly *free*, even though *as man* and *as* member *of a* family he becomes subject in the city to many laws, beyond the moral and domestic. And he is free because those laws being *essential* to the citizen do not diminish the *autonomy* in him, and all the while we can say that he is not constrained in his actions by others, other than from his being as *citizen*. If we wish to assign a name to all these forms of freedom, we could call *material* freedom that of inanimate substances; *spontaneous* or *instinctive* that of brute animals; *human* or of *will* that of man free from internal necessity; *moral* that of man not bound by *obligation*; *individual* if he goes exempt from every non-natural tie; *domestic* if from every tie outside of his own family; *civic* if from every tie external to his city; *national* if from every tie beyond the laws of the State to which he belongs.

VII. From that it can be seen that Bentham did not understand the idea of *law* under its true aspect, when he says: every law [is] an evil because it restricts freedom, and the legislator to be like the doctor reduced to choosing the lesser evil to avoid the greater. If he were speaking only about *penal* law, the observation would be fair; but taken in all of the extension that he took in this, he would oblige us to a strange consequence, that is we would have to call the gift of reason an evil for man, since his appetites and his will receive direction from it, from which he would be exempt if man were irrational.

No, the civil law does not *absolutely* restrict freedom; but restricts *an* inferior freedom, namely the liberty of the *individual man* and of the *domestic*, in order to render him *citizen*: it takes from man the liberty of solitude, harmonizing him in a social being, where nature calls him to share a greater good. If this is an evil, it will be an evil even teaching an ignorant person the truth since you take away from him the liberty to blunder; it will be an evil to fully satisfy a hungry person with food, since it takes away the freedom to eat when satiated. No, I repeat: a *just law* that leads man where nature calls him does not diminish but changes the species of liberty.

Thus also appears the inexactness of Montesquieu, who among the many ideas that he gives us of liberty, calling it now *security*, now *the feeling of security*, now *the right to not be constrained to that which the laws do not impose, and to be allowed [to do that] which these permit*. Always the base of every freedom is forgotten, which is, after all, always the *nature* of that *being* the liberty of which he talks about; when to a being whatsoever becomes imposed a necessity, *foreign to its nature*, then he ceases to be *free*, because he no longer has in himself the cause of his own action.

From that also can be deduced the diminution of liberty in an inferior order is as much a good to the extent [that] it is directed to and necessary for sharing in the goods of a superior order.

621. Now individuals reciprocally equal and independent, how can they constrain themselves to bonds of *stable* society? Every bond diminishes liberty, this diminution in the individual is *per se* an evil, the will cannot will an evil *per se*, therefore if it wills it, it wills it for some good that ensues. Every free association arises therefore from the longing to obtain a good. But this good that the *free* will expects is not either the *infinite* good, nor a *necessary* means of pursuing it, since the association in that case would not be *morally* free; but it would be a *dutiful* association. I conclude therefore that every association *freely* voluntary arises from the intent to obtain a finite *good*, a means of happiness in the mind of who associates himself.

But a finite good not imposing obligation, the association would not be *constant*; to establish the duration of it, what means can there be considering that the wills are not bound either by the order of nature, nor by rights of authority? One means only remains, and it is that each individual binds himself with the duties of loyalty. Therefore every free association must arise from a voluntary consensus, to be precise, a pact.

BIBLIOGRAPHY

Principal Primary Sources

Archivio della Civiltà Cattolica.
Civiltà Cattolica. 1850–present. Rome.
Pirri, Pietro. *Carteggi del Padre Taparelli d'Azeglio* [The letters of Father Taparelli d'Azeglio]. Torino: Bocca Librai, 1932.
   Note: Contains full bibliography of Taparelli's articles.

Relevant Editions of the Treatise

Taparelli, Luigi. *Saggio teoretico di dritto naturale appoggiato sul fatto* [Theoretical treatise of natural right based on fact]. Palermo, Stamperia d'Antonio Muratori, 1840–43. Updated and revised edition, Rome: Civiltà Cattolica, 1855. Used herein, Rome: Civiltà Cattolica, 1949.
———. *Corso elementare di natural diritto ad uso delle scuole*. Napoli: Tipografia all'Insegna del Diogene, 1845.
———. *Sintesi di dritto naturale*. Bologna: Nicola Zanichelli, 1940.

Relevant Articles

Taparelli, Luigi. "Sulla libertà di associazione." Palermo, 1848. Reprinted in Gabriele De Rosa, *I Gesuiti in Sicilia e la Rivoluzione del '48*, 211–45. Roma: Edizioni di Storia e Letteratura, 1963.
———. "Teorie sociali sull'insegnamento." *Civiltà Cattolica*, ser. I, vol. 1 (1850): 25–51, 129–57, 257–74, 369–84.
———. "I corpi morali sotto l'influenza del Teorema della libertà economica." *Civiltà Cattolica*, ser. I, vol. 10 (1852): 225–36, 368–80.
———. "Dell'armonia filosofica." *Civiltà Cattolica*, ser. II, vol. 2 (1853): 128–44, 253–73, 378–99

———. "Di Due Filosofie." *Civiltà Cattolica*, ser. II, vol. 1 (1853): 369–80, 481–506, 626–47.

———. *Esame critico degli ordini rappresentativi nella società moderna* [Critical examination of the representative orders in modern society]. Rome: Tipografia della Civiltà Cattolica, 1854. [Collection of Taparelli's articles in *Civiltà Cattolica*]

———. "Le due Economie." *Civiltà Cattolica*, ser. III, vol. 2 (1856): 609–20; ser. III, vol. 3 (1856): 257–72, 465–85, 611–24; ser. III, vol. 4 (1856): 397–417.

———. "Analisi critica dei primi concetti dell'economia sociale." *Civiltà Cattolica*, ser. III, vol. 8 (1857): 546–59; ser. III, vol. 9 (1858): 17–34.

———. "Agenti di produzione." *Civiltà Cattolica*, ser. IV, vol. 3 (1859): 401–13, 529–38.

———. "La libertà in economia: Conclusione." *Civiltà Cattolica*, ser. IV, vol. 11 (1861).

———. "Indirizzo di future trattazioni economiche." *Civiltà Cattolica*, ser. V, vol. 1 (1862): 146–57.

Relevant Translations

Jacquin, Robert, trans. and ed. *Essai sur les principes philosophiques de l'economie politique*. Paris: P. Lethielleux, 1943. Contains translations of Taparelli's articles "Le due Economie," 1856, "Analisi critica dei primi concetti dell'Economia sociale," 1857, and "Indirizzo di future trattazioni economiche," 1862.

Taparelli, Luigi. "The Influence of Catholic Prayer on Civilization." *Brownson's Quarterly Review*, vol. II (New Series), 1848: 345–80.

———. "Critical Analysis of the First Principles of Political Economy." Translated by Thomas C. Behr. *Journal of Markets and Morality* 14, no. 2 (2011): 613–38.

References

Actes du colloque international organisé par l'École française de Rome et le Greco n. 2 du CNRS. *'Rerum Novarum,' Écriture, contenu et réception d'une encyclique*. Rome: École Français de Rome, 1991.

Almodovar, António, and Pedro Teixeira. "The Ascent and Decline of Catholic Economic Thought, 1830–1950s." *History of Political Economy* 40 (annual supplement, 2008): 62–87.

Altholz, Josef. *The Liberal Catholic Movement in England: The "Rambler" and its Contributors, 1848–1864.* London: Burns & Oates, 1962.

Antonazzi, Giovanni. "L'Enciclica 'Rerum Novarum,' testo latino e autentica versione Italiana, Introduzione." In *L'Encyclica 'Rerum Novarum' e il suo tempo*, edited by Giovanni Antonazzi and Gabriele De Rosa, 45–74. Roma: Edizioni di Storia e Letteratura, 1991.

———. "Il laboratorio della *Rerum novarum*." In *I tempi della Rerum novarum*, edited by Gabriele De Rosa, 293–98. Rome: Istituto Luigi Sturzo, Rubbettino Editore, 2002.

Antonazzi, Giovanni, and Gabriele De Rosa, eds. *L'Encyclica Rerum Novarum e il suo tempo.* Rome: Edizioni di Storia e Letteratura, 1991.

Aquinas, Thomas. *De Malo.* Translated by Richard Regan. New York: Oxford University Press, 2003.

———. *De Ente et Essentia.* Translated by Robert T. Miller. New York: Fordham University, Medieval Sourcebook Online, 1997.

———. *On Kingship to the King of Cyprus.* In *Aquinas: Political Writings*, translated and edited by R. W. Dyson, 5–52. Cambridge: Cambridge University Press, 2004.

———. *Peri Hermeneias* [Commentary on Aristotle's "On Interpretation"]. Translated by Jean T. Oesterle. Milwaukee: Marquette University Press, 1962.

———. *Questiones Disputatae: De Potentia Dei.* Translated by the English Dominican Fathers. Reprint, Westminster, Md.: Newman Press, 1952.

———. *Quaestiones Disputatae: De Veritate, Questions 1–9.* Translated by Robert W. Mulligan, SJ. Chicago: Henry Regnery, 1952.

———. *Summa Contra Gentiles, Book I: God.* Translated by Anton C. Pegis. New York: Hanover House, 1955–57.

———. *Summa Contra Gentiles, Book II: Creation.* Translated by James F. Anderson. New York: Hanover House, 1955–57.

———. *Summa Contra Gentiles, Book III: Providence.* Translated by Vernon J. Bourke. New York: Hanover House, 1955–57.

———. *The Summa Theologica*. New York: Benziger Brothers, 1947–48.

———. *The Treatise on Law*. In *Saint Thomas Aquinas, The Treatise on Law: Summa Theologiae, I-II, QQ. 90–97*, translated and edited by R. J. Henle, SJ. South Bend, Ind.: Notre Dame University Press, 1993.

Aristotle. *Nicomachean Ethics*. Translated by David Ross. Edited by Leslie Brown. Oxford: Oxford University Press, 2009.

———. *Politics*. Translated by Ernest Barker. Edited by R. F. Stalley. Oxford: Oxford University Press, 1998; reprint 2009.

Aron, Raymond. *Montesquieu, Comte, Marx, de Tocqueville: The Sociologists and the Revolution of 1848*. Vol. 1 of *Main Currents in Sociological Thought*. Garden City, N.Y.: Anchor Books, 1968.

Aubert, Roger. *Le Pontificat de Pie IX (1846–1878)*. Paris: Bloud et Gay, 1952.

———. *Aspects divers du néo-thomisme sous le ponificat de Léon XIII*. Rome: Ed. 5 Lune, 1961.

———. "Internal Catholic Controversies in Connection with Liberalism." Chap. 20 in *The Church in the Age of Liberalism*, edited by Roger Aubert, Johannes Beckmann, Patrick J. Corish, and Rudolf Lill, 283–303. New York: Crossroad Publishing, 1981.

Behr, Thomas C. "Luigi Taparelli D'Azeglio, SJ (1793–1862) and the Development of Scholastic Natural-Law Thought as a Science of Society and Politics." *Journal of Markets and Morality* 6, no. 1 (Spring 2003): 99–115.

———. "Luigi Taparelli and Social Justice: Rediscovering the Origins of a 'Hollowed' Concept." *Social Justice in Context* 1 (2005): 3–16.

———. "Luigi Taparelli and Catholic Economics." *Journal of Markets and Morality*, 14, no. 2 (Fall 2011): 607–11.

———. "The 19th Century Historical and Intellectual Context of Catholic Social Teaching." In *Catholic Social Teaching: A Volume of Scholarly Essays*, edited by Gerard Bradley and E. Christian Brugger, 34–65. Cambridge University Press, 2019.

Berman, Harold J. *Law and Revolution*. Cambridge, Mass.: Harvard University Press, 1983.

Blum, Christopher Olaf. *Critics of the Enlightenment: Readings in the French Counter-Revolutionary Tradition*. Wilmington, Del.: ISI Books, 2004.

Boyle, OP, Leonard E. "A Remembrance of Pope Leo XIII: The Encyclical *Aeterni Patris*." In *One Hundred Years of Thomism, Aeterni Patris and Afterwards: A Symposium*, edited by Victor B. Brezik, CSB, 7–22. Houston: Center for Thomistic Studies, 1981.

Brennan, Patrick McKinley. "Subsidiarity in the Tradition of Catholic Social Doctrine." In *Global Perspectives on Subsidiarity*, edited by Michelle Evans and Augusto Zimmerman, 29–47. Dordrecht: Springer, 2014.

Calvez, Jean-Yves, and Jacques Perrin. *The Church and Social Justice: The Social Teaching of the Popes from Leo XIII to Pius XII (1878–1958)*. Chicago: Regnery, 1961.

Candeloro, Giorgio. *Il movimento cattolico in Italia*. Rome: Editore Riuniti, 1982.

Cassina, Cristina. "L'obsession interminable: La révolution française dans la littérature ultra-royaliste au début de la Restauration" [The unending obsession: The French Revolution in Ultraroyalist literature at the beginning of the Restoration]. *Storia della storiografia* 27, no. 1 (1995): 17–38.

Cessario, OP, Romanus. *A Short History of Thomism*. Washington, D. C.: The Catholic University of America Press, 2003.

Chadwick, Owen. *The Popes and European Revolution*. Oxford: Clarendon Press, 1981.

———. *A History of the Popes, 1830-1914*. Oxford: Clarendon Press, 1998.

Chafuen, Alejandro A. *Faith and Liberty: The Economic Thought of the Late Scholastics*. Lanham, Md.: Lexington Books, 2003.

Chenu, Marie-Dominique. *Toward Understanding Saint Thomas*. Translated by A.-M. Landry and D. Hughes. Chicago: Henry Regnery Company, 1963.

Clarke, W. Norris. "Action as the Self-Revelation of Being: A Central Theme in the Thought of St. Thomas." Chap. 7 in *Explorations in Metaphysics*. South Bend, Ind.: University of Notre Dame Press, 1994.

Coleman, SJ, John, ed. *The Development of Church Social Teaching*. New York: Paulist Press, 1986.

Collins, William R. *Catholicism and the Second French Republic, 1848–52.* New York: Columbia University, 1923.

Condorcet, Marquis de. *Outlines of an Historical View of the Progress of the Human Mind: Being a Posthumous Work of the Late M. De Condorcet.* Translated from the French. Philadelphia: M. Carey, 1796.

Conyers, A.J. *The Long Truce: How Toleration Made the World Safe for Power and Profit.* Dallas: Spence Publishing, 2001.

Coppa, Frank J. *The Papacy Confronts the Modern World.* Malabar, Fla.: Krieger Publishing, 2003.

Cubeddu, Raimondo. *Margini del liberalismo.* Soveria Mannelli (CZ): Rubbettino Editore, 2003.

Curci, Carlo Maria. "Il giornalismo moderno ed il nostro programma." *Civiltà Cattolica*, ser. I, vol. 1 (1850): 8–24.

———. "Il Socialismo plebeo ed il volterianismo borghese." *Civiltà Cattolica*, ser. I, vol. 1 (1850): 613–42.

Daniel-Rops, Henri. *The Church in an Age of Revolution.* Translated by John Warrington. London: J. M. Dent & Sons, Ltd., 1965.

Dante, Francesco. *Storia della 'Civiltà Cattolica' (1850–1891): Il laboratorio del Papa.* Rome: Edizioni Studium, 1990.

De Rosa, Gabriele. "Le Origini della 'Civiltà Cattolica." In *Civiltà Cattolica (1850–1945).* Naples: Landi, 1971.

———. *Storia del movimento cattolico in Italia.* Bari: Laterza, 1988.

Derré, Jean-René. *Lamennais: Ses amis et le mouvement des idées a l'époque romantique.* Paris: Librairie C. Klincksieck, 1962.

Dezza, Paolo. *Alle origini del neo-tomismo.* Milano: Fratelli Bocca, 1940.

Dreyer, Frederick A. *Burke's Politics: A Study in Whig Orthodoxy.* Waterloo, Ontario: Wilfrid Laurier University Press, 1979.

Droulers, Paul, SJ. *Cattolicesimo sociale nei secoli XIX e XX. Saggi di storia e sociologia.* Rome: Edizioni di storia e letturatura, 1982.

Dulles, SJ, Avery. "Centesimus Annus and the Renewal of Culture." *Journal of Markets and Morality* 2, no. 1 (1999): 1–7.

Ederer, Rupert J., ed. and trans. *Heinrich Pesch on Solidarist Economics: Excerpts from the Lehrbuch der Nationalökonomie.* Lanham, Md.: University Press of America, 1998.

Evans, Michelle, and Augusto Zimmerman, eds. *Global Perspectives on Subsidiarity.* Dordrecht: Springer, 2014.

Finnis, John. *Aquinas: Moral, Political, and Legal Theory*. Oxford: Oxford University Press, 1998.

———. "Subsidiarity's Roots and History: Some Observations." *The American Journal of Jurisprudence* 61, no. 1 (2016): 133–41.

Fortin, Ernest L. *Human Rights, Virtue, and the Common Good: Untimely Meditations on Religion and Politics*. Vol. 3 of *Ernest L. Fortin: Collected Essays*. Edited by J. Brian Benestad. Lanham, Md.: Rowman & Littlefield, 1996.

Gibson, Ralph. "Why Republicans and Catholics Couldn't Stand Each Other in the Nineteenth Century." In *Religion, Society and Politics in France Since 1789*, edited by Frank Tallett and Nicholas Atkin, 107–20. London: Hambledon Press, 1991.

Gilson, Etienne. *The Spirit of Thomism*. New York: P. J. Kenedy & Sons, 1964.

———. *Reason and Revelation in the Middle Ages*. Reprint, New York: Scribner's, 1966.

———. *Thomist Realism and the Critique of Knowledge*. Translated by Mark Wauck. San Francisco: Ignatius Press, 1986.

Golemboski, David. "Federalism and the Catholic Priniciple of Subsidiarity." *Publius: The Journal of Federalism* 45, no. 4 (October 1, 2015): 526–51.

Grasso, Kenneth, Gerard Bradley, and Robert Hunt, eds. *Catholicism, Liberalism, and Communitarianism: The Catholic Intellectual Tradition and the Moral Foundations of Democracy*. Lanham, Md.: Rowman & Littlefield, 1995.

Greeley, Andrew M. "What is Subsidiarity?" *America* 153, no. 13 (1985): 292–95.

Greenacre, Roger. "Subsidiarity in State and Church." *Contemporary Review* 260, no. 1517 (June 1, 1992): 287–91.

Haag, Henry. "The Political Ideas of Belgian Catholics (1789–1914)." In *Church and Society: Catholic Social and Political Thought and Movements, 1789–1950*, edited by Joseph Moody, 281–98. New York: Arts, Inc., 1953.

Hales, E. E. Y. *Revolution and Papacy, 1769–1846*. New York: Doubleday & Company, 1960.

Hayek, Friedrich, A. *The Mirage of Social Justice*. Chicago: Regnery, 1976.

———. *The Counter-Revolution of Science*. Reprint, Indianapolis: Liberty Fund, 1979.

———. *The Fatal Conceit: The Errors of Socialism*. Edited by W. W. Bartley, III. New York: Routledge, 1990.

Hearder, Harry. *Italy in the Age of the Risorgimento, 1790–1870*. London: Longman, 1983.

Helmreich, Ernst Christian, ed. *A Free Church in a Free State? The Catholic Church, Italy, Germany, France, 1864–1914*. Boston: Heath Publishers, 1964.

Henle, SJ, R. J., trans. and ed. *Saint Thomas Aquinas, The Treatise on Law: Summa Theologiae, I-II, QQ. 90–97*. South Bend, Ind.: Notre Dame University Press, 1993.

Heritier, Paolo. "Le personalisme libéral catholique dans l'Italie du XIXe siècle." In *Histoire de libéralisme en Europe*, edited by Philippe Nemo and Jean Petitot, 567–94. Paris: PUF, 2006.

Hittinger, Russell. "Recovery of Natural Law and the 'Common Morality.'" *This World* 18 (Summer 1987): 62–74.

———. *A Critique of the New Natural Law Theory*. Reprint, Notre Dame: University of Notre Dame Press, 1989.

———. "The Problem of the State in Centesimus Annus." *Fordham International Law Journal* 15, no. 4 (1991–92): 952–96.

———. "Social Pluralism and Subsidiarity in Catholic Social Doctrine." *Annales Theologici* 16 (2002): 385–408.

———. "Introduction to Modern Catholicism" and "Pope Leo XIII (1810–1903)." In *The Teachings of Modern Roman Catholicism on Law, Politics, and Human Nature*, edited by John Witte and Frank Alexander, 1–38 and 39–75. New York: Columbia University Press, 2007.

———. "The Coherence of the Four Basic Principles of Catholic Social Doctrine: An Interpretation." In *Pursuing the Common Good: How Solidarity and Subsidiarity Can Work Together*, edited by Margaret S. Archer and Pierpaolo Donati, 75–123. Vatican City: Pontifical Academy of Social Science, 2008.

Hobbes, Thomas. *Hobbes's Leviathan: Reprinted from the Edition of 1651*. Oxford: Clarendon Press, 1965.

Jacquin, Robert. *Taparelli*. Paris: Lethielleux, 1943.

———. "L'actualité du 'Droit Hypotactique.'" In *Miscellanea Taparelli*, edited by P. Ciprotti and J. D. Algeria, 191–205. Rome: Libreria Editrice Dell'Università Gregoriana, 1964.

John XXIII. *Mater et Magistra*. Encyclical Letter. May 15, 1961.

John Paul II. *Centesimus Annus*. Encyclical Letter. May 1, 1991.

Kant, Immanuel. "An Answer to the Question: What is Enlightenment?" and "To Perpetual Peace: A Philosophical Sketch." In *Perpetual Peace and Other Essays on Politics, History and Moral Practice*, translated by Ted Humphrey. Indianapolis: Hackett Publishing, 1983.

Kohler, Thomas. "Quadragesimo Anno." In *A Century of Catholic Social Thought*, edited by George Weigel and Robert Royal, 27–43. Washington, D. C.: Ethics and Public Policy Center, 1991.

Kraynak, Robert P. "The Origins of 'Social Justice' in the Natural Law Philosophy of Antonio Rosmini." *The Review of Politics* 80, no. 1 (Winter 2018): 3–29.

Kuhn, Thomas. *The Copernican Revolution*. Cambridge, Mass.: Harvard University Press, 1957.

———. *The Structure of Scientific Revolutions*, 2nd ed. In *International Encyclopedia of Unified Science*, vol. II, no. 2. Chicago: University of Chicago Press, 1970.

Langholm, Odd. *The Legacy of Scholasticism in Economic Thought*. Cambridge: Cambridge University Press, 1998.

Lebrun, Richard. "Joseph de Maistre and Edmund Burke: A Comparison." In *Joseph de Maistre's Life, Thought, And Influence: Selected Studies*, edited by Richard Lebrun, 153–72. Montreal: McGill-Queen's University Press, 2001.

Lecler, Joseph. "A propos de la distinction de la 'thèse' et de la 'hypothèse.'" *Recherches de Science Réligieuse* 41 (1953): 530–34

Legittimo, Gianfranco, "Sistemazione dottrinaria e programmatica." In *Sociologi Cattolici Italiani*, 30–50. Rome: Il Quadrato, 1963.

Leo XIII. *Quod Apostolici Muneris*. Encyclical Letter. December 28, 1878.

———. *Aeterni Patris*. Encyclical Letter. August 4, 1879.

———. *Rerum Novarum*. Encyclical Letter. May 15, 1891.

———. *Au Milieu des Sollicitudes*. Encyclical Letter. February 16, 1892.

Lewis, C.S. *The Abolition of Man*. Oxford: Oxford University Press, 1943.
Liddell, Henry George, and Robert Scott. *A Greek-English Lexicon*, 9th ed. Revised supplement by Henry Stuart Jones. First edition, 1843. Oxford: Oxford University Press, 1996.
Locke, John. "Second Treatise of Government." In *Locke: Political Writings*, edited by David Wooten, 261–386. Indianapolis: Hackett Publishing Company, 1993.
Macksey, Charles. "Aloysius Taparelli." In Vol. 14 of *The Catholic Encyclopedia*. New York: Robert Appleton Company, 1912.
Maistre, Joseph de. *Considerations on France*. Translated and edited by Richard A. Lebrun. Cambridge: Cambridge University Press, 1994. Original 1796.
———. *Essai sur le principe générateur des constitutions politiques et des autres institutions humaines*. Paris: Société Typographique, 1814.
———. *Du pape*. Lyons: Chez Rusand, 1819.
Malusa, Luciano. *Neotomismo e intransigentismo cattolico*. Milan: Ist. Propaganda Libraria, 1986.
Maritain, Jacques. *Man and the State*. Chicago: University of Chicago Press, 1951. Reprinted by The Catholic University of America Press, 1998.
———. *The Range of Reason*. New York: Charles Scribner's Sons, 1952. Online from the Jacques Maritain Center: https://www3.nd.edu/~maritain/jmc/etext/range.htm
Martina, SJ, Giacomo. *Pio IX (1851–1866)*. Rome: Editrice Pontificia Università Gregoriana, 1986.
Marx, Karl. *The Eighteenth Brumaire of Louis Bonaparte*. New York, Berlin: Mondial, 2005.
Marx, Karl, and Friedrich Engels. *Manifesto of the Communist Party*. Translated by Samuel Moore. Chicago: Charles H. Kerr & Company, 1906.
Masnovo, Amato. *Il neo-tomismo in Italia*. Milan: Soc. Ed. Vita e Pensiero, 1923.
McCool, Gerald. *Nineteenth-Century Scholasticism: The Search for a Unitary Method*. New York: Fordham University Press, 1989.
McInerny, Ralph. *Ethica Thomistica*. Washington, D. C.: The Catholic University of America Press, 1997.

Melé, Domènec. "Exploring the Principle of Subsidiarity in Organizational Forms." *Journal of Business Ethics* 60, no. 3 (2005): 293–305.
Menczer, Bela, ed. *Catholic Political Thought, 1789–1848 Selected Texts.* London: Burns, Oates and Washbourne Ltd., 1953.
Montesquieu Charles Louis de Secondat, Baron de, *The Spirit of the Laws.* Vol. 1 of *The Complete Works of M. de Montesquieu.* London: T. Evans, 1777.
Mucci, Giandomenico. *Carlo Maria Curci: Fondatore della Civiltà Cattolica.* Rome: Edizioni Studium, 1988.
Mulcahy, Richard E. "Subsidiarity." In Vol. 13 of *The New Catholic Encyclopedia*, ed. William J. McDonald, 762. New York: McGraw-Hill, 1967.
Munz, Peter. *The Place of Hooker in the History of Thought.* London: Routledge & Kegan Paul, 1952.
Mussolini, Benito. Speech before the Chamber of Deputies, May 26, 1927. In *Discorsi del 1927*. Milan: Alpes, 1928.
Nell-Breuning, Oswald. *Reorganization of Social Economy.* Translated and edited by Bernard William Dempsey. New York: Bruce Publishing, 1936, expanded 1937, reprinted 1939.
———. "Social Movements: Christian Social Doctrine." In *Sacramentum Mundi: An Encyclopedia of Theology*, vol. 6, edited by Karl Rahner, 114–16. New York: Herder & Herder, 1968–70.
Nitsch, Thomas O. "Social Economics: The First 200 Years." In *Social Economics: Retrospect and Prospect*, edited by Mark A. Lutz, 5–90. Dordrecht: Kluwer, 1990.
Novak, Michael. *The Catholic Ethic and the Spirit of Capitalism.* New York: Free Press, 1993.
Novak, Michael, and Paul Adams, with Elizabeth Shaw. *Social Justice Isn't What You Think It Is.* New York: Encounter Books, 2015.
O'Connell, Marvin R. "Ultramontanism and Dupanloup: The Compromise of 1865." *Church History* 53, no. 2 (June 1984): 200–17.
O'Neil, Charles. "Prudence the Incommunicable Wisdom." In *Essays in Thomism*, edited by R. E. Brennan, 85–203. New York: Sheed & Ward, 1942.
Paul VI. *Octogesima Adveniens.* Encyclical Letter. May 14, 1961.
———. *General Audience.* October 9, 1968.
———. *General Audience.* August 9, 1972.

Perego, Angelo. *Forma statale e politica finanziaria nel pensiero di Luigi Taparelli d'Azeglio*. Milano: A. Giuffrè, 1956.
Pinto, Ilenia Massa. "La Concezione Antica dell' Origine dello Stato e il Principlio di Sussidiarietà: Luigi Taparelli d'Azeglio" [The ancient conception of the origin of the state and the principle of subsidiarity: Luigi Taparelli d'Azeglio]. Chap. 4 in *Il Principio di Sussidiarietà: Profili Storici e Costituzionali* [The principle of subsidiarity: Historical and constitutional profiles] Naples: Casa Editrice Jovene, 2003.
Pius IX. *Quanta Cura*. Encyclical Letter. December 8, 1864.
Pius XI. *Divini Illius Magistri*. Encyclical Letter. December 31, 1929.
———. *Quadragesimo Anno*. Encyclical Letter. May 15, 1931.
Porro, Pasquale. *Thomas Aquinas: A Historical and Philosophical Profile*. Translated by Joseph G. Trabbic and Roger W. Nutt. Washington, D. C.: The Catholic University of America Press, 2016.
Poulat, Emile. Église *contre bourgeoisie: Introduction au devenir du catholicisme actuel*. Paris: Casterman, 1977.
Rommen, Heinrich A. *The State in Catholic Thought: A Treatise in Political Philosophy*. St. Louis: B. Herder, 1945. German original 1935.
———. *The Natural Law: A Study in Legal and Social History and Philosophy*. Rev. ed. Carmel, Ind.: Liberty Fund, 1998. German original 1936.
Rosmini, Antonio. *The Constitution under Social Justice*. Translated by Alberto Mingardi. New York: Lexington Books, 2007.
Rousseau, Jean-Jacques. "A Discourse on Political Economy." In *The Social Contract and Discourses by Jean-Jacques Rousseau*, translated by G.D.H. Cole. London and Toronto: J. M. Dent and Sons, 1920.
Sandonà, Luca. "Once Upon a Time: The Neo-Thomist Natural Law Approach to Social Economics." *International Journal of Social Economics* 40, no. 9 (2013): 797–808.
Schuck, Michael. *That They Be One: The Social Teaching of the Papal Encyclicals 1740–1989*. Washington, D. C.: Georgetown University Press, 1991.
Schumpeter, Joseph. *History of Economic Analysis*. New York: Oxford University Press, 1994.
Schütze, Robert. "EU Competences: Existence and Exercise." Chap. 4 in *The Oxford Handbook of European Union Law*, 5th ed., edited by Anthony Arnull and Damian Chalmers. Oxford: Oxford University Press, 2015.

Simon, Yves. *The Tradition of Natural Law*. Edited by Vukan Kuic. New York: Fordham University Press, 1992.

Smith, Adam. *Theory of Moral Sentiments*. Edited by Knud Haakonssen. Cambridge: Cambridge University Press, 2002.

Solari, Stefano. "The Corporative Third Way in Social Catholicism (1830–1918)." *European Journal of the History of Economic Thought* 17, no. 1 (February 2010): 87–113.

Sowell, Thomas. *Classical Economics Reconsidered*. Princeton: Princeton University Press, 1974.

Suarez, Francisco. *Defensio fidei catholicae et apostolicae adversus anglicanae sectae errores* [Defense of the Catholic and apostolic faith against the errors of Anglicanism]. 1613.

Tocqueville, Alexis de. *Democracy in America*. Translated by Harvey C. Mansfield and Delba Winthrop. Chicago: University of Chicago Press, 2000.

Torrell, Jean-Pierre. *St. Thomas Aquinas: The Person and His Work*. Translated by Robert Royal. Washington, D. C.: The Catholic University of America Press, 1996. Revised edition, 2005.

United States Catholic Bishops. *Economic Justice for All*. Washington, D.C.: United States Catholic Conference, Inc., 1986.

Vatican Council I. Dogmatic Constitution *Dei Filius*. 1870.

Veuillot, Louis. *De l'action des laïques dans la question religieuse*. Paris: Bureau de L'Univers, 1843.

———. *L'Illusion libérale*. Paris: Palmé, 1866.

Waterman, A. M. C. "Market Social Order and Christian Organicism in *Centesimus Annus*." *Journal of Markets and Morality* 2, no. 2 (1999): 220–33.

Weigel, George and Robert Royal, eds. *A Century of Catholic Social Thought*. Washington, D. C.: Ethics and Public Policy Center, 1991.

———, eds. *Building the Free Society: Democracy, Capitalism, and Catholic Social Teaching*. Grand Rapids, Mich.: Eerdmans Publishing, 1993.

Wippel, John F. "Metaphysics." In *The Cambridge Companion to Aquinas*, edited by Norman Kretzmann and Eleonore Stump, 85–126. Cambridge: Cambridge University Press, 1996.

INDEX

Acton, John Emerich Edward Dalberg, 136
Adams, Paul, 5n13, 87
administrative state, dangers of, 161, 191, 205n3. *See also* state power
Aeterni Patris (Leo XIII), 18, 35, 73, 78–80, 178–79, 185
Almodovar, António, 16n38
anticlericalism, 25, 74–75, 107
Antoine, Charles, 88, 144n4, 167n65
Antonazzi, Giovanni, 70n84, 107n59, 193n22
Aquinas, Thomas. *See* Thomas Aquinas
Aristotle, 8, 62; and Aquinas, 8, 14, 34, 38n47, 39, 41, 43–45, 46n24, 47, 52–55, 67, 81, 93n27, 98–99, 158, 183; decline of democracy, 191; hylomorphism of, 34, 45, 63, 82, 155, 177; *Nicomachean Ethics* of, 45n18, 47, 47n30, 62n71, 67n77, 83, 85–86, 99; philosophical anthropology, 44–45, 47, 52, 55, 67, 96, 158, 183
Aron, Raymond, 2–3, 7, 67

associations: charitable, 19, 70, 77, 92, 131, 135–36; consortia, 93, 111, 113, 131–35, 141, 186–87, 197, 201–19; deutarchy, 93–94, 104n52, 108, 110–12, 133–35, 186–87, 197; dutiful, 113–14, 118–22, 188, 197, 206–7, 224, 226–27, 231; ethnarchy, 94, 110, 113, 128, 135, 197; hypotactical, 93, 103–4, 109, 112, 168, 203, 206, 209–11, 217; natural, 113–16, 120, 122, 188, 197, 205, 224, 226–27; private, 101, 106, 108, 138, 168, 200; protarchy, 94, 104n52, 108, 110–13, 120, 128, 130, 133–35, 168, 187–88, 197; religious, 135–36, 138, 188, 202; unions (workers' associations), 135, 163, 170, 174, 194; voluntary, 105, 113–14, 116–17, 119–22, 128, 188, 198, 205, 207, 224, 226–27, 231
Augustine, 45, 96, 124–25
autonomy, 229; of the Catholic Church, 19, 23, 176; of consortia, 102, 112, 134; radical

notions of, 97, 122–23, 128, 136, 170

Bastiat, Frédéric, 16n38, 155, 156nn37–38, 159–60
beatific vision. *See* contemplation, intellectual, as man's highest function; end, ultimate
Beccaria, Cesare, 138n129
Behr, Thomas C., 5n11, 5n13, 11n28, 18n2, 154n32, 197n1
Bellarmine, Robert, 37
Benedict XVI (Pope), 92
Bentham, Jeremy, 8, 68, 156, 204n2, 230
Berman, Harold, 20n5
Biblical law, 19
Blum, Christopher Olaf, 27n21
Boethius, 39
Bonald, Louis de, 26–27
Bonaparte, Napoleon, 2, 17, 22–23, 26, 132, 174, 176
Brennan, Patrick McKinley, 16n39
bureaucracy, 20, 21, 131, 161
Burke, Edmund, 26–27, 135
Burlamaqui (Burlamacchi), Jean-Jacques, 35–36, 37n44, 213, 224

Calvez, Jean-Yves, 109n65, 143n4, 194n23
Cantù, Cesare, 205n3, 207n6, 208n8
capitalism, 22, 70, 80, 109, 139, 160, 193n21

Cassina, Cristina, 23n11, 26n17
Catholic Liberals, 16n38, 25, 30, 74, 123, 177, 183, 194. *See also* liberal Catholics
"Catholic Movement," 24, 69; liberal Catholic movements, 30, 184n8
Catholic Social Teaching (CST), 4, 87–88; historical development of, 19n3, 24–25, 107–9, 186; Taparelli's natural law science of society as cornerstone of, 6, 15, 16n38, 18, 32, 39, 69–80, 86, 92, 99–100, 106, 142, 174–77, 185, 187, 191, 193–95
Centesimus Annus (John Paul II), 92n25, 108n61, 193
Chadwick, Owen, 22n9, 23n10, 184nn7–8
charity, 70, 72, 76, 86n10, 92–93, 157–59, 163, 166, 168, 183, 191, 193n22, 197; social, 86n10, 92–93, 166, 183, 191
Chateaubriand, François-René de, 26–27
Chenu, Marie-Dominique, 40n1
church: as association, 72, 134, 156, 183; relation of to modern society and state, 17, 19–31, 39, 75, 78, 175–78, 184
Cicero, 96
citizenship, 115n76, 130, 202, 229–30
civil society, 111, 121n88, 131, 148, 164, 170, 188, 216, 229

Civiltà Cattolica (journal), 3n8, 4, 14n37, 18, 31, 36, 57–58, 68–73, 78, 100, 110, 123, 137n126, 153n29, 178, 181, 184, 194

class, 18, 20, 25, 83n4, 155, 157, 160, 177

Clement XIV (Pope), 32

Coleman, John, 100n46

Collegio Romano (seminary where Taparelli was rector), 18, 32–35, 39, 74, 79, 178, 181, 185

common good: contribution of new sciences to, 18; Epicurean concept of, 137–38; and property, 51n44, 148–49, 181; relation of authority to, 95n32, 102, 121–30, 133, 135, 169–70, 175, 212–16, 221–22; and rights, 96, 118n80; and subsidiarity, 94, 99, 104n53, 111, 113, 132–33, 135, 161, 164, 166, 187–89, 198, 202–3, 211–16; and social justice, 89–90, 149–50, 166; teaching of Leo XIII on, 76–78, 106; teaching of Pius XI on, 83n4, 84–85; teaching of Thomas Aquinas on, 48, 52–53, 108n61

common sense, 33, 62, 117

communism, 25, 76, 101, 107, 138n129, 139n132, 157

Comte, August, 2, 7, 9, 32

Condorcet, Marie-Jean-Antoine-Nicolas Caritat, Marquis de, 21n7, 27

conscience, 46n25, 85, 118n79, 155; education of, 11, 91n23, 107n59, 108n61, 116, 140, 145–46, 191; rights of, 29; rights and duties morally obliging us in, 15, 63, 83, 86, 90–91, 95–96, 98, 115, 142, 144–46, 151, 186, 188, 190. *See also* duty/duties

consortia. *See* associations; autonomy; liberty

contemplation, intellectual, as man's highest function, 45, 47, 96–97

Cousin, Victor, 32–33, 60–61, 62n70

Cubeddu, Raimondo, 16n38

Curci, Carlo Maria, 69–71, 74, 178, 181, 183

Daniel-Rops, Henri, 22n8, 26n17

D'Azeglio, Massimo, 18

death penalty, 216

Dei Filius (Vatican I), 73, 80

democracy, 8, 121n88, 126, 139n130; in America, 10–11, 14, 37, 87, 137n127, 191; response from Church, 29, 175, 178; teaching of Thomas Aquinas on, 54–55, 125–26

De Rosa, Gabriele, 25n14, 70nn83–84, 72n90, 193n22

Descartes, René, 27, 32–35, 178; anthropological dualism of, 7, 34, 45; *cogito* as faulty epistemological basis, 27; government based on, 22; universal doubt, 33, 59–60, 182

despotism, 8–9, 11–12, 30, 136–37, 191, 215, 227n17; administrative, 205n3; fearfulness of, 12, 139n130; selfishness as root of, 12, 191

deutarchy. *See* associations

development of doctrine, 19n3

dignity. *See* human dignity

Divini Illius Magistri (Pius XI), 89

Dreyer, Frederick A., 26n19

dritto ipotattico. *See* hypotactical right; subsidiarity

Droulers, Paul, SJ, 70n85, 71n87, 72

Duty/duties, 5; of associations, 94, 100–1, 102–4, 110–11, 114, 118, 122, 131–32, 141, 163, 210, 231; of authority, 53, 77, 129–30, 134, 165, 169–70, 198; economic, 47n30, 148–49, 162, 189; to help others (social charity), 13, 86n10, 92–93 114, 142–45, 186, 220–21; inhering naturally in the human person, 14–15, 99, 115–16, 119–20, 146, 150, 152, 167, 188–89, 199, 200; and rights (social justice), 14, 44, 76, 83, 86–87, 90, 91–92, 96, 98, 108n61, 117, 120, 133, 140, 141, 144n6, 146, 149–51, 153–54, 160–61, 169, 171, 185–87, 190; to oneself (especially self-preservation), 95, 98, 122, 140, 142, 147, 149–50, 152, 181, 185–86, 220. *See also* noninterference, moral obligation of

"eclectic" school, French, 33–34, 60, 174

economics, 154–73, 175, 177, 189, 193, 200; "Christian economics," 167n65; limits on state intervention in, 164–73, 175, 189, 193; medieval scholastics on, 159n44; naturalistic, 155–58, 170; social, 154, 157–73, 177, 189, 200

education: Catholic schools, 30–32, 75, 89, 153n29, 168, 178; moral, 140, 142, 146, 191; natural law basis of, 52, 115n76, 118, 227; role of government in, 109, 153n29, 168, 200; secularization of, 21, 28, 30, 115n76, 156, 171, 178

end, ultimate: as beatific vision, 46; in Aristotle, 47, in a pluralistic society, 64, 125, 159n45, 172; in realm of theology, 179

Enlightenment, 21, 25, 27, 60, 174; critique of religion of, 25

empirical science, true value of, 2–3, 7, 18, 37–38, 61, 97
empiricism, 9, 15, 38, 66, 68, 159n45, 179
equality, individual, 9–11, 13, 76, 86, 91–92, 108n61, 115n76, 126, 137–39, 142–43, 151–53, 155, 163, 190, 199
ethics: deontological, 63; eudaemonia, 47, 63, 64n73, 159n45; virtue, 42n5. *See also* Aristotle
ethnarchy. *See* associations
experience. *See* natural law

faith-reason relationship. *See* reason-faith relationship
family: calls for abolition of, 138–39; natural association of the, 6, 68n77, 72, 76, 105, 109, 112, 114–15, 120, 122, 127, 129, 134–36, 138–39, 153, 168, 183, 188–89, 204, 209–10, 224–26, 229–30
fideism, 29
Finnis, John, 98–99
flourishing, human: connection to natural law, 42, 48, 63, 91, 95, 157–58, 171, 179, 183, 186, 190, 192; political liberty as necessary to, 12, 83, 153, 164, 176, 191; pursuit of, 5, 14, 97
Fortin, Ernest L., 16n39, 18n2, 149n21, 193n22
freedom, religious. *See* religious freedom

freedom of association, human right of, 72, 96, 119, 121, 150, 153n29, 170, 178, 183
free will, 46, 134n122, 217, 224, 226, 228–31
French Revolution, 2, 12, 17, 19, 22–24, 26, 29, 40, 75, 131–32, 174, 178

Gallicanism, 21, 23, 28
Gibson, Ralph, 25n12
Gilson, Étienne, 40, 62n70
Gioberti, Vincenzo, 32, 223n13
God: duties toward, 53, 122, 212, 220; existence of as naturally knowable, 52, 91n23, 93, 155, 159n45, 179–80, 195; foreknowledge of, 46; as *ipsum esse*, 42, 228; as source of political authority, 99, 126, 222, 225; as source of reason, 41, 49, 79. *See also* contemplation, intellectual, as man's highest function
government, mixed forms of, 54, 125
Gregory XVI (Pope), 24, 29, 178
Grotius, Hugo, 8, 32, 35
Guizot, François, 173, 205n3, 208nn7–8, 223n13, 224n14, 227

Haag, Henry, 29n23
habits, 13–14, 85–86, 87, 90; of justice, 151, 185, 188–90
Hales, E. E. Y., 29n24

happiness: contemplation of the truth as highest form of, 96–97; on limitations of in this life, 47–48; "pursuit of happiness" as right, 5, 14, 90, 114, 121–22, 143, 150, 152; as ultimate goal of human will and perfection, 41, 45, 64n73, 129, 192

Hayek, Friedrich, 16nn38–39, 60n66, 85, 87, 148n19

Hearder, Harry, 28n22

hedonism, 190–91

Hegel, G. W. F., 32

Heineccius, Johann Gottlieb, 35

Heritier, Paolo, 16n38

Hittinger, Russell, vii, 16n39, 18n2, 42n5, 75n100, 88n16, 109n65, 193n22

Hobbes, Thomas, 1, 8, 31, 36, 68, 97, 119, 136n125, 139, 147, 177

honesty: "public," 163, 168, 191, 200, 225; virtue of, 93, 147, 158, 191, 197, 221

Hooker, Richard, 32

human action, 6, 11, 34, 43–44, 52, 56, 61, 79, 82, 90n22, 95n32, 116, 120, 145, 155–56, 162, 166, 179, 219; three motors of, 15, 98, 157–59, 164, 171, 190, 197

human being: as free and rational, 46, 49, 128, 144; as political and social animal, 67, 83, 167, 183

human dignity, 63, 68, 90, 104, 111, 168, 214

human freedom. *See* free will

human nature: belief in innate perfectibility of, 21; composite nature of, 5, 7, 15, 47–48, 61, 63, 82–83, 94, 97, 128, 143, 155, 190, 192; medieval Scholastic view of, 27; reversals on classical ideas of, 31

Hume, David, 136n125

hypotactical right (*dritto ipotattico*), origin of term, 102–4, 187. *See also* associations; subsidiarity

Immortale Dei (Leo XIII), 184n7

individualism: Taparelli's criticisms of, 82, 136, 188; Tocqueville on combatting, 12, 191

innate ideas, 43, 50, 191

intellect, 40–41, 43, 47, 59, 63n72, 144–45, 155n35, 158; and will, 46, 79, 95, 113, 122, 147

Investiture Controversy, 75, 176

Jacobinism, 22–23, 25

Jacquin, Robert, 4, 18n2, 35n40, 35n42, 57, 61–62, 89, 107–9, 143n4

Jesuits: French, 144; German, 16n38, 18, 84, 100, 102, 143n4; Italian, 4, 18, 35; and Pope Pius IX, 69–71, 183; suppression of, 32; Taparelli's work used in seminary education, 31, 177–78, 181

John Paul II (Pope), 19n3, 92, 108n61, 193
John XXIII (Pope), 108
Josephinism, 21, 23
justice: commutative, 141, 149, 169n71, 188, 192; distributive, 84, 104, 141, 149, 156, 188, 192; legal, 149, 188, 192. *See also* law; social justice
just war. *See* war

Kant, Immanuel, 21n7, 32–33, 42n5, 63n72, 97, 178
Ketteler, Wilhelm Emmanuel von, 98
Kraynak, Robert P., 143n4
Kuhn, Thomas, 2–3, 57, 59, 81, 82n2

Lacordaire, Jean-Baptiste Henri-Dominique, 28, 30, 177–78
laissez-faire liberalism, 5, 24, 70–73; among Catholics, 16n38, 25, 30; Taparelli's criticism of, 5, 55, 109, 136–38, 156–57, 189, 192, 194
laity, changing roles of, 30–31
Lamennais, Félicité de, 27–30, 32, 177–78
law: divine, 52, 93n27; eternal, 49, 180; positive, 51–52, 56, 147–48, 181, 230. *See also* natural law
Lebrun, Richard A., 26n18
Lecler, Joseph, 184n5

Legittimo, Gianfanco, 7n19
Leo XII (Pope), 28, 32, 178
Leo XIII (Pope), 4, 18–19, 32n29, 35, 69, 70n83, 73–80, 83n4, 106–7, 108n61, 149n21, 176–78, 184–85, 193–94
Lewis, C. S., 82n2, 155n35
Liberatore, Matteo, 16n38, 35, 69–71, 79–80, 167n65, 181, 183, 185
Libertas (Leo XIII), 19n3
liberal Catholics, 16, 25, 28–30, 73–74, 175; misreadings of Taparelli, 69, 123, 128, 183–84, 194. *See also* Catholic Liberals
liberty, 7, 9, 20, 190, 200, 224, 228–31; associational (of consortia), 5, 72, 131–36, 166, 183, 188, 198, 206, 211, 215–16; domestic, 138, 213–14; economic, 155–57, 161, 164, 166, 169n70, 189, 193; and equality, 9; false understanding of, 119, 137–38, 156, 159, 162, 165, 209; and justice/order, 11, 66, 111, 117, 140, 168; life, liberty, and the pursuit of happiness, 42, 76, 90, 113, 152, 187; political, 10, 12, 134n122, 212, 230; religious, 24, 72, 183; Taparelli's definition of, 134, 143. *See also* free will
Locke, John, 1, 8, 32–33, 36, 43, 51, 68, 123, 147–48, 177, 181, 191

Luther, Martin, private judgment as root cause of modernity, 27–28

Maastricht Treaty, 5, 110
Machiavelli, Niccolò, 31
Maistre, Joseph de, 25–27, 61, 177
Maritain, Jacques, 117–18
Marx, Karl, 2, 9–10, 32, 137, 139, 157
Massa Pinto, Ilenia, 5n11, 100n46
Mater et Magister (John XXIII), 108n61
materialist underpinnings of modern social theory, 14, 18, 21, 32, 48, 60, 63, 68, 72–73, 82, 95n32, 97, 143, 156, 170, 177, 179, 192
Mazzini, Giuseppe, 69, 138n129
McCool, Gerald, 33n34, 73n94, 79n108, 179n1
McInerny, Ralph, 47n29, 64n73
Menczer, Bela, 23n10
Messner, Johannes, 88
Metternich, Klemens von, 23
Michelet, Jules, 173
Mill, John Stuart, 2, 9, 32
monarchy, 8, 24–26, 54, 121n88, 127, 138n129, 227n17
Montalembert, Charles Forbes René de, 28, 30, 178, 184n5
Montesquieu, Charles de Secondat, Baron de, 7–9, 27, 61, 66, 68, 139n130, 181, 191, 192n20, 212n10, 230
Mussolini, Benito, 104, 106n57

Napoleon. *See* Bonaparte, Napoleon
naturalistic fallacy, 64n73
natural law, 39–56, 190–91; and *Civiltà Cattolica*, 71–73; definition of, 47n29, 49, 180; first precept of, 42n5, 52, 90–91, 143, 146, 154, 211, 220–21; God's importance for, 159; influence on CST, 19, 39, 73, 76–77, 106, 108n61, 185–87, 193–95; natural inclinations, 52, 157, 160, 197; relationship to social justice and subsidiarity, 2, 4, 92–97, 99, 102, 114, 116, 148–50, 166, 189; Taparelli's course on, 35–37; Taparelli's social science as based on, 6, 8, 10, 15, 17–18, 31, 56, 59, 62–66, 69, 71, 80, 82–83, 88, 145, 174–80, 182, 185; theory of authority, 123, 138n129; value of observation for reasoning about, 38n47, 62–63, 80, 147–48, 180, 182. *See also* Thomas Aquinas
natural right: competing understandings of, 16n38; movement from natural right to subjectively possessed natural rights, 95–98, 144–49, 177, 187, 198. *See also* rights
Nell-Breuning, Oswald von, 5–6, 16n38, 84, 87–88, 100, 102, 109n62, 143n4, 167n65

neoscholasticism, 2, 18, 19n3, 27, 31, 58n60, 71, 83, 88, 154, 175, 177. *See also* Scholastic revival
Neo-Thomism. *See* Thomism
Nitsch, Thomas O., 6n15
noninterference, moral obligation of, 91, 96, 99, 134–35, 142–44, 145n9, 186
Novak, Michael, 5n13, 16n39, 84, 85n7, 87–89, 106n57

Obligation, moral understanding of, 16n38, 63, 163, 183, 189–90, 199. *See also* duty/duties
Octogesima Adveniens (Paul VI), 108n61
oligarchy, 54

Paul VI (Pope), 108n61
peace, 53–54, 71, 113, 126, 148
Peace of Westphalia (1648), 21
Pecci, Vincenzo Gioacchino. *See* Leo XIII
Perego, Angelo, 130n109
Perrin, Jacques, 109n65, 143n4, 194n23
Pesch, Heinrich, 16n38, 88, 92, 143n4, 167n65; concept of solidarism in, 92n24
philosophy, contrast between Scholastic and modern, 58–61. *See also* neoscholasticism; Thomism
Pirri, Pietro, 18n2, 34n35, 37n44, 69n79, 143n4

Pius VI (Pope), 19
Pius VII (Pope), 22, 32
Pius VIII (Pope), 28, 178
Pius IX (Pope), 4, 18, 19n3, 69–74, 76, 80, 123n92, 128, 176–77, 181, 183–84
Pius XI (Pope), 4, 56n55, 80, 83, 85, 87–89, 92, 98, 100–1, 104, 105n55, 108n61, 185
Pius XII (Pope), 19n3, 56n55
Plato, 45–46, 96, 99, 172, 191
polyarchy, 94, 121n88
popular sovereignty, 123–27, 183, 194
Polybius, 191
Porro, Pasquale, 40n1
practical reason, 42n5, 46n25, 49–50, 52, 60–61, 64, 118, 140, 158, 179–80, 182, 186
private property, 51, 76–77, 80, 123, 147–49, 163, 181, 193
protarchy. *See* associations
Proudhon, Pierre-Joseph, 156n38
prudence, virtue of, 44, 50–51, 53, 118, 124, 133, 180, 183, 214
Pufendorf (Puffendorff), Samuel von, 8, 32, 36, 90n22

Quadragesimo Anno (Pius XI), 4–5, 80, 83–85, 88n13, 92, 98, 100–2, 104–5, 108, 109n62, 131n111, 143n4, 185, 187
Quanta Cura (Pius IX), 72–73, 80, 123n92, 176

Quod Apostolici Muneris (Leo XIII), 75–78, 80

reason–faith relationship, 41–42, 59, 73, 179
Reid, Thomas, 33, 62
regime form: Catholic indifference to, 95n32, 124, 175; unchosen by individual, 120–21
religion: as a support to good government, 10–12, 25, 27–28, 72–73, 160, 163; reconciling to a new age, 2, 32; wars of, 21
religious freedom, 30, 72, 75, 168, 175. *See also* liberty
"religious question," 19–24, 31
Rerum Novarum (Leo XIII), 4, 18–19, 70, 72, 80, 84, 106–7, 108n60, 133, 163, 176–77, 179, 193–94; as turning point in CST, 19, 107, 149n21, 185, 194
Revolutions of 1848, 2n4, 30, 69–72, 174, 183
rights: abstract versus concrete, 5, 51n44, 90, 116, 118, 121, 126, 148–50, 152, 181; animal, 145n9; human, 15, 56n55, 87, 90, 129, 131–32, 150; inalienable, 146, 150, 183, 189; social, 91, 131, 144, 146, 149–51, 187; subjective, 4, 6, 15, 63, 80, 86–87, 96–98, 116, 142, 144–51, 177, 187. *See also* duty/duties; freedom of association; natural right

Romagnosi, Gian Domenico, 172, 202, 207n5, 209n9, 223n13, 228
"Roman question," 71
Rommen, Heinrich, 16n39, 38n47, 105n54, 133
Roothaan, Jan, 143n4
Rosmini, Antonio, 143n4
Rousseau, Jean-Jacques, 8, 27, 36, 97, 136n125, 138n129, 147, 177; on the General Will, 1, 105, 115n76, 123, 187; social contract, 1, 76, 115n76, 119, 123, 139
Royalists, 23–25, 28, 30
Royer-Collard, Pierre Paul, 173

Saggio teoretico (of Taparelli): genesis of, 35–37; Pius XI's recommendation of, 89, 181; publication history of, 3, 57, 66, 177; structure of, 55–58, 182, 185; selected text of, 201–31; unjustly dismissed by scholars, 4, 8, 61n68, 143n4
Sapientiae Christianae (Leo XIII), 19n3
Schuck, Michael, 19n3
Scholastic revival, nineteenth-century, 39–55. *See also* neoscholasticism
Schütze, Robert, 5n12, 110n66
Second Vatican Council, 108
self-defense, right of, 147. *See also* duty/duties

self-interest: materialistic versions of, 5, 37, 71, 82, 93, 95–96, 139, 143, 156–58, 159–60, 167; "rightly understood," 9–13, 117, 142–43, 157, 159, 190, 197
separation of church and state, 20, 28, 178
Simon, Yves, 82n2
Smith, Adam, 31, 143
social contract theory, 1, 16n38, 66, 97, 115, 119–20, 123, 141, 147, 187, 210. *See also* Rousseau, Jean-Jacques
socialism, collectivist, 72, 75–78, 88, 92n24, 136–38, 155, 157, 174, 189, 192–93
social justice, 83–93, 199–200; background for Taparelli's definition of, 42, 116, 143n3; and the common good, 89; critiques of, 16n38, 84, 86, 87–88; as distinct from distributive justice, 84, 104, 141, 149, 188, 192; elaboration in CST, 4, 84, 92; first law of, 153; origins of term, 2; as personal virtue, 89–91, 113, 149–54, 185, 189; and subordinate associations, 101, 113–14; Taparelli's theory of, 5, 86–87, 90, 98, 140, 141–43, 149–50, 158, 163–64, 166–68, 177, 183, 185–86, 188–89
"social question," 2, 77, 88, 160, 174
social science: naturalistic, 2–3, 15, 81–82, 137, 160; normative and realist, 2–3, 15, 18, 51, 58, 62, 97, 140, 159, 174–95
society, concept of, 67–69. *See also* civil society
Society of Jesus. *See* Jesuits
Socrates, 46, 96
solidarity, ethical principle of, 86n10, 92–93, 98, 106n61, 113–15, 118, 135, 142, 166, 171, 183, 186, 191–92
Sordi, Domenico, 35, 181
Sordi, Serafino, 32, 35, 178, 181
soul: as formal cause, 45; immortality of, 46; relation to body, 34, 162
sovereignty, popular. *See* popular sovereignty
speculative reason, 43, 47, 50, 55, 62, 118, 140, 179, 182, 186. *See also* practical reason
Spedalieri, Nicola, 224
subjective rights. *See* rights
state power: limits on intervention of in economy, 164–73, 175, 189, 193; modern centralization of, 17, 101, 131–32, 161, 172, 175, 191
Suarez, Francisco, 35, 37, 126, 147, 181
subsidiarity, 198, 200, 201–19; appearance in CST, 16nn38–39, 143n4, 106–8; development by Taparelli of principle of, 4–6, 72, 84n5, 174–75, 177, 187; genealogy of idea of,

93–113; principles in practice, 131–40, 154, 164, 166; as regulative principle of social justice, 87, 110, 168–72, 183, 185, 189; Taparelli's definition of, 4–5, 87, 102–4, 116, 141, 187, 206
suffrage, universal, 28, 74n97, 124, 178
Syllabus of Errors (Pius IX), 72–73, 123n92, 128, 176, 184

Taparelli, Luigi: Aristotelian-Thomistic anthropology of, 7, 34, 63, 82–83, 128, 154–55, 162, 175, 177, 179, 189, 192–93; caricature of as reactionary, 4, 14n37, 16; context for theory of social order, 2–3; contrast between scholastic and modern philosophies of, 58–61; conversion to scholastic philosophy, 32–38; thesis-and-hypothesis reasoning of, 6, 38, 61–64, 176, 180, 184, 194
Teixeira, Pedro, 16n38
Thomas Aquinas, 8, 15, 18, 31–32, 34–35, 37–55, 59–60, 67, 79, 81, 83, 85–86, 90, 91n23, 93n27, 98, 106, 125–26, 130, 147–49, 155, 158–59, 175, 177, 179–80, 183, 185; on best form of government, 54; definition of law of, 130n109; on justice, 85–86; metaphysics of being and epistemology of, 40–45, 59, 179; moral philosophy of, 45; on natural law and politics, 15, 45, 48–55; on private property, 147–49, 181; psychology and anthropology of, 45–48; on source of authority, 123–26; on subsidiarity, 98–99; on virtue, 14
Thomism: Aristotelian-, 2–3, 15, 33, 59–60, 62, 68, 93, 169n71, 174; flexibility with respect to practical conclusions, 39–40, 44, 55, 179; influence on CST, 73, 80, 185, 193–94; Taparelli's role in reviving, 16, 31–36, 69, 71, 79, 178–81, 193
Thoreau, Henry David, 164
Throne and Altar paradigm, 12, 21–25, 28–29, 176
Tocqueville, Alexis de, 2, 9–14, 87–88, 101, 136, 137n127, 139n130, 140, 190–91
Torrell, Jean-Pierre, 40n1
Trent, Council of, 31, 178
Traditionalists, 22, 26–29, 33, 40–41, 58n60, 61, 71, 177–78
Troppau Doctrine, 23
tyranny, 9, 54, 78, 89, 121, 134–35, 137, 167, 198; on the deposition of tyrants, 53, 121

Ultramontanism, 25, 28–30, 184n8
unions. *See* associations

universal destination of goods, theory of, 147–48, 181
usury, 169n71
utilitarianism, 95, 137, 138n129, 139, 157, 170, 225n16

Vatican II. *See* Second Vatican Council
Veritatis Splendor (John Paul II), 19n3
Veuillot, Louis, 25, 30–31
virtue, 14

Vitoria, Francisco de, 32, 37
Voltaire, 27

wage, just, 163
war, 54, 56, 118, 227; just war, 54, 118, 227; as man's natural state, 136n125
Wippel, John F., 41n2
Wolff, Christian, 8

Zigliara, Tommaso Maria (Cardinal), 70, 185